MW00775565

Godhead and the Nothing

Godhead
and
the Nothing

Thomas J. J. Altizer

STATE UNIVERSITY OF NEW YORK PRESS

Published by
State University of New York Press, Albany

© 2003 State University of New York

All rights reserved

Printed in the United States of America

No part of this book may be used or reproduced in any manner whatsoever
without written permission. No part of this book may be stored in a retrieval
system or transmitted in any form or by any means including electronic,
electrostatic, magnetic tape, mechanical, photocopying, recording, or otherwise
without the prior permission in writing of the publisher.

For information, address the State University of New York Press,
90 State Street, Suite 700, Albany, NY 12207

Production by Marilyn P. Semerad
Marketing by Michael Campochiaro

Library of Congress Cataloging-in-Publication Data

Altizer, Thomas J. J.
    Godhead and the nothing / Thomas J. J. Altizer
        p. cm.
    Includes bibliographical references and index.
    ISBN 0-7914-5795-8 (alk. paper) — ISBN 0-7914-5796-6 (pbk. : alk. paper)
    1. Death of God theology.   2. Nihilism—Religious aspects—Christianity.
   I. Title.

BT83.5 .A427 2003
230—dc21   2002036481

10 9 8 7 6 5 4 3 2 1

For Lissa McCullough

Contents

PREFACE

While this book is in genuine continuity with my theological work over the past forty years, it attempts to open new vistas, and most particularly does so to make possible a full theological thinking about an actual absolute nothingness, one which our history has known as the Nihil, and one which has never been fully entered by theological thinking. Our new era, a new postmodern world, can be known as an era of nihilism, certainly nihilism is more powerful now than ever previously, and yet we have no real theological understanding of nihilism, and this despite the fact that the Nihil or the Nothing has been a fundamental theological category for theologians as diverse as Barth and Tillich. Absolute nothingness is an ultimate ground of a purely apophatic mysticism, and it is even more primal in Mahayana Buddhism, just as it has been resurrected in the deepest expressions of a uniquely modern imagination. Nietzsche is the only Western thinker who has fully thought an absolute nothingness, although that nothingness is a deep even if elusive ground of Hegelian thinking, and of all of the fullest expressions of modern dialectical thinking and vision. Genuine or full dialectical vision and thinking finally realizes a *coincidentia oppositorum* between its opposite poles. This is true in both ancient and modern dialectical movements. While often attempted in modern dialectical theology, this goal has not yet been achieved, but it is a goal which can be understood as our most challenging contemporary theological project.

My theological thinking has continually been engaged in this project, but only in this book is that thinking fully focused upon the Nothing, and above all upon the primal or ultimate relationship between the Nothing and the Godhead itself. Heidegger's *Being and Time* is deeply grounded in the Nothing, although here the Nothing as such is not unveiled. In his 1929 essay, "What is Metaphysics?," he could affirm that the Nothing originally belongs to Being, but this is a primal motif which he was unable or unwilling fully or actually to develop. A comparable lacuna occurs in Barth and Tillich, just as it does in the ancient world in Augustine himself. Indeed, Augustine is that thinker who discovered an actual nothingness, a nothingness which he could know as being incarnate in sin. But ontologically Augustine could only know evil as a privation of Being, therefore he could not know evil as an actual nothingness, thereby leading to an Augustinian and Western dichotomy between the nothingness of evil and the full actuality of sin. Hence the deep paradox of an evil that is a sheer or pure nothingness and nevertheless a full actuality in sin, or an evil that is ultimately real even while being absolutely unreal, or an evil that is a pure illusion and yet overwhelmingly real in and as that very illusion. Both our philosophy and our theology have been unable to resolve this paradox, but it is resolved in our greatest modern imaginative enactments, which from Dante through Joyce have fully envisioned an absolute evil or an absolute nothingness, one which is overwhelmingly real, but only real as that nothingness itself. This is a fully actual nothingness which does not enter philosophy until German Idealism, but then it creates a philosophical revolution, and a revolution in which Being itself is inseparable from an absolute nothingness.

Unfortunately this is a revolution which has yet to enter theology, nor has it entered any twentieth century philosophical understanding of God or the Godhead, and while the fullest or deepest expressions of twentieth-century philosophy have either suspended or dissolved all thinking about everything which we once knew as God, this is accompanied by a comparable suspension of all genuine thinking about evil. Our common twentieth-century understanding of both evil and God is more prosaic and banal than ever before, and is truly challenged neither by philosophy nor theology, but only by the purest expressions of our imagination. Few thinkers have been able fully to enter the realm of the imagination, and perhaps no theologians, and nothing is a deeper barrier to this goal than our given understanding of God, or every understanding of God which is actually manifest and real. Not until the advent of postmodernity does an actual language of God fully and finally disappear. This is accompanied by a freezing of theology itself, as for the first time theology has seemingly ceased to evolve, and can only perpetuate itself in its ancient expressions, even if these are now more empty than ever previously. Theology has virtually disappeared from our university world; it is manifest in the mass media and our periodicals only in its most banal expressions, as theological thinking can now only be a deeply solitary thinking, and one if only thereby truly invisible today.

Perhaps the most decisive way to awaken theology in our world is to center upon its deepest "other," one which can be understood as the Nothing itself, a Nothing which is surely the opposite of everything which we once knew as God, and a Nothing whose full advent is inseparable from a uniquely modern realization of the death of God. Just as Nietzsche could know that death as releasing an absolute nothingness, theologians could commonly know that death as embodying the purest nihilism, a nihilism unknown until this advent, but one ever more comprehensively real thereafter. This new nihilism is one in which the Nothing is fully embodied, and so fully embodied that the

Nothing has ceased to be manifest as the Nothing and the Nothing alone. Now it is inseparable for us from everything else, and most clearly inseparable from that absolutely new and absolutely total exteriority which is now engulfing us. That exteriority is inseparable from a new interior emptiness, one affecting every dimension of our existence, and one which can be called forth as a new embodiment of the Nothing, but now an embodiment far more universal than ever previously in our history. Every real response to that embodiment is finally a theological response, for the naming of the Nothing has always been a theological naming, even if a reverse or inverted naming, for the Nothing is ultimately inseparable from the Godhead itself. Already this is deeply known by a pure mysticism, certainly known by the deepest mysticism of the ancient and the medieval worlds, but it is not fully actualized in either pure thinking or the imaginative vision until the advent of the modern world.

Theology itself is torn asunder by that advent, one effecting a deep divorce between ecclesiastical theology and philosophical theology, and a comparable divorce between theology and the imagination, or at the very least an ultimate disjunction between all inherited theology and all truly new expressions of the imagination. For the first time a chasm opens between philosophy and theology, for even if all of our major early modern thinkers are theological thinkers, dogmatic theology becomes either invisible or wholly transformed in that thinking, as a new autonomous thinking ever more fully unthinks every previous theological thinking. While this can be known as a process of genuine secularization, it does not end philosophical theology; it far rather wholly transforms it, and in German Idealism philosophy and theology become fully conjoined. Although this had occurred in Spinoza and Leibnitz, only in German Idealism is a full and comprehensive philosophical theology reborn, and reborn as a philosophical theology that turns the world of theology upside down. At no point is this reversal more fundamental than in Schelling's and Hegel's discovery of an actual nothingness at the center of the Godhead, a nothingness alone making possible what we most deeply know as freedom, a discovery reborn in Heidegger, but reborn in Nietzsche, too, whose revolutionary enactment of the pure nothingness of the Godhead is a realization of an absolutely new freedom or what he could proclaim as the Will to Power or Eternal Recurrence.

There is a deep continuity in German philosophy between Leibnitz and Heidegger, one fully drawn forth by Heidegger himself. There is no such continuity in our theology, a theology that ever more fully retreats from pure thinking, or from all genuinely modern thinking, and above all retreats from a uniquely modern philosophical theology. That theology is either unknown in the theological world today or is assaulted as the purest atheism, and while Barth and Tillich could encounter the Nothing, that is not occurring theologically today, hence the necessity of this book. While nihilism is at the forefront of contemporary philosophy and literary theory, it is absent from our theological thinking as such, and this despite the fact that our deeper naming of the Nothing has always been a theological naming, for the Nothing is truly unknown apart from a theological horizon. One might surmise that Heidegger refrained from a full exploration of the Nothing because of a realization that this could only be a truly theological venture, and if Nietzsche is that philosopher who has most fully unveiled the Nothing, this can be understood as a truly theological unveiling, even if it is one wholly reversing theology itself. True, Sartre centered his greatest work upon the Nothing, but here Sartre's language, too, is a reverse theological language. He abandoned this language in his later work, but then he became silent about the Nothing. Is it possible that theology can only actually speak today by centering upon the Nothing, and not upon that absolute nothingness which an apophatic theology can know as primordial Godhead, but rather upon that actual Nothing which was so deeply born in modernity, and is perhaps truly universal in our new world?

It is possible that theology is now our most forbidden thinking, that thinking least tolerated in all of our worlds, even being absent as theology itself from our seminaries and churches, only being accepted when it is an ethical theology; but an ethical theology today is divorced from all understanding of God, and hence has ceased to be a genuine theology. Yet this condition is inseparable from a new world in which thinking has ceased to challenge the world, or to deeply challenge it, as a new conservatism reigns triumphantly, real opposition has ceased to occur, and not only politically, but also throughout all of our institutions, and even throughout all of our publications except for those with only a miniscule circulation. If ours is the most conservative world since the advent of modernity, it could be that the absence of theology from our world could be a deeply positive sign, or a positive sign to theology itself, just as it could be that nothing could more subvert our world than a genuine theological thinking, and a theological thinking calling forth that which is most "other" than our world. Of course, such an "other" could truly unveil our world, and unveil it perhaps by speaking it most openly. If a speaking of an absolute nothingness could be such a speaking, this need not be simply a negative speaking, but far rather one making possible a movement through our absolute nothingness to its own reversal.

At bottom, such a movement has always been primal in Christianity, and in Buddhism, too, but only a Christian theological thinking will occur in this book; while that is a major limitation, it is one inevitable in everything now possible as theological thinking. What is most needed today is a fundamental theological thinking, one centered upon the Godhead itself, and centered upon that which is most challenging or most offensive in the Godhead, one which has truly been veiled in the modern world, except by our most revolutionary thinkers and visionaries. If we allow Blake and Nietzsche to be paradigmatic of those revolutionaries, nowhere else does such a centering upon God or the Godhead occur, although a full parallel to this occurs in Spinoza and Hegel; but the language of Hegel and Spinoza is not actually offensive, or not in its immediate impact, whereas the language of Nietzsche and Blake is the most purely offensive language which has ever been inscribed. Above all this is true of the theological language of Blake and Nietzsche, but here a theological language is a truly universal language, one occurring in every domain, and occurring as that absolute No which is the origin of every repression and every darkness, and a darkness which is finally the darkness of God, or the darkness of that Godhead which is beyond "God." Only Nietzsche and Blake know a wholly fallen Godhead, a Godhead which is an absolutely alien Nihil, but the full reversal of that Nihil is apocalypse itself, an apocalypse which is an absolute joy, and Blake and Nietzsche are those very writers who have most evoked that joy.

So it is that an evocation of an absolute nothingness can be a way to an ultimate joy, one known both to a Buddhist and a Christian mysticism, and one strangely reborn in full modernity, but reborn only in the most revolutionary expressions of modernity. Certainly this is a *coincidentia oppositorum*, one which we have yet to understand theologically. This book attempts to make a step in that direction, and while this step may only be a misstep, even missteps can point the way, a way now seemingly invisible in our labyrinth. This book has all too indirectly been under the impact of the radically new thinking of D. G. Leahy, who has also been one of its primary critics, just as it has also been enriched by the deep probing of Robert Detweiler and Ray L. Hart. Lissa McCullough and Brian Schroeder, who have been foremost among many critics of my recent work, have also contributed to this book. Moreover, they edited a book on my theology while I was completing this book, a truly challenging critique, and one that almost derailed this project. I have also truly benefited from the copy editing of Lisa Metzger, an editing that was genuinely challenging, and often theologically astute. *Godhead and the Nothing* is dedicated to Lissa McCullough, who is that younger theologian who works most in its spirit, even if her work is leading her in different directions.

CHAPTER 1

↶

The Name of God

Is it possible that there is an actual name of God for us, a name that we can speak or evoke, and speak so as to name the nameless, or to evoke what we have been given as the most ultimate of mysteries? While there are innumerable names of God in our languages, mythologies, and traditions, we now know that there is no possibility whatsoever of reconciling these into a common name of God, or a universal image of God, or a universal concept of God. Hence every truly universal or natural theology has long since disappeared from our world, a disappearance which is also a disappearance of a common understanding or a common meaning of God. In our century there has not been a major philosopher who could think clearly or decisively about God, and at no other point is there a greater gulf between contemporary philosophy and all previous philosophy. There is no truly major work of twentieth-century art or literature which can openly envision God, or which can fully call forth a God who is not a truly distant, or empty, or alien God. To actually or fully to speak of God in our world is to evoke a wholly mysterious, or vacuous, or annihilating presence. And what is most manifestly missing in our world is an actual pronunciation of the name of God in a genuine moment of affirmation, or in a full moment of life and energy and body, or in a moment when we are truly awake.

Now it is true that a genuinely mystical naming of God has inevitably been a naming of mystery, and the deeper the mystical naming the deeper the evocation of nothingness, dark night, and abyss, so that a mystical naming of God is finally a calling forth of unknowing, and the deepest possible unknowing, or the deepest possible silence. While such silence truly can be known as grace, nothing is more rare in our world than such a silence, so that if the silence of God is indeed the grace of God, it would appear to be more absent from our world than from any other world, and absent if only because a pure silence has virtually disappeared from our world. If only at this point our

world truly is a Godless world, and perhaps most openly Godless in our very
pronunciations of the name of God, pronunciations which are mispronunciations, and mispronunciations above all when firmly spoken as the name of
God, or uttered as the name of God and the name of God alone. This is just
what is impossible in the purest imaginative and conceptual languages of our
century, for if the name of God and the name of God alone is now truly
unspeakable, our pronunciations of the name of God will inevitably be mispronunciations, and mispronunciations precisely to the extent that they can
be heard.

Yet it is overwhelmingly difficult for us to refuse to pronounce or to
evoke the name of God, or to renounce a ground which is an ultimate ground.
Even when groundlessness is truly comprehensive, as it is in the nihilism
which has so dominated our century, an ultimate ground is evoked in calling
forth an ultimate nothingness, and therein the name of God is inevitably
called forth. For it is called forth in the very evocation of an ultimate or
absolute nothingness, and thereby such nothingness becomes the name of
names, and if only thereby the name of God. Is it simply not possible for us
to escape or to transcend a necessity for the naming or the evocation of the
name of names, not possible to erase or to dissolve our naming of God? For
this occurs even in our deepest and purest atheism, an atheism surely impossible for anyone who is actually liberated from God. Our philosophers have
inevitably, even if indirectly, evoked God when all conceptions of God are
seemingly impossible, and our poets have inevitably called forth God even
when envisioning an ultimate chaos or an ultimate nothingness, and our
common language even in its most prosaic expressions has never been a truly
Godless language (unless this is true in a new electronic language, or a truly
new anonymous language, a language in which anonymity is all in all).

Now it could be said that our deepest twentieth-century images of God
are images of the anonymity of God, the total anonymity of God. Here a new
humanity is truly an image of the anonymous God, a nameless humanity even
as an anonymous God is nameless, but a namelessness truly evoked in a
uniquely twentieth-century imagery. So it is that our purer naming has named
namelessness itself, thereby it has named the anonymous or the nameless
God. This is manifestly not a mystical naming of God, for this naming precludes every possible mystical communion, or every possible truly mystical
transfiguration. But it does not preclude something very like a mystical union,
a union with the depths of abyss or of nothingness itself. While such a union
is surely not a mystical union, it echoes the highest expressions of our mysticism in its call for a total transfiguration, and a transfiguration possible only
by way of a full union with the depths of anonymity itself. Such a union is
manifest for all to see in the greatest landscape paintings of Monet and
Cézanne, and even in the late landscapes of Van Gogh, wherein the very

incarnation of chaos in the dazzling space before us poses an inescapable call for union with that chaos, a union wherein an exterior and an interior chaos are inseparable and indistinguishable, just as the interior and the exterior wholly pass into each other in all of the greatest expressions of truly modern painting. We greet such painting with joy. An ultimate call to full liberation is clearly present, and its very presence calls for a transfiguration of our interiors that dissolves every possible or every manifest "I," as a new seer is truly born, but a wholly anonymous seer, a seer transcending every possible center. A fully comparable transformation is present in our uniquely modern literature, as a uniquely modern center or subject is ever more decisively negated and reversed, but this negation is a fully transfiguring negation, even if it calls forth a centerless or anonymous subject. This is that new or anonymous subject that can only know an anonymous God, but in truly knowing and realizing anonymity, it realizes a truly anonymous God, and therefore a totally nameless God. This naming of namelessness is nevertheless a genuine naming, a naming of an ultimate and final anonymity, and thus a naming of the anonymous God.

Thereby the name of God itself becomes anonymous, even as it is in our deepest mystical naming. Just as each naming is a naming of abyss or of a dark night, each naming calls for an ultimate transfiguration, a transfiguration which is the deepest possible union, and the deepest possible union with the depths of abyss. This is a condition necessitating our mispronunciation of the name of God. Even as an actual name of God is absent in our deepest modern thinking about God, just as it is unseeable in our purest modern imagery of God, such namelessness is nonetheless the name of God for us, and one calling forth an ultimacy every bit as great as did our previous naming of God. So, too, this is a condition which has brought to an end everything that we once knew as metaphysics and theology. This is not the consequence of modern secularism or modern positivism, but rather the consequence of our deepest modern naming of God, a naming of an absolute anonymity or an absolute nothingness, and therefore the unnaming of everything that we once named as God.

What could an absolute anonymity possibly mean, and above all an absolute anonymity of God? How does it differ from a mystical apprehension of a divine nothingness, or from a simply literal anonymity? First, it is to be noted that the absolute anonymity which our world has come to know is a consequence of a long historical evolution, one beginning with the epiphany of Yah or Yahweh to wandering nomads in the ancient Near East, only gradually evolving to a full and genuine monotheism. That monotheism expressed itself in diverse and conflicting traditions, a diversity releasing profound conflicts between these traditions, a radical discord continually calling forth the most powerful religious orthodoxy in the world, but no less so continually generating our most powerful religious heresies. Only in our own time are we coming to understand the integral and essential relation of heresy and orthodoxy in this radical polarity, one which is surely a decisive source of the immense power of this monotheistic tradition, and one which has been most overwhelming at those very points or moments when this tradition has realized its greatest power.

Radical breakdowns and transformations are also characteristic of this tradition, such as occurred in the first exile of Israel, or even in the exodus itself, for exodus and exile have been primal expressions of this tradition throughout its history. So, too, this tradition has generated deep orthodoxies and deep heresies which are truly paralleled by no other religious tradition. This is most manifestly true in Christianity, which is the only major tradition that begins with a profound internal opposition, one which we now know to be present in the earliest expressions of Christianity, and one which is dormant only in the weakest or least creative expressions of Christianity. Already in primitive Christianity there were deeply discordant forces, which generated the very advent of the Great Church or the Catholic Church, whose orthodoxy was born in response to what it could know as demonic heresies. While this orthodoxy only evolved gradually, it is fully paralleled in the evolution of Christian heresy, thus making possible the greatest conflict in ancient Christianity: an ultimate war between Christian Gnosticism and the Great Church.

Indeed, that conflict can be understood as an archetypal model of the opposition between heresy and orthodoxy, one illuminating the very identity of orthodoxy and heresy, for each only fully became itself by way of its opposition to the other, and each is inseparable from the other, and inseparable if only because each is finally meaningless apart from the other. In this perspective, heresy and orthodoxy are essential to each other, and if Gnosticism was overwhelmingly powerful in the ancient Christian world, a uniquely modern heresy is comprehensively powerful in our world, a heresy which can be understood as a genuine heterodoxy, and most clearly so in its very inversion or reversal of the orthodox Christian God. Nowhere is this so clear as it is in our deepest modern philosophical "atheists": Spinoza, Hegel, and Nietzsche, each of whom truly reversed the absolute transcendence of God. This reversal is impossible apart from a reversal of theological orthodoxy itself, yet it is a reversal of a uniquely Christian orthodoxy, a reversal of a transcendence of God known in Christianity and in Christianity alone. Only in Christianity is there a consciousness of the pure and total transcendence of God. This consciousness only gradually evolved, above all in Western as opposed to Eastern Christianity, as can be seen in the evolution of the consciousness of God from Augustine through Occamism and beyond. This culminates in a consciousness of the absolute transcendence of God which is pure transcendence and transcendence alone. Yet this is the very transcendence that is open to being absolutely transformed into its very opposite, a transformation occurring not only in our deeper philosophical atheism, but far more luminously in the ultimate imaginative enactments of late modernity, one already beginning in Blake, and continuing even into our own time, imaginative enactments realizing an absolute abyss, and an absolute abyss which is apocalypse itself, even if a wholly negative apocalypse.

But this is that pure transcendence which is reversed in a uniquely modern atheism, an atheism impossible apart from this very transcendence, and hence an atheism essentially related to that transcendence, so that our atheism is a true heterodoxy, and as such inseparable from Christian orthodoxy. A full and actual atheism can only be found in the modern Western world. It is not realized here until the late sixteenth century, but then it ever more gradually becomes a comprehensive atheism, as fully manifest in the historical ending of Christendom. That ending impacted upon the world as a whole, initiating a new and comprehensive secularism, yet that secularism can be and has been understood as being in essential continuity with the Christendom that generated it, and just as it is only Christianity among the world religions which has released a true or full secularization, it is only Christianity which has embodied both interiorly and historically a deep and ultimate dichotomy. This is not only a dichotomy between "flesh" and Spirit, or between the kingdom of darkness and the kingdom of light, but also a dichotomy between sin and grace, wherein grace is realized as penetrating into the deepest depths of sin. Only thereby is it a uniquely Christian grace. Consequently, it is Christianity and Christianity alone which knows grace itself as a dichotomous grace, and dichotomous precisely by way of its integral and essential relation to its very opposite. If here a genuine *coincidentia oppositorum* occurs, this is one releasing the deepest power of each opposite, and only thereby can what Christianity knows as apocalypse occur.

In this perspective, it is inevitable that Christianity should have generated that secularism that is seemingly its very opposite, and if Christianity has historically transformed itself more than any other religious tradition, its own deep dichotomy can be understood as a primal ground of this transformation, a primal ground most decisively present in the uniquely Christian vision of God. Theologians have commonly affirmed the uniqueness of the Christian God, again and again affirming that this uniqueness lies in the absolute Yes of the Christian God. Yet that Yes in a deeper Christian consciousness and thinking is inseparable from the absolute No of God, hence the unique dichotomy of the Christian God, and one fully realized in the fullest historical expressions of Christianity. So it is that Christendom is the most dichotomous world in history, and the Christian consciousness the most dichotomous expression of consciousness itself, one realized in that subject which is a purely self-divided, or self-alienated, or dichotomous, subject, and precisely thereby inseparable from its ground in the uniquely Christian God. While Buddhism can know selfhood itself as a pure nothingness, neither Buddhism nor any other non-Christian world can know selfhood as a dichotomous selfhood, or a center of consciousness which is a truly dichotomous center, for as Nietzsche knew so deeply this is a center that is a uniquely Christian center, even if Nietzsche could also know it as a universal center in its purely repressive power.

Thus Nietzsche could know the death of God as the ultimate source of an absolute Yes-saying or a total joy, a death realizing an absolutely new consciousness, for he could know an old consciousness, or all historical expressions of consciousness, as inseparable from a pure *ressentiment*, a *ressentiment* which is No-saying itself, and a No-saying which has only truly been named in the Christian naming of God. Nietzsche is deeply Augustinian in so comprehensively knowing the universality of a total guilt or a total alienation—indeed, at this point, more Augustinian than Augustine himself, for that alienation and guilt is only fully manifest with the death of God, a death hurling us into a universal abyss of nothingness. But it is precisely the transfiguration of that abyss which is the sole source of an absolute and total Yes. Perhaps in Nietzsche more than in any other thinker we can see the integral and essential relationship between an absolute Yes-saying and an absolute No-saying, and if only thereby Nietzsche is a full and genuine theologian, but a uniquely Christian theologian, and if no other thinker has more fully made manifest the universality of a total impotence and guilt, no other thinker has pronounced and enacted such an absolute Yes and Amen. So it is that Nietzsche can justly be known as a Pauline thinker, but a reverse or inverted Pauline thinker, as the Christian consciousness is now not simply torn asunder, but truly and purely reversed. Although Nietzsche could finally know his own time as the advent of a "second Buddhism," it is so only as a pure nihilism, a nihilism which is the consequence of the death of God. Just as he could unveil the advent of Christianity in *The Antichrist* as the advent of nihilism, he could know the death of God as the historical fulfillment of that very nihilism, for this is that one expression of total No-saying which can be and is being transfigured into its very opposite. Now if Nietzsche is our purest heretic, or our most heterodox thinker, his very heresy is a genuine heterodoxy, inseparable from that orthodoxy which it reverses, just as it is inseparable from a Western and Christian world, or that world realizing itself in the most dichotomous consciousness in history. Has that world now truly ended, ended in its deepest ground, or is it now totally present as it never was before, even if invisibly so, and totally present in an abyss which is now seemingly invisible as such, but precisely thereby most integrally actual to us? Is it simply accidental that it is our time which has most fully known Nietzsche as a prophet for us, our time which is most comprehensively open to our darkest seers, and our time in which joy itself is most fully manifest as a mirage? Is it only in our time that the very word "God," or its counterparts, is either wholly silent or wholly mispronounced, and is this a decisive sign or emblem of our world, one bearing our unique signature, and thereby unveiling, if only at this point, our very anonymity?

Yes, our most actual consciousness is an anonymous consciousness, but that very anonymity veils an ultimately dichotomous center, one manifestly called forth when our anonymity is dislodged, and one inescapable in either our speech or our action, so that ours is certainly not an innocent anonymity, even if it can induce a new and comprehensive passivity. That very passivity is another decisive sign of our unique condition, one not only manifest in our new and vacuous imaginative or fantasy worlds, but equally manifest in a new passivity of thinking itself, a passivity clearly embodying our new world, thereby foreclosing the possibility of genuinely challenging that world. For the first time in our history, no ultimate challenge now confronts us, or none which can engage our world. If such a challenge is occurring, this could be only in a subterranean mode, one invisible and inaudible, or virtually so, for it is in fantasy alone that deep challenge is now openly manifest, a fantasy inevitably sanctioning that which it seemingly challenges. Has there ever been a time when fantasy is so comprehensive as it is in our new world, or ever a time in which there was such an overwhelming gulf between the "real" and the imaginative? This gulf forecloses the possibility of that which we once knew as the imagination, just as it has ushered in a totality of reification which not even a Marx or a Kierkegaard could foresee.

That very reification is anonymous precisely as a new reification, for it is vastly distant from everything which we once knew as "matter" or "thing." "Matter" is now just as distant from us as is "spirit," and if this has ushered in a new Gnosticism, that very Gnosticism is inseparable from our new materialism; if this is a rebirth of an ancient or Hellenistic dualism, it wholly transcends that dualism by ending any possible relation between "matter" and "spirit." It could be said that a genuine or purely dualistic thinking is impossible in the West. It is certainly absent in any genuinely Western thinker. Yet dualism has dominated our Western tradition or traditions as it has no other tradition, as fully manifest in Christianity itself, and at no other point has Christianity more openly been at war with itself. Has all such dualism now truly ended, or is it even more powerful in a subterranean form? A dualism so pure that neither opposite is manifest as a real or actual opposite, as every echo of its own other here vanishes, but vanishes in such a way as to irrevocably seal this very opposition.

Perhaps a truly new, even if invisible, dualism offers us a way into what we have come to know as the anonymous God, a God so anonymous as to be unknowable or inactual to us as a true or pure otherness or transcendence, yet precisely thereby inactual to us as a divine or ultimate immanence, and if Christianity and the West have known a deeper polarity between immanence and transcendence than any other tradition, that very polarity has seemingly disappeared for us, and disappeared in a new and comprehensive anonymity. Yet that very anonymity could veil an ultimate dualism, an ultimate opposition or dichotomy between immanence and transcendence, one so ultimate that it is invisible and silent to us, and invisible and unknowable just because neither transcendence nor immanence as such is truly manifest or actual to us. Now what our history has known as immanence, or as an ultimate or absolute immanence, is the immanence of a pure or absolute transcendence, so that when that transcendence is invisible and unhearable, so, too, is such an immanence, an immanence inseparable from its own transcendence, or from its own ground in an absolute transcendence. Even Nietzsche could only know an absolute immanence as a total transfiguration of an absolute transcendence, and even that late modern poetry and painting embodying the purest immanence is unhearable and unseeable apart from the echo or horizon of absolute transcendence, so that when that horizon or echo is stilled, a pure and total immanence likewise disappears and becomes silent.

A new silence is no doubt a decisive key to our world, and if what we once knew as both transcendence and immanence is now silent, this need not mark only an ultimate absence or void. It could well be the site of a truly new distance or chasm between immanence and transcendence, one so overwhelming as to dissolve or obliterate any possible relation between them, and therewith to dissolve any manifest presence or sign of either transcendence or immanence. Such a condition, and such an ultimate condition, could be understood as a truly new dualism, but a dualism so radical and so total that neither pole is now hearable or in sight, for when the chasm between these polarities is uncrossable, then so, too, becomes unspeakable and invisible the horizons of their respective poles. A genuine parallel to such a condition is present in ancient Gnosticism, when the name and the image of "God" becomes unhearable and unseeable as Godhead itself, and the name and the image of body and world passes into an abyss of chaos or nothingness. In the ancient world, only Gnosticism could purely know such an absolute abyss as the very center of both God and the world, or the Creator and body itself, an abyss alone making possible a passage into Godhead itself, or into a primordial pleroma that is absolutely distant from every other horizon. Here, true immanence can only be identical with absolute transcendence, and if no real difference is possible between them, no openness is possible to any other horizon, and therefore world itself becomes invisible and unhearable.

Innumerable critics know our world, or our uniquely new world, as a rebirth of Gnosticism. Yet it is a reverse or inverted Gnosticism, one knowing immanence and immanence alone, and therefore a new immanence, a new immanence that is every bit as vacuous and unnamable as an ancient Gnostic transcendence, and one that is equally distant from any possible body or world. Therein it is profoundly different from that immanence celebrated and embodied in modern poetry and painting, for if that immanence is a truly incarnate immanence, the new immanence open to us is a truly disembodied one; or, insofar as it is embodied, it could only be so in a new vacuity or a new emptiness, one which is untouchable and unseeable, and only actually embodied as vacuity itself. Certainly that vacuity resonates with an ancient Gnostic vacuity, but it nevertheless deeply differs from it, and does so as a nameless vacuity, one invisible and unheard, or unheard and invisible as an actual vacuity, for its very namelessness is a true anonymity foreclosing all possibility of attention to itself. Gnostic naming is truly unique in the world in terms of the very violence of its naming. Only Gnosticism can know body itself as a truly bottomless abyss, or can know the Creator not simply as an absolutely alien abyss, but as a purely negative abyss, with no possible origin except a purely negative origin, and therefore no possibility whatsoever of transfiguration. Now this is just what our abyss or vacuity is not, and cannot be if it is a truly nameless or anonymous vacuity, and thus a vacuity with no possible origin, or no origin upon our horizon. And if ultimate origin has vanished for us, we know a truly new silence, and so far from being a pure or primordial silence, that silence is a truly actual silence, and an actual silence precluding the very possibility of a primordial silence.

Gnosticism can know an absolute gulf between a primordial plenum and the very actuality of the world. No such gulf is possible for us, we can hear no genuine echoes of a primordial silence, and cannot if only because we can hear an actual silence, and even if that actual silence is an actual anonymity, and an anonymity which is all in all, that very anonymity speaks or is actual as itself, thereby foreclosing the possibility of a hearing which is truly the hearing of a primordial ground, or the hearing of a primordial ground which is not fully empty and vacuous. So it is that our vacuity is not truly a Gnostic vacuity. Indeed, it is its very opposite, and its opposite if only because it is so finally closed to every opposite which is the opposite of itself, or every opposite which is an actual opposite. Gnosticism is the purest dualism that has ever appeared upon a Western horizon, and its very distance from us unveils the impossibility of such a dualism for us. Yet it does not preclude the possibility that ours is a truly new dualism, a silent and invisible one, if only because opposites as such are invisible to us, an invisibility which could mask their very presence in a new vacuity so vacuous and anonymous as to be without any trace of opposition itself. Could that disappearance of manifest or actual opposites be a decisive sign of the advent of a new God?

Late modernity can be understood as a longing for a new God. Just as a Gnostic Godhead was a truly new Godhead in its world, such an advent could be possible for us, but it could occur only in a night just as deep if not deeper than a Gnostic darkness, and precisely because we have so irrevocably lost everything that we once knew as light. Nothing is more artificial and unreal in Gnosticism than its renewal of ancient mythological languages and imagery, and nothing could be more unreal in a new Godhead than its epiphany by way of any manifest symbolic languages or imagery. This is just what is impossible in any truly new epiphany, an impossibility which is fully manifest today. So it is that truly new epiphanies of the Godhead are inseparable from full and total negations or dissolutions of every previous divine or ultimate epiphany, negations which are fully actual both in the prophetic revolution of Israel and in Buddhism itself, and if this is a negation which truly occurred in that axial revolution which ended the primordial world, another axial revolution could be at hand today, but only insofar as it effects such a dissolution or negation. Here, we can understand the necessity of a new polar or dualistic ground, one not only establishing a chasm between old aeon and new aeon, but one realizing a dichotomous chasm in Godhead itself, a chasm between its primordial and its apocalyptic poles, and a chasm which is crossed in an absolutely new epiphany of the Godhead, an epiphany inevitably ending that chasm itself. Only that crossing could truly end this polar ground, and if that is a crossing which we can only await, until its advent for us we must inevitably know a deeply dichotomous ground, and know it even if it is invisible and unhearable to us.

Apocalyptic faith is a participation even now in an ultimate ending and an ultimate beginning, and hence a participation in a *coincidentia oppositorum*. Here omega is truly omega only insofar as it effects an absolute ending, and alpha is truly alpha only insofar as it embodies that ending. Thus absolute beginning *is* absolute ending, just as absolute ending *is* absolute beginning, as so luminously called forth both by Joyce's *Finnegans Wake* and by Hegel's *Science of Logic*. If this pure coincidence could occur between our most ultimately discordant writing, that very coincidence is a primal witness to the continuity between ancient and modern apocalypticism, or between an original Christianity and its deepest inversions or reversals. So, too, there is an ultimate opposition both in the *Science of Logic* and in *Finnegans Wake*, and an opposition between true and truly absolute polarities, but an opposition which is finally realized in a transfiguration of these polarities, even if this is invisible and unheard apart from the horizon of this transfiguration. Indeed, this very transfiguration occurs only in a world that embodies an ultimate opposition, a world which can be known as a truly apocalyptic world, and apocalyptic precisely by way of this opposition. Both Blake and Hegel could know such an opposition as the very center of Godhead itself, but one which is revealed or is manifest only with the advent of a final apocalypse. Hence it is unknown not only in the pre-Christian world, but in Christendom itself, and is only released with the ending of Christendom.

So it is that there is a true coincidence between absolute beginning and absolute ending, or a true coincidence between apocalyptic beginning and apocalyptic ending, and just as an eternal movement of eternal return is a dissolution of every possible ending, a full and final apocalyptic movement is an ending of every possible beginning except an apocalyptic beginning. That is a beginning which dawns not only in ancient apocalypticism, but in modern apocalypticism, too, a dawning which is the dawning of a final ending, and a final ending only manifest in the most ultimate darkness. Hence apocalypticism and Gnosticism are truly parallel to each other at this crucial point, and even as a profound conflict between these polarities occurred in early Christianity, a fully comparable conflict is occurring in our world, but only insofar as a final darkness is manifest and real. That is a darkness foreclosing the possibility of an actual remembrance, recall, or renewal. Here the renewal of former epiphanies of God can only finally be empty and unreal, hence they only occur in retreats from this darkness, retreats annulling or reversing that ultimately new epiphany which is here at hand, as witness the dissolution or reversal of apocalypticism in ancient Christianity, a reversal effecting the most radical transformation of a new world which has ever historically occurred. Unless such a reversal has occurred of a uniquely modern apocalypticism, and if this has ushered in a truly new passivity, that passivity is nowhere more fully manifest than in our contemporary pronunciations of the name of God.

Yet if there is no possibility for us of an historical recall or renewal, the possibility is therein established of a truly new repetition, a repetition of that which lies truly beyond our history and consciousness, and above all beyond everything which we can know as consciousness and history today. Hence anonymity, and a total anonymity, could be an essential ground of such a repetition, an anonymity releasing us from all that we have been given as history and consciousness, and only thereby is the possibility realized of an ultimately new repetition. Nonetheless that repetition would truly be repetition, but now repetition in the Kierkegaardian sense of a truly forward movement. This is opposed to the backward movement of recollection, and it is only when a backward moving recollection is truly and finally foreclosed that such a repetition becomes possible. Thus if we cannot truly or actually remember or recollect God, this could make possible a genuine repetition of God, but only a repetition that is the opposite of every possible recollection, or the opposite of every recollection of an historical epiphany of God, and of every recollection of primordial Godhead itself. Now if this is just the recollection that has perished with the modern realization of the death of God, that death could be a repetition of the Godhead, and one itself effecting the dissolution of all recollection of God, a dissolution apart from which no absolute repetition would be possible.

A purely apophatic mysticism can know such a dissolution, but so, too, does full apocalypticism know that dissolution, and if apocalypticism is a forward moving repetition rather than a backward moving recollection, it is not only a reversal of the primordial movement of eternal return, but a reversal of every historical epiphany of God, or a reversal of every historical epiphany which can be recollected or renewed. A truly apocalyptic crisis inevitably effects such a reversal, and if Christianity dawns with apocalyptic crisis, Christendom ends with a rebirth of apocalyptic crisis, and a rebirth ending every genuine recollection of God. Yet that ending does not preclude the repetition of God or the Godhead. It far rather makes it possible, or makes it possible as an absolute repetition, and just as this occurs in the very beginning of Christianity, it could be occurring today, and occurring in the very invisibility of this repetition, or its invisibility apart from the center of this repetition itself. Apophatic mysticism can be known as a profoundly backward movement, a backward movement to primordial Godhead, but apocalypticism is inevitably a profoundly forward movement, and one possible only by way of a liberation from primordial Godhead, or a liberation from every undifferentiated primordial Godhead, or every primordial Godhead freed of a potentiality for its own ultimate transfiguration.

At no point is Christianity more unique than in its dissolution of an undifferentiated primordial Godhead. Even if such a Godhead was not manifest in the West until the advent of Christianity, as most purely apprehended by Plotinus, this is the Godhead that has continually posed the gravest and most ultimate temptation to Christianity, a temptation fully realized in Gnosticism, which is perhaps the purest of all challenges to Christianity. While that challenge has certainly been reborn in our world, it may well be most powerful when most fully disguised, as it can be disguised in a refusal to evoke or pronounce the name of God, and above all when this refusal occurs independently of a purely iconoclastic ground. But is this an actual possibility in our world? For even if our world has more comprehensively known the anonymity of God than any other world, such an anonymity is surely not an evocation of or a witness to an undifferentiated Godhead, and cannot be if only because the namelessness of anonymity is itself a form of naming, and is so in its very naming of namelessness. Hence it is a response to a void or an abyss, one impossible in an undifferentiated Godhead, a Godhead transcending all possibility of an actual naming, including the naming of namelessness itself. The very image of anonymity, or of a full anonymity, is a response to an actual emptiness, a response to an emptying that has actually occurred, therefore it could not possibly be a response to an undifferentiated Godhead, or to a primordial totality of any kind.

Now just as the symbol of an absolute Nothing is the deepest symbol of full or late modernity, and one which does not enter either conceptual thinking or the imagination until the advent of that modernity, this certainly cannot be understood as a symbol of a primordial and undifferentiated Godhead, and cannot be if only because it so forcefully calls forth the full actuality of absolute nothingness itself. Nor can this absolute nothingness be confused with a mystical absolute nothingness, just as it cannot be confused with a simple or literal nothingness, it rather can be understood as being truly unique to our world, or unique in its very epiphany or manifestation. All too significantly no such nothingness is actually known in any Western theological tradition, and while it has at least indirectly entered a uniquely modern Christian theology, it has never done so fully or decisively, and this despite its deep impact upon both Kierkegaard and Heidegger, to say nothing of Hegel, Schelling, and Nietzsche. So, too, an absolute nothingness has been deeply and comprehensively envisioned by Blake, Goethe, Dostoyevsky, and Mallarmé, just as it has purely and even totally been called forth by Joyce, Kafka, Stevens, and Beckett. Yet it has not yet been theologically understood, and not yet fully confronted theologically, and this despite the fact that those thinkers and visionaries who most fully engaged an absolute nothingness thereby clearly established truly new theological horizons.

We can also understand that nothing has more fully dislodged our apprehension or naming of God than has the epiphany of an absolute nothingness. Here lies another historical analogy with ancient Gnosticism, for Gnosticism could finally know the absolute nothingness of both the world and the Creator. But our is a nothingness that is the very opposite of what Gnosticism knows as the Godhead, a Godhead and primordial Godhead which is the Pleroma or the All. So Gnosticism is vastly removed from what full modernity knows as the absolute Nothing. Neoplatonism and scholasticism can know evil as a pure nothingness or a privation of Being, and thus cannot know the actuality of evil, nor can they know absolute nothingness itself, a nothingness which does not enter Western thinking or the Western consciousness itself until the advent of full modernity. This was surely a revolutionary event, and it is inseparable from an eschatological or apocalyptic crisis of the West, a crisis truly known by every thinking and every vision which has been open to an absolute nothingness, and now a crisis fully embodied in a postmodern world. Hence nihilism is inseparable from that world, a full nihilism impossible apart from an embodiment of absolute nothingness, and a comprehensive nihilism unknown in every previous world.

So it is that the very name of God is more precarious in this world than in any other world, but is it possible that to know the anonymous God is to know the name of God for us, and is such anonymity inevitably a mask of absolute nothingness itself? Then we could understand that nothing is more forbidden to us than an actual or full pronunciation of the name of God, just as we could then understand that nothing could be more fully liberating for us than a final release from every possibility of evoking God. Yet it is also possible that there is no hope for such liberation apart from a passage through absolute nothingness itself. Then the naming of God would be essential for us, and if the name of God for us could only be a name of absolute nothingness, that name could finally be liberating for us, even if it now inevitably calls forth a truly abysmal voyage. If such a voyage is now inevitable for us, even if fully disguised by the deep anonymity of our world, and even if seemingly impossible because of that comprehensive passivity now engulfing us, it is nevertheless evoked by the name of God, and by that very name of God which we have now been given.

CHAPTER 2

⁓

Primordial Sacrifice

We know that the deepest and most universal movement of archaic religion is the movement of sacrifice, one which is the ultimate foundation of all cultic ritual, if not the innermost movement of ritual itself, and which can preserve itself even in an abatement or transfiguration of ritual, as in a Confucian *li* or in a tragic plot. Our deepest gestures can be apprehended as echoes of a primordial movement of sacrifice, or are so when they are truly responses to another, responses sanctioning the "other," whom in that very sanction becomes an other who is "for us." It is precisely the deepest and most primordial "other" that is sanctioned in the movement of sacrifice, for the sacrificial victim is ultimately deity itself, and a deity whose ultimate actualization is inseparable from the movement of sacrifice. One could question whether it is possible ever truly or finally to escape a sacrificial movement, or to do so in a genuine moment of life. If this movement occurs again and again in both our deepest and our most common dramatic enactments, is it just thereby that drama is inevitably real for us, and one calling for a ritual response, a ritual response which is a ritual participation, or an anamnesis that is a repetition and renewal of a primordial sacrificial act? Now even when such a primordial act is wholly interiorized in consciousness, as it is in the birth of mysticism throughout the world, it does not thereby lose its original sacrificial movement, but rather realizes it wholly within, and does so in its very emptying or reversal of consciousness itself.

Deep ritual is inseparable from mystery, and even from the most ultimate mystery, and it is just thereby an enactment of mystery, for every true cult is a mystery cult, and every such cult is a continual enactment of sacrifice, and at bottom an enactment of primordial sacrifice. Nothing is more veiled in this mystery than is primordial sacrifice itself, and while its deep power is unquestionable, its actual role in our lives is seemingly impenetrable, just as its profound effect upon our history is so deeply controversial. This is most manifestly true of a uniquely Western culture, and just as Greece and Israel are ultimate sources of that culture, we may discover in each an ultimate conflict between a truly and even absolutely new consciousness and world and a primordial ground or world. In each, regressions to an archaic world occur most powerfully in renewals of primordial sacrifice, and even as Baalism and the mystery cults were a deep threat both to a new Israel and a new Greece, it was only by way of a comprehensive transformation of primordial sacrifice that Greece and Israel each became most uniquely themselves. This is the transformation that has perhaps most challenged our critical understanding both of a new Greece and a new Israel. If our deepest modern discoveries of Greece have occurred in German thinkers and scholars, and above all in Hegel, Nietzsche, and Heidegger, here is unveiled a uniquely Greek *agon* and *ananke*, each inseparable from primordial sacrifice, and just thereby the power of each ultimately challenges our understanding. Yet nowhere else is primordial sacrifice more fully manifest, since an iconoclastic Israel decisively shattered that sacrifice, but no less so because archaic sacrifice throughout the world is so cryptic and elusive to the modern hermeneut.

Greece alone has given us a literature openly embodying primordial sacrifice. This occurs most fully in Greek tragedy, and, as Hegel would teach us, in Greek comedy. Just as tragic enactment was originally and perhaps universally a transposition of ritual or liturgical enactment, the tragic hero or heroine is a sacrificial victim, or is so when tragedy is most fully or most actually itself. Hegel was the first thinker to think deeply about tragedy, for in the perspective of both Hegel and Nietzsche, Aristotle's understanding of tragedy fails to rise above the level of the ancient tragic chorus, and Hegel is our only thinker who could discover a truly tragic ground in both Christianity and Greece. This is precisely the point at which Hegel could understand that the Classical world passes into the Christian world. If Hegel is our only truly modern thinker who could realize a genuine continuity between the Classical and the Christian worlds, it is Hegel and Nietzsche who most deeply understand primordial sacrifice, even as it is the very movement of sacrifice that calls forth their deepest thinking. This is the movement that deeply engages Hegel's attention even in his earliest thinking, but it is only the mature Hegel who realizes a purely conceptual embodiment of primordial sacrifice, for it is the movement of sacrifice or pure or absolute negation which is the deepest center and ground of both the *Phenomenology of Spirit* and the *Science of Logic*.

While the movement of sacrifice occurs throughout the *Phenomenology*, its conclusion most clearly calls forth absolute sacrifice, the Calvary of absolute Spirit, for in absolute knowing the self-knowing Spirit knows not only itself, but also the limit or negative of itself, and to know one's limit or one's inherent negativity is to know how to sacrifice oneself (807). Of course, such

absolute knowing is the consequence of a vast internal and historical movement, one which is most clearly recorded in the history of religion, a movement from primordial religion to the absolute religion of Christianity, yet it
most luminously occurs in Greek religion, or in what Hegel can know as
religion in the form of art. Most revealing here are the Greek mystery cults,
for it was Hegel and not Nietzsche who philosophically discovered Dionysus.
Just as Hegel can declare in the Preface to the *Phenomenology* (47) that the
"True" is the Bacchanalian revel in which no member is not drunk, he can
unveil the Greek mystery cult as the site at which the absolute Idea or Notion
is first decisively unveiled. This occurs in the cultic enactment of the sacrifice
of the mystery god, one wherein the worshiper and the god pass into each
other, and do so by mutually surrendering their distinctive selfhoods or centers. In this sacrifice the human center gives itself to the consciousness of the
divine Being descending to it from its remoteness, and the divine Being
through this act realizes the actuality of self-consciousness (714).

Thus the mystery cults truly were a preparation for Christianity, and not
only a preparation but an actual enactment of the movement of incarnation.
While the mystery cult initially is only a secret fulfillment, or an imaginative
rather than an actual one, it must become an actual deed, one whereby consciousness realizes itself as a pure self-consciousness. Yet this occurs only by
way of the mediation of the sacrifice of the divine Being, descending from
its universality into individuality, and thus becoming united with reality itself
(716). Therefore the act of the mystery cult begins with the pure surrender of
its enactor, one reflecting its individual act into the universal or into the divine
Being, rather than into herself or himself. Conversely, the divine Being perishes in its immediacy in this act, for the sacrifice of the sacrificial victim is
a symbolic and liturgical enactment of the sacrifice of God. That such a
sacrifice is truly possible is only because the divine Being must have already
sacrificed itself *in principle*, for primordial sacrifice is a reenactment or renewal of an absolute sacrifice. If it is not until the Greek mystery cults that
an absolute sacrifice is open and clear, thereby we can know that true sacrifice
is a surrender as complete as is death itself, but this is a renunciation in which
consciousness truly becomes itself, for it is precisely in true sacrifice that
consciousness becomes the unity of itself and its opposite (507).

Hegel is most innovative, however, in his understanding of Greek comedy, a comedy which he alone can know as necessarily calling forth the birth
of Christianity, one wherein an actual self-consciousness exhibits itself as the
fate or the destiny of the gods. Just as the feasting on the sacrificial offering
in the mystery cults unveils the mystery of the gods, comedy is an ironic
unveiling of the gods, but simultaneously a complete emancipation of immediate individuality from a universal order or necessity. In Greek comedy,
there occurs a vanishing of the gods into an evanescent mist, yet now this

necessary and inevitable destiny is united with self-consciousness. The gods vanish in the negative character of this new individual selfhood, but here selfhood is not the negative emptiness of this disappearance, but rather preserves itself in this very nothingness, abiding with itself as its own sole actuality, and thereby the religion of art is consummated and has completely returned into itself (747). No longer is there an unconscious union with the deity, as in the mystery cults. On the contrary, the actual self of the comic actor coincides with what he impersonates, just as the comic spectator is completely at home with this drama, and can know himself or herself as playing within it. Thus comedy is the return of everything universal into self-certainty, wherein there occurs a complete loss of fear and *Angst*. This is a form of self-consciousness over against which there is nothing whatsoever in the form of essence, for here Spirit itself loses its own consciousness (748).

Yet this twilight of the gods issues in the birth of the absolute religion, and the birth of Christianity is the advent of absolute self-consciousness; this advent is inseparable from the individual and historical realization of absolute sacrifice, the Calvary of absolute Spirit. This crucifixion is the absolute self-negation or self-emptying of the Godhead itself, one realizing itself in the deepest depths of consciousness, depths which realize themselves in the full and final advent of the totality of self-consciousness. Here, the individual and historical realization of absolute sacrifice is apocalypse itself, for not only is this sacrifice the center of history, but it is the apocalyptic fulfillment and ending of history, or is so in that absolutely new and final historical destiny which this sacrifice and this sacrifice alone releases. Moreover, this absolute and apocalyptic destiny is now realized as the destiny, and as the necessary and inevitable destiny, of consciousness itself, for the depths of consciousness realize themselves only by way of the internalization and interiorization of this movement of absolute sacrifice. Absolute sacrifice or absolute negation is necessarily realized in the very movement and actuality of consciousness, a consciousness which finally can be itself only by being "for-itself," or only by being identical with its own true opposite or "other."

That which is seemingly most alien to our interior consciousness, the movement of sacrifice, and of an absolute sacrifice, is now unveiled both as our innermost destiny and as the deeper actuality of consciousness itself. Consciousness could not truly be itself apart from this actuality, or it could not be manifest or real as that which is most deeply occurring within ourselves. So far from being passive or quiescent, or from being simply and only itself, true or real consciousness is an ultimate movement or enactment. It embodies an absolute act, and an absolute act which actualizes itself by becoming ever other than itself, by becoming ever other from its own immediacy or givenness, or its own center or "I." Thus it is that the movement of sacrifice is the innermost center and ground of consciousness itself. Indeed, it is absolutely necessary in the calling forth of self-consciousness, a self-consciousness which can truly be itself only by actually realizing its own inherent other. Yet this movement is only possible and real because an absolute sacrifice has already occurred, a sacrifice which is our deepest and most ultimate origin or beginning, and which we necessarily enact by truly or actually becoming ourselves.

At the very least, echoes recording a primordial sacrifice lie deeply buried within ourselves. Freud could discover the unconscious only by discovering the Oedipus complex, a complex which is the consequence of the very advent of consciousness; and this is an advent which is the consequence of a primordial sacrifice. So, too, Nietzsche could discover ressentiment as the consequence of an original repression, an original repression which is a primordial sacrifice, and a sacrifice giving birth to our very interior, and to that interior which we know as the "I" or the center of consciousness. This is the "I" that Nietzsche knows as the "bad conscience," a wholly guilty or wholly repressed "I." This "I" is the very center of a uniquely modern imagination, a doubled or dichotomous "I," one which can act only by acting against itself, or which can realize itself only by negating itself. This self-negation is a self-sacrifice, and thereby one clearly renewing primordial sacrifice. But we must never lose sight of the Hegelian realization that if an actual sacrifice is possible and real for us, and truly actualized in our deeper movements of consciousness, then this is only because the Godhead must have already sacrificed itself, a sacrifice which is our deepest origin and ground.

This ground is ever called forth in our most actual moments, moments which are actual only in their self-negation or their self-emptying. That self-emptying realizes an actual interior emptiness, but that emptiness makes possible a full engagement or a full presence. Here fullness and emptiness are inseparable, as we are fully present only by being fully absent or "other" from ourselves. This is just what we have known as sanctity or sainthood, a sanctity only possible by way of a deep self-emptying, a self-negation or a self-emptying of everything that is simply given to us, or everything that is simply and only ourselves. Therefore sanctity and sacrifice are inseparable. The saint is certainly not a simply natural or simply innocent being, but one who is the consequence of a deep and continual self-emptying, and whose most integral acts embody self-emptying. Saints are neither known nor manifest apart from their acts, and if such acts induce our deepest veneration, and do so even when they occur in seemingly secular realms, we respond to them not simply as moments of true power, but as moments embodying our deepest even if most elusive ground. Hence they inevitably call forth not only veneration but worship, a worship which can only truly be given to Godhead itself, but which is irresistible when we encounter moments of genuine self-emptying. Thereby we are recalled to our ultimate origin, an origin that could only be an absolute sacrifice, but an absolute sacrifice that is an original or primordial sacrifice, and one actually recalled or renewed in our deepest and most actual moments.

Now it is of fundamental importance to realize that we are not simply called to sacrifice, but *recalled* to sacrifice. Only recall can be actual for us. This is a recall to that which has not simply occurred, but has ultimately occurred, an ultimacy actually present when we are recalled to primordial sacrifice. We can observe the power of such recalling simply by noting the sheer intensity of our response to Freud or Nietzsche, or to Dostoyevsky, Kafka, or Beckett, for the very enactment of primordial sacrifice inevitably overwhelms us, and does so most deeply when it is dissociated from our given religious traditions, or our apparent or manifest religious worlds. A pure power is present here which is absent from everything that we can actually know as "God," a power not only irresistible but which we deeply seek. We seek it even knowing its profoundly destructive power, and perhaps precisely because of its ultimately negative power. While that power is seemingly wholly beyond us, it is nevertheless profoundly within us, and even if such power is seemingly unnamable, it calls forth not only our deepest silence, but also our purest speech. While such speech finally defies even our deepest hermeneutics, such a hermeneutics is possible only within the horizon of this speech, only within the horizon of a language that is pure darkness and pure light at once.

If only in the perspective of this challenge, we can be aware of a realm beyond the domain of our existing religious language, certainly beyond anything which we can know as theological language, and even beyond everything which we have been given as mythical language. There are, of course, ancient myths calling forth primordial sacrifice as the original event of creation, but these have been dissipated in our religious traditions, and above all in our monotheistic traditions, wherein an original sacrificial movement has been wholly transformed into an act of absolute power. We now know that this profound transformation occurred in the original exile of Israel, although it was inaugurated by the prophetic revolution itself. This revolution is inseparable from an absolute negation of archaic religion, and therewith a negation of primordial sacrifice, even if this is a negation that preserves and transcends that sacrifice which it negates. Yet not until exile does Israel know Yahweh as that creator who alone is the Creator. It is also not until the exile that Israel transforms an archaic sacrificial cultus into the writing of the Torah, thus giving birth for the first time to scripture itself. It is scripture which most disguises primordial sacrifice, even if that sacrifice remains a deep although hidden ground of scripture, and most hidden in the very advent of a pure and total monotheism.

Deep traces of this ultimate transformation are recorded in the Bible, and perhaps most clearly in the Book of Job, surely the most radical and heretical book in the Bible. Even if its original text was deeply transformed by priestly editors, it remains inexplicable how this book could have become canonical. The Creator or El Shaddai of the great bulk of the Book of Job is the God of absolute power and absolute power alone, or that God who is Creator and only Creator, wholly divorced from everything that Israel knew as hope and redemption, and therein divorced from the covenantal and legal traditions of Israel. Only this divorce makes possible the final epiphany of the Creator to Job. All too significantly now the name of the Creator is Yahweh and not El Shaddai, but a Yahweh deeply isolated from everything that Israel had previously known as Yahweh, as this Yahweh appears out of the deepest and most ultimate void. Now every possible myth and ritual is annulled. While this is a genuine resolution of the deep tragedy of Job, it is wholly divorced from the dramatic dialogues of the book, just as it is divorced from every possible human response, except the response of absolute submission, a submission which is an ultimate silence, and the only such silence recorded in scripture. But this is a silence inseparable from an epiphany of absolute power, as the liturgical movement of sacrifice is now transformed into its very opposite, and the act of God can now be known and realized only as an act of absolute power and absolute power alone.

No major Biblical book is more absent from the New Testament than is the Book of Job, although there are Christian hermeneuts who can know Paul as a reborn Job. Paul would appear to be truly Jobean in knowing the absolute wrath and the absolute judgment of God, for even if this judgment is now an apocalyptic judgment, here it is only the God of absolute No-saying who can be truly known apart from what Paul knows as faith in Christ. Historically, Paul's genuine letters are extraordinarily important, for not only do they give us the first ancient record of a full and genuine self-consciousness, but the Pauline "I" is wholly divided against itself, torn asunder by an ultimate conflict between the "I" of *sarx* or "flesh" and the "I" of *pneuma* or Spirit, this conflict is the consequence of what Paul knows as the ultimacy of the Crucifixion, an absolute sacrifice which is the one source of redemption or justification. Now it is just the interior realization of that sacrifice which issues in the advent of the Pauline "I," or even in the full and final advent of self-consciousness itself. Hegel is the deepest modern disciple of Paul, and Augustine his deepest ancient disciple, for it was Augustine and Hegel who realized revolutionary understandings of self-consciousness, and did so as genuinely Pauline thinkers.

Yet it is Hegel who most deeply knows the revolutionary advent of self-consciousness as the consequence of the full and final enactment of an absolute sacrifice. This absolute sacrifice inaugurates the third and final age of the Spirit, but an age of the Spirit which is the consummation of all previous history, and most clearly so a consummation of the history of religion, which has always been an anamnesis or renewal of primordial sacrifice. This sacrifice is most deeply why Christ is the primordial Logos, a primordial Word embodying the primordial sacrifice—a sacrifice lying beyond our mythical and theological horizons—and it is just when this Word is evoked apart from such horizons that it releases its deepest power. This is a power doubtless present in the Eucharist, just as it is in every genuine act of sacrifice, but we have no theology unveiling such a power in the Eucharist, just as we have no literary theory unveiling the power released by literary enactments of sacrifice. For it is ritual itself which is most unknown in our hermeneutics, ritual which is the deepest cipher in all our languages of understanding. The pure ritual act would appear to lie beyond all language whatsoever, unless it is captured in an anti-language, a reversal of all existing language, and a reversal recovering or recalling a primal rite, the rite or ritual of primordial sacrifice.

Hence the deepest recall is one recalling us to the deepest primordial act, this is that act which is "the beginning," a beginning which is certainly not a primordial paradise, a paradise which we have wholly lost, and thus one beyond all possibility of recall. Nor is our longing for death, as Freud believed, a longing for an original inorganic condition, or a longing for nothingness. It is far rather a longing for a deep and ultimate enactment, an enactment which occurs in primordial sacrifice, a sacrifice whose plant or animal or human sacrifice is ultimately the sacrifice of deity itself. For it is the "blood" of this sacrifice that is the deepest source of what we most deeply know as an ultimate or absolute power. We have long known, and above all since Durkheim, that it is ritual sacrifice in all its forms that most deeply sustains or grounds society. Deep breakdowns of society almost invariably issue in orgies of violence that can be understood as compulsive repetitions of primordial sacrifice. If the terror of our deeper political revolutions is just such a compulsive repetition, this is a terror occurring in the very advent of our most secular societies, thus all too ironically recording the genuine universality of primordial sacrifice. Repression itself can be understood as a consequence of primordial sacrifice, as it is in the great modern discoverers of repression, Nietzsche and Freud, a primordial sacrifice which is our most primordial act, and not only a primordial but an ultimate act, an act which our deepest and purest ritual calls forth as the act of Godhead itself.

This is that one act in which human and divine action are wholly conjoined. While our deepest mysticism calls forth such a union, it does so by way of an interiorization of primordial sacrifice, just as our deepest tragedy enacts a comparable union by its very enactment of primordial sacrifice. The ultimate *agon* of the tragic hero or heroine is a conflict with the depths of the divine realm itself, just as the *ananke* of a tragic destiny is a movement of primordial sacrifice, and one wherein the tragic victim is the very embodiment of sacrificial deity. Once we grasp such a movement as the very essence of tragic action, then we can understand that tragedy has not died in the fullness of modernity, it has rather become even more deeply interiorized, finally culminating in the dissolution of self-consciousness itself, which can be understood as a sacrificial and therefore tragic dissolution.

Precisely in this fulfillment, however, a primordial sacrifice is even more open and clear than it is in classical tragedy. Now the tragic stage returns as a full sanctuary, a sanctuary enacting a pure sacrifice, but now a sanctuary in which every actual trace of deity has disappeared, or every deity has disappeared which is not the very act of sacrifice and of sacrifice alone. Hence the paradox that our most deeply modern literature and drama is sacred and profane at once; purely sacred in its deepest enactment, yet purely profane in its horizon and world; deeply atheistic in its language and imagery, and yet deeply sacred in its ultimate enactments, enactments it is true which are deeply negative enactments, and precisely thereby embodiments of primordial sacrifice.

Once we realize this, we can recognize that there are depths for us beyond what we can know as God, and if the God whom we actually know is the consequence of repression, this could well be the consequence of the repression of primordial sacrifice. And this could very well be a repression which is released or abated in our deeper moments, moments in which we recall primordial sacrifice, and thereby renew or reenact that sacrifice. "God" is then truly absent for us, but only because primordial Godhead is recalled, but a Godhead which is the absolute act of sacrifice, and an act which we reenact in our deepest moments of recall. All such moments are the very opposite of passive moments, the opposite of a pure quiescence or a pure innocence, and thus the opposite of everything that a mythical language and symbolism can know as paradise. This is a paradise that is dislodged by the deeper movements of ritual action, just as it is in our deeper moments, and if it is the very act of death or sacrifice which is the deepest ritual act, this is an act immediately dissolving or reversing everything that we can know as a mythical or religious realm, or everything that we can imagine as paradise. Deep ritual is inevitably offensive to the world in which it is enacted, it releases a power going far beyond everything that we can understand, just as it disrupts every human sanction and rule.

No greater assault upon priestly power and cultic ritual has ever occurred than in the prophetic revolution of Israel, yet the prophetic call can be understood as a ritual call. All too significantly the fullest Biblical account of a prophetic call occurs in the recording of the original vision of Isaiah (Isa. 6), when Isaiah sees the Lord sitting on a throne in the Temple, with seraphs above Him chanting, "Holy, holy, holy is Yahweh Sabaoth." Isaiah is cleansed and forgiven when one of the seraphs touches his mouth with a live burning coal which it has taken from the altar, whereupon Yahweh calls Isaiah to his prophetic vocation, and does so with the injunction that he must speak to his people so that they cannot possibly understand, making the mind of the people dull, stopping their ears and shutting their eyes, lest they comprehend with their minds and repent and be healed. Who could imagine a more offensive calling, or a greater assault upon all understanding? Yet this is the very prophetic call that the synoptic gospels record as being renewed in Jesus. We know that Jesus did speak in a language that his people, and even his disciples, could not possibly understand, and did so in his parables, parables transformed by the synoptic gospels, and transformed by so fully diluting their original offense, the original challenge of the parables. Nevertheless, it is clear that this is a challenge to lose oneself, to sacrifice oneself, but now a sacrifice occurring not in a cultic act but in the actuality of the world itself. Of course, this is also true in the original prophetic oracles, but Jesus' parabolic language is a far more common language than is the language of those oracles, indeed, it is the most common or prosaic language ever employed by a prophet, and it calls for an ultimate enactment in the brute immediacy of our actual lives. This very call is an ultimate offense, and even as it occurs in a wholly common or vernacular language, it calls for an absolute enactment in the sheer immediacy of our most common acts, and the enactment for which it calls is sacrifice itself, but now a sacrifice occurring in a sanctuary which is the world.

Nevertheless, this very call for sacrifice, and for an absolute sacrifice, as so clearly manifest in the Sermon on the Mount, realizes the ritual action of sacrifice, but now sacrifice is fully incarnate in world itself, and in the brute immediacy of the world. All of the parables of Jesus are parables of the Kingdom of God, a kingdom that in the eschatological proclamation of Jesus is immediately at hand. While in the parables themselves the Kingdom of God is silent and unspoken, it nonetheless is spoken in that silence, and spoken in a parabolic language and action calling for an immediate enactment of the Kingdom of God. That kingdom is not the "rule" or the "reign" or the "sovereignty" of God, but rather a reversal of all such power, a reversal which is the sacrifice of God, a sacrifice enacted in the ritual action of primordial sacrifice, but now enacted in the most common events of life itself. Hence the parables of Jesus are profoundly offensive to their hearer, but incredibly powerful in that very offense. This power is seemingly irresistible to its real hearer, but is inevitably lost or reversed when it is respoken in a traditional or established language, and above all so when it is respoken in the traditional language of religion. This is just what occurs in the synoptic gospels, so that only a deep deconstruction of the language of the gospels could call forth anything echoing the original power of the parables, and thereby the parables become most offensive to everything that we know as "God."

The New Testament itself is most deeply centered in the Crucifixion, a crucifixion which passes into ritual action in the Eucharist, which is itself centered in an *anamnesis* or renewal of the Crucifixion (I Cor. 11:24), just as

the Crucifixion is the very center of Paul's eschatological proclamation. Yet
this is the very crucifixion which is never embodied in the dominant expressions of Christian theology, a theology refusing the death of God in the
Crucifixion, and thus a theology annulling the absolute sacrifice of the
Crucifixion, and annulling it by knowing only the absolute sovereignty and
the absolute transcendence of God. All such theology is inevitably closed to
the parables of Jesus, or can know the parables only as allegories of an
eternal regeneration or deification, thereby fully reversing the parables, a
process already beginning in the synoptic gospels. What is most reversed here
is the actual movement of sacrifice or self-negation, for now the destiny of
the believer is wholly in the beyond, in the absolute glory of Heaven and
Heaven alone. Just as the Christ of Passion thereby becomes the Christ of
Glory, the Christian is eternally elected to that glory, a glory that is the very
opposite of sacrifice or crucifixion. Nothing could so deeply veil or reverse
primordial sacrifice, and if that sacrifice now becomes confined to cultic
action, or to the lives of the saints whose sanctity is precisely their
otherworldliness, or to the devotion of the faithful whose piety lies wholly in
an interior feeling, it would be difficult to imagine a greater reversal of Jesus,
or a greater reversal of primordial sacrifice.

If the deepest power of Catholicism lies in the Eucharist, and the deepest
power of Protestantism in its purely eschatological proclamation, then the
deepest power of literature may well lie in its most immediate or most actual
language, and thereby in that language that is most distant from a non-literary
language. Even if the purest language of a Kafka or a Beckett is literary and
non-literary at once, it thereby realizes a realism wholly beyond our common
language, and just as Kafka was the first writer to discover a truly parabolic
language, this is a language that is overwhelmingly realistic to us, and realistic as absolute judgment, a judgment that first passes into a common language
in the parables of Jesus. Such judgment can be understood as a primordial
sacrifice, as it certainly was by Kafka himself, a sacrifice continually enacted
in his writing, and a sacrifice which is a primal source of the power of his
writing, even as it is a primal source of the power of Beckett's writing. If only
through the writing of a Beckett or a Kafka, we can gain some awareness of
the original power of the parables of Jesus, and it is just because this is a purely
negative power that it can be so immediately overwhelming. If Jesus had a
greater impact upon his hearer than did any previous prophet or speaker, we can
thereby understand his language as a purely negative language, as primordial
sacrifice passes into the pure immediacy of speech itself.

Thus that crucifixion which is the destiny of Jesus is already being
realized in his eschatological and parabolic speech, and if an absolutely new
actuality is thereby born, one which Hegel could understand as absolute self-
consciousness, this is a self-consciousness that is fully united with its opposite, an absolutely new life which is an absolutely new death, and precisely

thereby an absolute recall or anamnesis of primordial sacrifice. Thus it is an absolute anamnesis of absolute sacrifice, the sacrifice of Godhead itself, one foreshadowed by the mystery cults and by Greek tragedy, and even foreshadowed in the whole world of ancient and primordial religion, but only fully and actually occurring in that Jesus who is the primordial Word, or that word which is the absolute and final renewal of primordial sacrifice. So it is that Jesus is the ultimate Victim, that victim whose life *is* death, so that we can never truly recall him as a man or a person. Even if this is true of every ancient hero, only in Jesus can we recall an absolutely singular or unique event, an event that is called forth in every actual sacrifice, in every actual and final perishing or loss. Thus Jesus is the name of absolute sacrifice, and the name of primordial sacrifice when it becomes fully actual and real, and even if Jesus is a universal humanity, such a humanity could only be a sacrificial victim, and a sacrificial victim precisely in its deepest actualization.

Hegel was not alone in understanding the fullness of self-consciousness as the consequence of an original fall, an original self-negation or self-emptying of absolute Spirit. The seeds for this deeply modern understanding of self-consciousness were established by Augustine's new understanding of the original fall, one which is the origin of the full actualization of the individual will. Even if that will as a fallen will is a purely negative will, it is precisely in the abasement or breaking of that will that a redemptive grace occurs, a redemptive grace that is an eternally predestined grace, and inseparable as such from an original fall that is a *felix culpa* or "fortunate fall." Just as Augustine could deeply conjoin and unite predestination and freedom, for it is predestination alone which makes freedom possible, even as our freedom is an inexplicable mystery apart from predestination, the full actualization of our freedom is the actualization of original sin, hence the profound negativity of our fallen will. Not until Nietzsche does predestination pass into a full philosophical understanding, and does so in Nietzsche's understanding of the origin of self-consciousness or the deeply interior "I," an origin that is the origin of ressentiment, a ressentiment which is an absolute No-saying, and an absolute No-saying most deeply directed against itself. This is that No-saying whose true opposite is an absolute Yes-saying, a Yes-saying which is the absolute affirmation of Eternal Recurrence, and a Yes-saying wholly transcending the No-saying of ressentiment, but one only possible by an actual reversal of that No-saying. This is why Nietzsche is the most deeply Augustinian of modern thinkers, and is so precisely in understanding the total negativity of the individual will, but a negativity absolutely essential for a reversal of that will.

Augustine knows that reversal as an absolute grace only made possible by an absolute predestination. But Nietzsche knows an absolute predestination as an absolute eternal recurrence, one wholly reversing the individual will. Even as an Augustinian grace wholly reverses the fallen will, a fallen will born in original sin, the interior "I" for Nietzsche is born in an original repression. For both Augustine and Nietzsche, our interior "I" is born in an original self-negation, but it is precisely because this is a predestined self-negation that it is a liberating or redemptive self-negation, and even if an original repression or an original self-negation expands and deepens itself as interiority evolves, the very self-lacerations of this repression are clearly a renewal of an original repression or fall. But so likewise are they a renewal of an ultimate primordial sacrifice, one occurring in the very advent of repression or self-negation. A repression is an absolutely self-negating act, but just therein a sacrificial act, even if this act can only truly be known or realized as a sacrificial act through an absolute affirmation of either predestination or eternal recurrence.

Nietzsche and Hegel, above all other thinkers, could understand an absolutely self-negating act as an absolutely sacrificial act. Nietzsche could reverse Hegel's understanding of self-consciousness by understanding it as an absolutely negative self-consciousness, but an ultimate and final negativity only revealed or made manifest by the final and irreversible death of God. This irreversible death of God is unknown to Hegel, who finally knows the death of God as the resurrection of God. Thus it is Nietzsche, and not Hegel, who most deeply knows the absolute sacrifice of God, and an absolute sacrifice of God unveiling the absolute negativity of the "I" of self-consciousness, for once the irreversible death of God has wiped away our whole horizon, and we are now straying as through an infinite nothing, an absolute groundlessness is our own, and is our own most deeply in our deepest center. Only now can we know our "I" as the "I" of ressentiment, of a pure No-saying, and that No-saying actualizes itself in an absolute and final self-negation, but a self-negation alone making possible an absolute act of Yes-saying. Yet is this not an actual understanding of an original and absolute self-sacrifice, and as an absolute sacrifice the sacrifice of Godhead itself, that very Godhead which Nietzsche could understand as the absolute and total No-saying of God, but a total No-saying most deeply and most profoundly directed against itself? Hence such No-saying is inseparable from the actual sacrifice of God, and equally inseparable from the sacrifice of ourselves. Further, if that sacrifice is only fully possible when we fully and finally realize ourselves as an absolute negativity, that is the very negativity which Augustine discovered as the one and only way to an absolutely redemptive grace.

The truth is that Hegel's philosophical discovery of an absolute self-negation, and a self-negation or a self-emptying which *is* absolute Spirit, was a profound renewal of the Crucifixion. Nietzsche's discovery of an ultimate *coincidentia oppositorum* between an absolute Yes-saying and an absolute No-saying was equally a renewal of the Crucifixion, and at no other point is there a deeper coincidence between Hegelian and Nietzschean thinking. Moreover, both Hegel and Nietzsche are deeply Augustinian thinkers. Each centered their thinking upon self-consciousness, a self-consciousness philosophically and theologically discovered by Augustine, and whereas Hegel's understanding of self-consciousness is wholly positive and Nietzsche's wholly negative, this polarity is first present in an Augustinian philosophical and theological revolution, a deep polarity which finally breaks asunder in full modernity. Yet that is the very crisis fully calling forth a primordial sacrifice, one fully called forth in the deepest expressions of our imagination, and in the deepest of expressions of our thinking, too, and so much so that we can only evade the ultimacy of primordial sacrifice by stilling our mind and imagination.

Surely the profound self-negation which we have come to know is in deep continuity with primordial sacrifice, but would it even be possible apart from an original and absolute primordial sacrifice? Certainly not for either a Freud or a Nietzsche, and certainly not for Hegel as well, and all of these thinkers are united in centering their thinking upon the renewal or recall or anamnesis of that sacrifice. Only such an anamnesis could be a source of light in our darkness, and it is just such an anamnesis that releases our deepest power. True, this could only be a wholly negative power, but it is just thereby an anamnesis of primordial sacrifice, and even an anamnesis of the "blood" of that sacrifice, a blood that in the consecrated bread and wine of the Eucharist is the very body of the Crucified God. Just as that body could only be a sacrificial body, the deepest recall can only be the recall of an absolute primordial sacrifice, and a sacrifice enacted in us in the very moment of this recall. Nothing else could account for the overwhelming power of tragedy for us, a tragic power that is deepest in its purest negativity, but only such negativity could have a profoundly transforming effect. Our participation in tragedy is a truly liturgical participation, a participation in deep ritual action, a ritual action which is the tragic plot, and which is clearly a renewal or anamnesis of primordial sacrifice.

The catharsis that the sacrificial action of the tragedy effects is a catharsis of our deepest negativity, because this action is the repetition and renewal of the primordial sacrifice of God. If the tragic hero or heroine is a face or mask of sacrificial deity, it is our participation in that tragic destiny that effects catharsis, and thereby tragic action as such is eucharistic action, and is so precisely by being an anamnesis of primordial sacrifice. So it is that anamnesis is not simply and only a cultic reenactment, or, if so, it is a cultic reenactment which is a universal reenactment or renewal. At no other point is primordial sacrifice more fully manifest as a universal sacrifice, and a universal sacrifice which is a *recalling* of primordial sacrifice, and of that primordial sacrifice which is an absolute sacrifice. That is the sacrifice which is most inescapable in our actual lives, or that absolute and primordial act which we have most deeply repressed, and if it returns in our deeper moments and our deeper acts, it returns as a truly negative power, but nevertheless a negative power which is a transfiguring power, and transfiguring precisely as an absolutely sacrificial act.

Only in primordial sacrifice are we given an archetype of a purely negative power which is nonetheless and precisely thereby an ultimately transfiguring power, and if sacrifice is the most universal movement in the history of religions, and one preserved even if transcended in our great religious revolutions, primordial sacrifice is thereby a deep and ultimate ground, perhaps our deepest ground. While that ground can be and has been known as the deepest ground of repression, as the deepest ground of an absolute No-saying, it and it alone can be truly reversed in an absolute Yes-saying, a Yes-saying impossible and unreal apart from such a reversal. So that not only is an absolute Yes-saying inseparable from an absolute No-saying, but an absolute No-saying is precisely thereby inseparable from an absolute Yes-saying, so that when we truly recall primordial sacrifice we just thereby recall or renew an absolute transfiguration. This is just the movement occurring in a genuine anamnesis, or in a pure movement of ritual, a ritual movement deeper than all mythical imagery and action, and more universal than any possible mythical language. If religious revolutions commonly effect a genuine demythologizing, a genuine "deritualizing" is simply impossible, or can occur only insofar as ritual itself is either veiled or disguised. While it is true that ritual can be deeply interiorized, as it is in mysticism throughout the world, this can certainly be understood as a deepening rather than a dissolution of ritual, and all too significantly a genuinely mystical movement is inevitably a sacrificial movement, although now the transfiguring power of ritual is open and clear.

Mystical movements are commonly if not universally a return to a primordial power, and to a primordial power of regeneration or re-creation. Here a primordial movement of eternal return is deeply interiorized, even if this occurs by way of a reversal or dissolution of consciousness itself. Such a reversal occurs in all full participation in ritual action, just as every ritual movement is at the very least a shadow or reflection of the primordial movement of eternal return. Thus ritual action is necessarily both circular and cyclic, for it is an anamnesis of a primordial eternal return. Yet that eternal return is regeneration itself, and a cosmic or universal regeneration, but a regeneration occurring only through primordial sacrifice, or only through a primordial "death." That is the death that is renewed in our deepest and purest ritual, hence such ritual is inevitably a sacrificial ritual, and if it thereby renews primordial sacrifice, that is a renewal that is regeneration. So it is that the Christian Eucharist is a renewal of a universal mass or sacrifice, and while the destruction of the Temple ended cultic sacrifice in Judaism, it seemingly deepened it in Christianity. If nothing is more powerful in the patristic Church than eucharistic sacrifice, it is here that salvation or eternal life in that church is most open and manifest. The eucharistic action is a movement of anamnesis or renewal—the renewal of the Crucifixion, yes, but just thereby an anamnesis of primordial sacrifice, and if only here Christianity knows the Crucifixion as primordial sacrifice.

Hence the extraordinary importance of the very movement of *recall*, a recall that is certainly not remembrance, it is far too deep for that and it ultimately recalls a primordial event, one going beyond any possible memory, or any possible conscious memory. If our deepest memory could only be an unconscious memory, it can only be recalled through a purely negative act. Certainly anamnesis is such an act, or is so in its ritual movement of sacrifice; if anamnesis is remembrance, it is a remembrance of the deepest sacrifice, and yet the ultimacy of this sacrifice issues in a pure joy, and a joy inseparable from the very violence of sacrifice, indeed, from the very horror of sacrifice. Just as Easter can only be celebrated as the consummation of Holy Week, Easter is inseparable from the Passion of Good Friday, and that is the passion which is the center of the Eucharist. Only the anamnesis of that passion makes possible for the Christian a participation in eternal life; thereby the Christian knows an absolute sacrifice as eternal life, an eternal life which thereby is regeneration, and a regeneration which is primordial regeneration, and therefore primordial sacrifice. Thus primordial sacrifice is the deepest center of Christianity, and it is just thereby that Christianity is the expression of a universal movement and world. Nowhere is Christian universality more manifest than in the Eucharist, and most purely so in the anamnesis of the Eucharist, an anamnesis which is a truly universal anamnesis, for nothing is more universal in our world than is primordial sacrifice.

$\backsim$

Primordial Evil

Perhaps evil is the most ultimate of all mysteries. Evil finally defies the comprehension of all our philosophies and theologies, and above all so when it is understood as being quite simply nothingness, and precisely thereby is not finally understood at all. At no point is Western thinking more distant from Eastern thinking than in its refusal of the problem or mystery of evil. In Western thinking, it is as though evil is quite simply an illusion, or at best a pure ignorance, an ignorance or illusion wholly dissolved in pure thinking. As opposed to Eastern thinking, such ignorance or illusion cannot be deep or ultimate, cannot be possible in a purely logical or purely rational thinking. Thereby, too, Western thinking is deeply opposed to the Western imagination, and at no point is Western literature more distinctive or unique than in its centering upon an ultimate or absolute evil, an evil fully opaque to the Western mind, or is so until the full advent of modernity. German Idealism was the first philosophy fully to incorporate the Western imagination, and all too significantly it is in German Idealism that there is first drawn forth a conceptual understanding of the actuality of evil, one decisively occurring in Schelling and Hegel. Heidegger regarded Schelling's *Treatise on Freedom* as the acme of the metaphysics of German Idealism, a metaphysics which is a "system of freedom" as present in Schelling's treatise, but here an absolute freedom is present only in God, and present only in the becoming of that Godhead that strives against the "darkness" or "evil" of itself. This is a darkness which Schelling can speak of as "that within God which is not *God himself*" (359), but it is the very ground of God's existence, and one releasing a primordial longing to give birth to itself.

Here, as elsewhere, Schelling is under the deep impact of Eckhart and Boehme, and can even speak of that "Nothing" which has long since been the cross of reason (373 n. 2), a "Nothing" which is the second principle of darkness or the spirit of evil, for it transcends that dark principle that had

31

made possible the original creation. In God, too, there would be a depth of darkness if He did not make it His own and unite it with Himself, and it is this union which makes possible both the love and the glorification of God (399). This is that love which is the absolute freedom of God, but it is finally a human freedom, too, or is so when we exist "in God" (347). Hegel differed most deeply from Schelling in realizing an absolute negativity as the very center of his thinking, a center making possible the first philosophical under-standing of the death of God, and while Hegel follows Augustine and Chris-tian tradition in understanding evil as a withdrawal into self-centeredness, he wholly transcends that tradition in understanding this withdrawal as occurring *from the beginning* in the "externalization" and "alienation" of the Divine Being. For Absolute Being becomes its own "other," thereby it withdraws into itself and becomes self-centered or "evil"; but this is that self-alienation which leads to death, a death which is the death of the abstraction or alienation or "evil" of the Divine Being (*Phenomenology of Spirit*, 778–80). So it is that Hegel can understand the "Bad Infinite" or Abstract Spirit as the consequence of God's own self-alienation, an alienation which is an absolute self-alienation, and one which is the ultimate ground of all alienation. Hence even in the *Science of Logic* Hegel can unveil all abstract spirit as "Evil" (I, One. 3, c).

Now it is truly remarkable that so little attention is given to evil in Western philosophy. One could search in vain in our philosophical dictionar-ies and encyclopedias for a serious treatment of evil, and in the twentieth century (as opposed to the nineteenth century), no major philosopher has even examined the question of evil as such. This is despite the fact that, in our common understanding, evil has never been so incarnate as it has been in the twentieth century. So, too, the twentieth-century imagination has far more profoundly and more comprehensively been immersed in an absolute evil or abyss or nothingness than all previous expressions of the imagination. Whereas Dante's *Inferno* is inseparable from the *Purgatorio* and the *Paradiso*, and Milton's *Paradise Lost* is inseparable from an apocalyptic redemption, the redemptive moments of a uniquely twentieth-century imagination can only be realized in the depths of darkness or abyss. Is our darkness so deep that it defies all conceptual understanding whatsoever, and is this the reason why the question of evil is perhaps our most forbidden question, that very question which embodies a truly apocalyptic darkness?

Finally, the question of evil is inseparable from the question of the origin of evil. The Christian symbol that most clearly illuminates this question is the *felix culpa* or the "fortunate fall," one deeply reborn in the very advent of modernity, as epically enacted in *Paradise Lost*. Here, only an original fall makes possible redemption, or an apocalyptic redemption, and not only an original but a total fall, a total fall whose dialectical correlate is a total redemption. This is a symbolic core underlying Hegel's dialectical philosophy, too, for only an original or primordial self-negation or self-emptying of Spirit makes possible the evolution or self-realization of Spirit itself, one wholly alienating Spirit from itself, as the "in-itself" and the "for-itself" of Spirit become wholly divided and self-estranged, and yet this is the very condition that makes possible a reconciliation of Spirit with itself. This is the reconciliation that Hegel could know as "theodicy," and an absolutely necessary theodicy, one wherein "evil" or an absolute self-division and self-estrangement are absolutely necessary for apocalypse. This apocalypse is the absolute transfiguration of Spirit, one wholly and absolutely transcending the totality of an original or primordial Spirit, and only the self-negation or the self-emptying of that totality makes possible such an absolute transfiguration of Spirit itself.

In the perspective of the history of religions, nothing is more distinctive of the New Testament than the role therein of an ultimate or absolute evil, just as it is the New Testament and not the Hebrew Bible which openly and clearly speaks of Satan, damnation, and Hell, even as Jesus is the first prophet who is recorded as both naming and engaging in an ultimate conflict with Satan, a conflict inseparable from his eschatological proclamation and enactment of the Kingdom of God. Inevitably Christianity realized a totality of damnation or eternal death which was previously unknown in the world. As Nietzsche knew so deeply, only Christianity embodies a total guilt or a total ressentiment, and if this makes possible a realization of the depths of sin and the fall, it likewise calls forth full visions of Satan and Hell which are unique to Christianity, unless they are called forth in such historical consequences of Christianity as Gnosticism and Islam. But so also are they called forth in a post-Classical Western literature, and above all so in full modernity, which if only at this point is in manifest continuity with ancient and medieval Christianity, and far more so than is modern Christian theology. Our only modern theology that is fully directed to the question of damnation is Karl Barth's *Church Dogmatics*, but it denies the very possibility of damnation as a consequence of Christ's atoning death: "By permitting the life of a rejected man to be the life of His own Son, God has made such a life objectively impossible for all others" (II, 2, 346). Would it be possible to imagine a theology more fully removed from our deepest imaginative realizations?

Almost immediately in Christian history an apocalyptic Kingdom of God was transformed into the absolute sovereignty and the absolute transcendence of God. Theologically this could be known as the absolute passivity and the absolute immutability of God, a "simplicity" of God foreclosing all possibility of an actual transfiguration of Godhead itself, thereby making impossible the "death" or transfiguration of Godhead in the Crucifixion. True, Paul could know such a "death," and know it as the deepest ground of a truly new faith, but when Pauline thinking passes into a full theological understanding in

Augustine, death can only be a human and never a divine actuality. Although Augustine can declare in his treatise on the Trinity that it is correct to speak even of "God being crucified," but only owing to the weakness of our flesh and not to the power of the Godhead (I: 28). Perhaps Luther's discovery of the ultimacy of this "death" was his most revolutionary act, but such a death does not fully pass into pure thinking until Hegel, and then it creates a genuine philosophical revolution, one revolving about an absolute negativity, and an absolute negativity that is finally the source of all movement and life.

Yet absolute negativity can also be known as absolute evil, and even if an Hegelian negativity is absolutely positive and absolutely negative at once, this is the first time that absolute evil enters pure thinking itself, a presence making possible the first philosophical understanding of the death of God. Now it is of extraordinary significance that it is not until the advent of modernity that either thinking or the imagination can either know or envision the death of God. If imaginatively this first occurs in *Paradise Lost*, here the atoning death of Christ cannot be envisioned as the death of Godhead itself, which is perhaps the deepest reason for Milton's Arianism. Nevertheless, it is only the Son of God's free acceptance of death that calls forth an ultimate epiphany in which the Son is manifest as being most glorious; in him all his Father shines substantially, and in his face "Divine compassion visibly appear'd," and an infinite love and grace (3: 138–42). While Milton refused to envision the deity of the Son as being equal to the absolute deity of the Almighty, the Son as the newly anointed King of Heaven shares an eternal bliss that is equal to the Father's. This is just the bliss that the Son abandons to save the world from utter loss, so that the Messiah is more by merit than by birthright the Son of God, and in response to the Son's free acceptance of crucifixion the Almighty can declare that in the Son love has abounded more than glory, and his humiliation will exalt his incarnate humanity so that here shall reign "Both God and Man, Son both of God and Man, anointed universal King; all Power I give thee, reign forever" (3: 315–18). Hence an apocalyptic glory is only made possible by the crucifixion, wherein eternal death is transfigured into an apocalyptic eternal life, but only by the absolute humiliation and death of the Son of God.

Already in *Paradise Lost* we may discover a full coincidence of eternal death and eternal life, one which can be understood as a rebirth and renewal of the New Testament itself, for it had largely if not wholly been dissolved by the great body of Christian tradition. So it is that Luther could respond to that tradition as a demonic transformation of the Christ of Passion into the Christ of Glory, and thus as a dissolution of the Crucifixion itself, or a transformation of crucifixion into resurrection, and hence an annulment of the death of Christ. In his deeper faith and thinking, Luther could know the death of God in the Crucifixion, which is precisely why this crucifixion is Crucifixion, but this realization is lost in Protestant dogmatics, until it is clearly called forth dogmatically for the first time in Milton's *De Doctrina Christiana*. If only at this crucial point, *Paradise Lost* and *De Doctrina Christiana* are in full correlation with each other, thereby a totality of death and of eternal death is called forth for the first time in the Christian imagination. Not only is this enactment a decisive sign of the full advent of a uniquely modern world, but a modern world unreal and unrealized apart from a journey through eternal death.

Dante's *Inferno* is the initial germination of this new world, for not until the *Inferno* does a deep and eternal darkness enter the Western imagination. Just as this darkness is absolutely essential to the ultimate transfiguration of the *Purgatorio* and the *Paradiso*, so likewise is such a darkness essential to everything which we have actually known as reconciliation or rebirth. Unlike all comparable enactments in the ancient world, or in the pre-Christian world, eternal life is realized only through eternal death. Here, not only is eternal death absolute evil itself, but it is only through such death that absolute evil is namable or manifest. While absolute evil may well have first penetrated the horizon of consciousness in the birth of apocalypticism in ancient Iran, it was only a fully developed apocalypticism in Hellenistic Judaism that brought forth a purely negative dichotomy between the kingdom of light and the kingdom of darkness, and only the birth of Christianity that called forth an eternal life that is realized only through eternal death. Only then is Hell fully namable as Hell, or Satan fully namable as Satan, and if these are truly apocalyptic realizations, they are possible only by way of the full advent of what Jesus alone could name and enact as the Kingdom of God.

Such a dialectical coincidence of eternal life and eternal death can truly be known as a *coincidentia oppositorum*. Even if a *coincidentia oppositorum* is universal in the history of religions, it is deeply muted—if not dissolved— in the great body of Western religious tradition, and this despite the fact that it lies at the very origin of Christianity, just as it was resurrected or renewed in the very advent of modernity. This is a coincidence unknown to all of our theologians, but it was deeply known by Hegel and imaginatively enacted by Blake. If both Blake and Hegel are consequences of a deeply Western mystical tradition, this is most clearly manifest in their enactments of a dialectical identity of eternal life and eternal death, but one only possible by way of an absolute opposition between the opposing polarities of a wholly self-divided or self-estranged Godhead. Already Lurianic Kabbalism knows a self-contraction or *tzimtzum* of primordial Godhead or *En Sof*, even as Boehme knows an ultimate opposition between the light and the darkness of the Godhead, an opposition only possible through the self-division of Godhead itself. Both Blake and Hegel were profoundly affected by a Boehmian tradition, and perhaps by a Kabbalistic tradition as well, and above all so in knowing a deep self-division or self-alienation in Godhead itself, one wholly opposed to the theological traditions of the West, and to Western philosophical tradition as well.

Now this is just the context that makes possible a renewal or even discovery of absolute evil, yet here absolute evil is inseparable from absolute good, even as eternal death is inseparable from eternal life. If the mature and revolutionary Blake could envision God as Satan, just as Hegel could know the orthodox Christian God as the "Bad Infinite" or Abstract Spirit or a pure "Being-in-Itself" wholly other than a pure "Being-for-Itself," these dichotomies themselves are inseparable from the realization of a final or apocalyptic *coincidentia oppositorum*. While an apocalyptic *coincidentia oppositorum* may well have been a deep underground of Christianity throughout its history, and was surely a fundamental ground of the very birth of Christianity, it is never called forth in Christian theology as such, and never appears in a post-Heraclitean Western philosophy until Hegel. Hegel could claim that every fragment of Heraclitus is present in the *Science of Logic*, a science of logic which is the first and only purely dialectical logic in the West. For only dialectical thinking and vision can know a *coincidentia oppositorum*, and if even the thinking of Marx and Marxism could be grounded in Hegelian logic, that is yet another decisive sign of the truly subversive role of dialectical thinking in the West. This subversive role is even more comprehensively present in the dialectical expressions of the Western imagination, which have perhaps been the deepest challenge to all forms of Western orthodoxy.

Now there can be no question that dialectical vision is profoundly offensive, and most clearly so in its ultimate sanctioning of absolute evil. Absolute evil is here absolutely necessary for the realization of an absolute good. Satan and the Son of God are dialectical polarities in *Paradise Lost*, each essential to the other, and so, too, are Christ and Satan essential to each other in Blake's mature vision, but this vision, unlike Milton's, culminates in a *coincidentia oppositorum* of Satan and Christ. Perhaps nothing is or could be more offensive than Blake's revolutionary vision, but that vision is as totally affirmative as any other, and is philosophically paralleled only in Nietzsche's vision of Eternal Recurrence, which likewise calls forth an absolute affirmation of good and evil at once. The truth is that good and evil flow into each other in such vision; each thereby loses its distinctive or unique identity. This is the consequence of the deepest and most ultimate affirmation, an absolute affirmation of all and everything, and therefore an affirmation of "evil," or an affirmation of an ultimate totality comprehending everything whatsoever. Nor can we think that here evil is affirmed only insofar as it is simply and only "nothing," for at no point are the visions of both Nietzsche and Blake more unique than in their very embodiment of an ultimate or absolute Nothing, a Nothing which is

Godhead itself, yes, but it is precisely the "death" or absolute transfiguration of that Godhead which is the triumph of an absolute apocalypse.

Now if both Blake and Hegel could understand that Godhead *from the beginning* has withdrawn into an "externalization" and self-alienation, and one only reversed by a universal process of self-negation or "Self-Annihilation," it is vitally important to gain some understanding of such a "beginning," a beginning wherein creation is fall, but is nevertheless a *felix culpa* or "fortunate fall." Here, evil itself has its origin in the regressive movement of the Godhead, and from the very center of that Godhead, so that evil is not the consequence of a lower or alien Creator, as in Manicheanism and Gnosticism, but rather the consequence of the fullness of Godhead itself. This is why evil is ultimately an absolute evil, wholly inexplicable when it is understood as being anything less than that. And this is just why it is not until Schelling, Hegel, and Nietzsche that we have been given a philosophical understanding of evil, or not until Dante, Milton, and Blake that we have been given deep and comprehensive imaginative visions of evil. Non-dialectical minds will inevitably refuse such vision and understanding, for non-dialectical thinkers are bound to the ultimacy of what Hegel understands as the "Given," a given wholly isolating consciousness from its ground, and thereby foreclosing the very possibility of an ultimate or radical thinking and vision.

While it is true that mythical and mystical visions throughout the world have known creation as fall, these visions are wholly alien to our monotheistic traditions, or have arisen within them only as profoundly heretical subversions. The very vision or understanding of an absolute evil is just such a subversion, for it inevitably challenges or assaults what these traditions have known as God. Nor can we imagine that such assaults occur only in a premodern world, or a prescientific world. Never have they been so comprehensive as they are in the twentieth century, and it is precisely a uniquely twentieth-century imaginative language that most comprehensively embodies a vision of the totality of evil, nothingness, and abyss, a purely negative abyss which is absolute in that very comprehensiveness. This is just the context in which our twentieth-century philosophy and theology appear vacuous and unreal, or is so when it cannot speak of nothingness or the abyss, and therefore cannot evoke evil. Such a refusal of evil as a genuine question is surely a refusal of the very actuality of the world. Indeed, one can observe in the very history of philosophy and theology a progressive diminution of the question of evil. Perhaps at no other point do their histories more fully coincide. Yet when philosophy first deeply engages the question of evil in German Idealism, this is precisely the point at which philosophy fully becomes theology, and thereafter a non-philosophical theology progressively regresses into a fully dogmatic and ecclesiastical form.

Now if the question of evil truly has become a deeply forbidden question in the twentieth century, it has done so in a world that Nietzsche could foresee as a profoundly nihilistic world. This world embodies a totality of nothingness that is unique in history, so that a nothingness which our theological traditions could once know as evil itself would appear to be the very horizon of our new world, one numbing if not dissolving our deepest questions, as witness the virtual absence of God in twentieth-century philosophical language. It is not insignificant that both God and evil are so fully absent from our thinking, for each may well be deeply and profoundly related to the other; perhaps are deeply related in post-classical Western thinking, and if this thinking was inaugurated by Augustine, and was so by his very conceptual discovery of the subject of consciousness, it was Augustine who called forth a subject of consciousness that is inseparable from a total and interior guilt, even if this is a subject or self-consciousness that is only possible by way of the presence of God. If Descartes is the true founder of modern thinking, this occurs though a deep transformation of this Augustinian ground, for a uniquely Cartesian radical doubt releases an inward evidence in thought itself, which it is impossible to doubt, and which alone makes possible the truly new Cartesian judgment, *cogito ergo sum*. For the first time the subject or "I" of thinking is indubitably certain, and certain in itself and in itself alone, and not certain only when it is united with the "I" of God. If this truly new *cogito* now becomes the foundation of thinking itself, thinking for the first time becomes an absolutely autonomous thinking, so that the thinking subject is absolutely isolated from anything standing outside of itself.

Even though Descartes himself was certainly not an atheist, and could believe that scholastic philosophy would have been rejected as clashing with faith if his philosophy had been known first (letter to Mersenne, 31 March 1641), there can be little doubt that the truly autonomous philosophy which he inaugurated would inevitably culminate in a deep and pure philosophical atheism. Both Pascal and Kierkegaard knew this deeply, and unlike all atheisms in our ancient worlds, ours is a truly comprehensive atheism, and is so even in dissolving the question of God. Yet is this dissolution inevitably a dissolution of the very possibility of thinking about evil? If a new subject of thinking is an absolutely autonomous subject, does that very autonomy preclude all possibility of apprehending an ultimate ground which is not finally identical with itself, hence finally dissolving every possible "other," or every "other" that is truly alien to itself? Thereby not only would all transcendent "otherness" disappear, but so likewise would vanish all interior "otherness," so that in the wake of this disappearance, both God and evil would become unnamable, or could be evoked only in a silence in which no actual naming or language is possible.

Yet once again we must take note of the ubiquity of evil in a uniquely modern imaginative language, thereby our imaginative language is truly other than our purely conceptual language. If it is only in Dante that an imaginative and a conceptual language truly coincide, a reversal of this coincidence is ever more truly drawn forth in modern imaginative language, culminating with a ubiquity of nothingness in the deepest and purest expressions of late nineteenth and twentieth-century imaginative languages. Our deepest mystical languages have ever evoked a pure and total nothingness, one which Eckhart could know as Godhead itself, and one present in that purely apophatic Dionysian mysticism first appearing in the West in Erigena. If this is a mysticism reborn in the Boehemian tradition, it is surely renewed in German Idealism, and may well have been a deep ground of Nietzsche's revolutionary discovery of the pure actuality of a total nothingness. Every "I" truly perishes in such a nothingness, but so likewise do good and evil, or God and the world, as consciousness itself is truly reversed, even as it is in the deepest expressions of ancient mysticism. But now a truly new nothingness is at hand, for now it is actually and not only interiorly ubiquitous. And just as ancient mysticism could know a deep and ultimate joy, a uniquely modern "nihilism" can know a comparable joy, as clearly enacted by Nietzsche, and as present in the ecstatic imaginative embodiments of late modernity, which Nietzsche alone foresaw, but these embodiments are nevertheless inseparable from embodiments of nothingness, or embodiments of what the theologian can only know as evil.

Is evil, then, an inevitable ground of what we can most deeply realize as joy, one unnamable and invisible from any other horizon, but one inevitably present in pure joy? If a pure nothingness is inevitably present in deeply mystical realizations, is a comparable nothingness necessarily present in our deepest imaginative realizations, and in our moments of pure joy as well? Nietzsche could understand joy as a pure and total affirmation, even as Spinoza understood it as a pure activity, as opposed to a pure passivity. Just as both Spinoza and Nietzsche could know a deep identity of mind and will, this is an identity dissolving every possible teleological meaning or order, but only thereby is true freedom possible, or a full and genuine act of the mind or will. Evil perishes in every such act, so that for Spinoza evil is simply an illusion, but Spinoza knew that all but the truly enlightened are deeply bound to illusion. Nietzsche knows this illusion as ressentiment, a ressentiment which is a truly and purely negative will, and one most deeply directed against itself, so that it is the very origin of the "bad conscience," a bad conscience that at bottom is the very subject or center of consciousness. This is that interior subject or "I" which perishes in a pure and total affirmation, an interior subject wholly absent in Spinoza's thinking, so that Spinoza could know an integral subject or center of thinking known by no other thinker, one in which there is a pure harmony between body and mind. Only that harmony makes genuine freedom or joy possible, but in this perspective every other possible center of subject could only be known as "evil."

Yet it is the dissolution of that "evil" which is the realization of joy. Joy could never be present in anything which we could know as a naturally given, or anything which we could envision as innocence. It is always the consequence of a deep act, or what Spinoza knew as pure activity, and the deeper the activity the deeper the reversal of passivity, a passivity which truly is "evil," or truly is death. Yet we pass through that death in realizing joy, and if it is left behind in a moment of joy, it is nevertheless essential to joy, or essential to the actual realization of joy, a joy which is alien both to the natural and to the angelic or ideal orders, but not alien to what the Christian most deeply knows as Godhead itself. Even Spinoza knew what scripture speaks of as the love or the glory of God, but that love is the very opposite of a pure passivity or a pure quiescence, so that, all too ironically, Spinoza, the first truly modern Biblical interpreter, could unveil a scholastic understanding of God as the very reversal of scripture. If this occurred through Spinoza's "atheism," this is an atheism that knows the totality of God, and knows the totality of God as absolute act or activity. Nietzsche knew a comparable act and activity, and knew it as Eternal Recurrence, and an Eternal Recurrence also reversing a pure passivity into a pure activity. This alone is joy itself, but it is possible only in confrontation with the deepest darkness and abyss. Even if Spinoza is innocent of any possible abyss, he unveils a deep ignorance and illusion which are its counterpart, and only the dissolution of that ignorance makes possible a genuine joy.

That ultimate joy that Spinoza knew, and one here uniquely released in pure thinking itself, is one in which the individual subject of thinking is wholly absent as such, even as an individual subject is inevitably dissolved in the deepest expressions of mystical vision. Spinoza knew an eternal or "third" kind of knowledge, an intellectual love of God issuing in pure joy, a blessedness in which the mind is endowed with perfection itself (*The Ethics*, V, P 33). That perfection is the perfection of what Spinoza knows as "Substance" or Godhead itself, a perfection which is the glory or love of God, and so far from being a divine passivity, that perfection is absolute power, a power whose modal expression is the very power of the world. Just as the finite and the infinite are deeply and purely united in Spinoza's understanding of "Substance" or God, so, thereby are united the absolute power of God and the power of the world, and a power of the world which is never so pure as it is in genuine thinking itself. Such thinking banishes all contingency, and therefore dissolves everything that possibly could be apprehended as evil. Only then is true joy possible, and if this joy is the consequence of the disappearance of any possible contingency, it is a joy proceeding from an absolute necessity. While this necessity dissolves everything that we can know as the freedom of the individual will, only thereby is true freedom realized, which is the freedom of purely knowing and therefore purely willing the absolute necessity of God. God is the name of absolute necessity, but that is the name of an absolute love and glory, a glory fully manifest as the consequence of the dissolution of all illusion, and a glory wholly transcending everything that we can know as the individual subject or "I."

Now the truth is that Spinoza's thinking embodies a truly reverse understanding of evil, evil is not simply an illusion, it is overwhelmingly real in virtually every mind, and is concretely manifest whenever we apprehend contingency, or apprehend any final cause or any teleological order whatsoever. Thus everything that once was known as belief in God can here be known to be evil. It is inevitably the source of a deep passivity, a passivity not only making genuine thinking but genuine life impossible. Hence it is not only a deep ground of tyrannical government and oppressive society, but is also a primal, if not the primal, source of what Nietzsche would later understand as repression and ressentiment. There is a true *coincidentia oppositorum* between Nietzsche and Spinoza. No genuine thinkers are so humanly opposite and opposed, and yet they are the only great thinkers whose thinking ultimately coincides, and most clearly coincides in their understanding of both joy and freedom, a freedom and a joy which are the very opposite of passivity or "evil," and only that joy is finally real. Inevitably Nietzsche and Spinoza are known as our deepest atheists, or our most subversive thinkers, the ones most fully calling forth the evil of everything that is a given for us, and only a deep and comprehensive reversal of that given makes possible a genuine life, but that reversal is blessedness or joy itself.

It is not insignificant that Spinoza is so reluctant to employ the word "evil," or that Nietzsche can fully speak of evil only in his continual call that we go beyond good and evil. For Nietzsche, the very apprehension of evil binds us to its dark power, therein we become what we behold, and are what we seemingly know. Nevertheless, Nietzsche is deeply Augustinian in knowing the ubiquity of evil, or the ubiquity of evil in everything that we know as the subject of consciousness or the "I," and if nothing is more distinctively Western and Christian than such a self-consciousness, nothing is more absent in Spinoza. Yet Spinoza is perhaps our most isolated thinker. It is simply impossible to imagine a Spinozist tradition or school. Here he is manifestly far distant from Nietzsche, and even if modern Western philosophy is now unthinkable apart from Spinoza, no one could possibly share his pure thinking, just as nowhere else can we discover such a conception of God. From Spinoza's own perspective, one could imagine that this is a decisive sign of the ubiquity of evil or illusion, and while all imagination is dissolved in Spinoza's thinking, within this horizon all other thinking is finally fantasy, so if at only this point Spinoza knows the totality of fall. No Western philosopher understood ignorance or illusion more deeply than did Spinoza, just as no other philosopher has realized such pure thinking. Here thinking as thinking is totality itself. While this is true of Hegel, too, the very comprehensiveness of Hegel's thinking, and even of his purely logical thinking, precludes the possibility of a thinking which is thinking and thinking alone, or a thinking transcending all historical actuality. Yet Hegel was profoundly inspired by Spinoza, and above all so in his radically new understanding of an absolute negativity, and even if he deeply reacts against Spinoza's dissolution of the subject of consciousness, he fully accepted Spinoza's revolutionary understanding of "Substance," even if inverting it in his revolutionary understanding of "Substance" as "Subject." But that very inverted continuity gives deep witness to the profound historical potentiality of Spinoza's unique understanding of "Substance" or God, and Spinoza can truly be known as the father of a uniquely Western atheistic pantheism or pantheistic atheism, one profoundly reborn in full modernity, and fully reborn in all our deep or comprehensive thinking.

Spinoza, Hegel, and Nietzsche are all philosophers of totality. As opposed to all ancient and Eastern thinkers, they know totality as actuality itself, an actuality that is the very opposite of that absolutely primordial passivity or quiescence that our Eastern and ancient worlds have known as totality, for it is the actuality of world itself, as for the first time in history *this* world is known and actual as totality itself. At no point is this new world more clearly manifest than in that new and radical freedom which it embodies, a freedom inseparable from a new and totally embodied necessity, but a truly new freedom of absolute affirmation. This absolute affirmation embodies an absolute responsibility, for it is a responsibility for everything whatsoever, for everything that occurs. So it is that evil itself must here be affirmed, or must be affirmed insofar as it is actual in the world, insofar as it is actuality itself. Unlike in scholasticism, here evil is not affirmed only insofar as it is good, but rather affirmed in its own inmost actuality, in its own actuality in the world. For once world or finitude itself is known as totality, then it can only be accepted as itself, can only be affirmed as itself, and not affirmed only insofar as it points beyond itself, or embodies an otherness which is the otherness of itself. With the perishing of every possible beyond, or every pure transcendence which is transcendence alone, or every infinity which is not the infinity of finitude itself, finitude or the world can only be accepted or affirmed as itself, and affirmed and accepted in its ownmost actuality, in its actuality as itself.

Such an affirmation is clearest and most overwhelming in Nietzsche's absolute Yes-saying, a Yes-saying which is an absolute affirmation of Eternal Recurrence, or an absolute affirmation of an absolute immanence. That is precisely that immanence that Spinoza, Hegel, and Nietzsche all know as totality itself, an immanence only manifest with the dissolution or disappearance of a pure transcendence, or with the final realization of the death of God.

Not only do each of these thinkers know that death, although they know it in radically different ways, but each realizes a new and total affirmation as a consequence of that death, and for each, such affirmation is a total affirmation of finitude itself, of the world itself, a world which here as world is eternity itself. Spinoza, Hegel, and Nietzsche are all philosophers of eternity, and not of a transcendent or other-worldly eternity, but rather of an absolute immanent eternity, which is an immediate and totally present eternity, and totally present in the full actuality of the world. Only when that actuality is totally affirmed is this eternity actual and real, and this is an affirmation demanding and embodying a total affirmation of every moment, and of every actual moment. So as opposed to an archaic eternal return in which every moment is an eternal now, this is an absolutely immanent eternal return that is absolutely here and now. Nietzsche, Hegel, and Spinoza are all philosophers of eternal return, but theirs is a pure inversion and reversal of every ancient and primordial eternal return, and is so in its very calling forth of the eternity of an immediate actuality.

That actuality certainly comprehends "evil," or everything that we can know and experience as evil, and even if it ceases to be evil in that affirmation, it is nevertheless evil in itself, or evil in its own enactment. To totally affirm the world is to affirm that enactment, is to affirm everything that has actually occurred. Thus an absolute affirmation of the world is a pure and total acceptance of an absolute responsibility for the world; that responsibility is true freedom, a freedom most purely known by Nietzsche and Spinoza, and most comprehensively known by Hegel. It is known here by that absolute theodicy which is the Hegelian "system," a theodicy in which the real as real is absolutely rational, just as it is for Spinoza, but to know that "reason" is to know theodicy itself, is to know the absolute goodness of the world. Yet this is a goodness inseparable from everything that we can know as evil, from everything that has actually occurred in the world as evil, for it is inseparable from everything that has occurred, and only an acceptance of the deepest horrors of evil can make possible a total acceptance of the world, a total affirmation of the world. This is precisely why a total acceptance of the world is an absolute affirmation of eternal return, and not the eternal return of a transcendent infinity, but the eternal return of the deepest actuality of the world as world.

Eternal recurrence or eternal return is fully manifest in every purely religious apprehension, in every truly sacred world, but so likewise is it fully manifest in a uniquely modern atheism. If this is a true *coincidentia oppositorum*, nowhere is it more fully manifest than in the deepest thinking of Spinoza, Hegel, and Nietzsche, our most God-obsessed philosophers, and precisely thereby our deepest atheistic thinkers, and our only Western philosophers who have given us genuine conceptions of evil. For even if a conception of evil is wholly absent in Spinoza, he nevertheless gives us a purely negative conception of evil in his conception of contingency as necessity (*The Ethics*, II, P 44). For Spinoza, only our imagination or fantasy can regard things as contingent, and if only such fantasy can know evil, that which fantasy knows as evil pure reason knows as necessity. Nor do Hegel and Nietzsche differ from Spinoza at this crucial point, and just as Western Christian theology ultimately knows the necessity of evil in its primal dogma of predestination, a predestination which in the Augustinian tradition *is* creation, Spinoza, Hegel, and Nietzsche all know predestination as eternal return, just as they know it as creation, and a creation comprehending everything whatsoever that is actually real. So to affirm that creation is to affirm everything that has occurred, and to affirm the absolute necessity of everything that has occurred. Only that occurrence is true *theodicy*, a theodicy which is eternity itself.

Here, evil as evil could only be a primordial evil, an evil not only present *from the beginning*, but present "in the beginning," in the beginning or advent of eternity itself. This eternity is the absolute necessity of everything whatsoever, and therefore the absolute necessity of everything that we have known as evil, of everything that has been manifest or actual as evil to us. For even if this can occur only in our fantasy or illusion, in knowing a totally present and totally actual absolute necessity we know the deep and final necessity of everything occurring in the world, and thus of everything that we have named as evil, or of everything that bears the image of evil to us. That, too, must here be absolutely affirmed, and is affirmed in knowing the pure necessity of a pure contingency, or the pure necessity of everything that occurs. Both Nietzsche and Spinoza could know the full affirmation of that necessity as redemption or blessedness, but such redemption is a full and total sanctioning of evil, or a sanctioning of all that evil that has occurred in the world. Now such evil is "good," or is absolutely necessary, and is absolutely necessary because it is a primordial ground of the world, or an ultimate ground of the world as world, or the world as pure actuality itself. Apart from that "evil" there could be no possible joy, and no possible freedom, a freedom and joy only possible in an absolute affirmation, or in an absolute knowing, a knowing and an affirmation which is inevitably a willing of "evil," or a willing of that necessity which we have imagined as evil.

Certainly our deepest Western imagination has truly imagined evil, or has imagined a pure abyss or a pure nothingness, and even if such an abyss or nothingness is truly alien to Spinoza, it is not alien to Hegel and Nietzsche, both of whom incorporated our Western imaginative traditions into their thinking. At no other point is there a greater distance between Spinoza and Hegel and Nietzsche, unless it occurs in the deep absence of the pure subject from Spinoza's thinking, an absence that precludes the possibility of all genuine acts of the imagination, and if that is an absence making possible the very purity of Spinoza's thinking as thinking and thinking alone, that is an absence making impossible the naming of evil. As Nietzsche knew so deeply, not only can evil only be named by our ego or "I," but that "I" is inseparable from evil, or from a profoundly interior negativity, an interior negativity born in the very advent of consciousness and consciousness alone (*Genealogy of Morals*, II), which is to say in the very advent of everything that we can know as "in the beginning," a beginning which is the beginning of a pure and absolute negativity, just as it is for Hegel, and therefore beginning itself is the beginning of a primordial evil.

Just as such a primordial evil is a genuine absolute, it is inevitably called forth in a truly absolute thinking, or in a truly absolute modern Western thinking. Even if such an evil is wholly invisible in Spinoza's thinking, it fully becomes visible with the full activation of the modern Western subject of thinking, and just as this occurs in Hegel's realization of Spinoza's thinking, it likewise occurs in Nietzsche's incorporation of Spinoza's thinking. So, if only in his successors, Spinoza is a thinker of primordial evil, and if the pure harmony of Spinoza's joy is surely unique, or unique among thinkers, this could only be because of the absence therein of primordial evil. This absence precludes that ultimate conflict which Hegel and Nietzsche so deeply know, a conflict which is ultimately with primordial evil, but only such conflict makes possible either full joy or full freedom. Perhaps an Hegelian joy is most deeply present in the *Science of Logic*, a science finally transcending all abstract spirit and all abstract reason (*Verstand*), but paradoxically enough this also occurs in a virtually opposite form in *Thus Spake Zarathustra*, which is the deepest embodiment of a purely Nietzschean joy. Neither the *Science of Logic* nor *Thus Spake Zarathustra* could be either possible or real apart from an absolute conflict with primordial evil, and if each finally ends that evil, or intends to end it, each is only truly real in this conflict itself, a conflict certainly and absolutely impossible in everything that our ancient worlds know as either a primordial totality or Godhead itself.

CHAPTER 4

⤸

Evil and Nothingness

Christian scholasticism from its very beginning has known evil as the "privation of being," or quite simply as nothingness itself. Perhaps the last spokesman for this tradition was Karl Barth, who while strongly maintaining that nothingness is not nothing, and is indeed the "shadow side" of creation, or that which God does not will; nothingness does "live" by that non-willing, although it is real only by reason of the *opus Dei alienum*, the divine negation and rejection. Barth can even identify nothingness as the "past," the ancient menace or nonbeing which defaced the divine creation, but which is consigned to the past in Jesus Christ. If our thought is conditioned by the obedience of Christian faith, we have only one freedom, namely, to regard nothingness as finally destroyed, and to make a new beginning in remembrance of the One who has destroyed it (*Church Dogmatics*, III, 3, 364). Barth insists that there can be no possible conflict within God Himself, for any God in conflict with itself is bound to be a false God, but the activity of God does take place in a definite opposition, in a real negation, and "nothingness" is that from which God separates Himself and in the face of which He asserts Himself and exerts His positive will. For God elects, and therefore rejects what He does not elect; so likewise God wills and therefore opposes what He does not will, for the Yes of God is No to that to which He has not said Yes. God is Lord on the left hand as well as the right. He is the Lord of nothingness, too, and because nothingness is on the "left" hand of God, it really "is" in this paradoxical manner. Indeed, in the free grace of God, in God's election, God has made the controversy with nothingness His own, thereby God knows nothingness. But through the resurrection of Jesus Christ, nothingness has lost its perpetuity, and thereby and only thereby nothingness is finally destroyed.

If our only freedom is to know that nothingness has finally been destroyed, that freedom is faith itself, a faith in which an actual opening to nothingness is impossible, and impossible because now nothingness is absolutely unreal. This impossibility and this impossibility alone is what Barth could know as apocalypse, an apocalypse which is an eternal election, and an election which is creation itself. If Barth finally identifies creation and apocalypse, that is an identification which is at the very center of the orthodox Christian tradition, one continually calling forth the nothingness of nothingness itself, and only in that nothingness of nothingness is God truly God. Hence evil itself is finally an illusion, an illusion actual as such only in sin, but the forgiveness of sin is a dissolution of that illusion, and thereby a realization of the nothingness of nothingness, and thus a realization that God *is* God. We need not deny that the radicality of Barth's theology is only made possible by a uniquely modern nihilism. But so, too, the power of Christian scholasticism is inseparable from the power of ancient paganism. If Barth is inescapably a scholastic in his affirmation that God is the No to nothingness, he is thereby scholastic in understanding the finality of the nothingness of nothingness, even if he is anti-scholastic in understanding that this is effected only by the resurrection of Jesus Christ.

Now it is precisely evil as evil that disappears in every such affirmation, so that Barth could maintain that as a consequence of the resurrection damnation is impossible, an impossibility which is the impossibility of nothingness, or the impossibility of nothingness in that apocalypse which is the resurrection. Perhaps at no other point are our orthodox theologies more fully united. It is as though the very affirmation of God is not only inseparable from but identical with the denial of nothingness, and the deeper the affirmation of God the deeper the denial of nothingness. Here, every orthodox Christian theology is a dialectical theology, and if the Yes of God is the No to nothingness, this is known by every orthodox theology, and even known by the orthodoxies of Judaism and Islam. Yet so likewise is it known by our philosophical orthodoxies, all of which realize a dissolution of nothingness, and do so in their very knowledge of Being, which is surely a major if not the major reason why the scholastic theologian can know that Being is God. If this is impossible for Barth, and impossible for Luther, Milton, and Kierkegaard as well, this is the impossibility of a nothingness which could be even a shadow of God.

The very name of God in Barth's theology can be known as the No to "nothing," thus the actual name of God is Jesus Christ, that Christ who has finally annihilated nothingness. In the wake of that annihilation, all are elected to grace. So it is that the "left hand" of God is finally a sheer nothingness, one which can be known as such in faith, and if this is that freedom that alone is known as freedom in faith, this is that freedom that is deliverance from nothingness, a nothingness which has now wholly and finally been annihilated. But the annihilation of nothingness is the annihilation of evil, an evil which "is" no more, and is no more because it has finally been destroyed by Christ, and is only present in a "past" or a "non-being" which is now anni-hilated. Faith can know nothing of nothingness, and therefore can know nothing of evil, an evil or nothingness against which the No of God is directed. If the victory of the resurrection has annihilated that nothingness, this is eternally enacted in God's willing of election or predestination, an election which is the very Yes of God, and the No of God is said and enacted only for the sake of this Yes. So it is that the No of God is finally the Yes of God, and is so already in that creation which is election; the "left" hand of God is finally the "right" hand, and the "shadow side" of creation is finally unreal. This, of course, is what Christian orthodoxy has always maintained, an orthodoxy fully reflected in Christian scholasticism, and if here evil is a nothingness that is a "privation of Being," evil as evil simply cannot and does not exist, and, insofar as it is, it is caused by the good (*Summa Theologica*, I, 49, 1).

If Aquinas is our most truly and most fully systematic theologian, he surely is so in his understanding of evil. Even if this understanding is largely inspired by the radical Neoplatonism of Pseudo-Dionysius, it is also inspired by that new Aristotilianism which he largely created, as manifest in that deep emphasis that he places upon the causation of evil. While here evil does not effect anything of itself, it is effective by virtue of the good annexed to it, for following Augustine he affirms that evil exists only in good, and every actual being is a good, so that the absence of good, taken in a privative sense, is an evil. But the subject of evil is good, for again following Augustine, he affirms that there is no possible source of evil except the good, and only good can be a cause because nothing can be a cause except insofar as it is a being, and every being, as such, is good. Evil has a cause by way of an agent, but only accidentally and not directly, so that evil as a deficiency of being is accidental to the good, and the good is the cause of evil only as an accidental cause. In voluntary acts the defect of the action comes only from an actually deficient will, and the defect itself is not a fault for fault follows only from a deficient will, so that evil has only an accidental and not a direct cause. Above all this is true because the supreme good is the cause of every being, therefore God is only an accidental cause of evil, just as it is equally true that nothing can be essentially evil, even as nothing can be wholly and perfectly evil. No being can be called evil by way of its participation in evil, but only by a privation of participation. This and this alone is the reality or actuality of evil, so that evil as evil is simply and only an illusion.

Luther responded to such scholasticism as the very voice of Satan or the Antichrist, but just as a full scholasticism was reborn in both Lutheranism and Calvinism in the seventeenth century, and reborn in Anglicanism, too, where it was profoundly resisted only by Milton himself, scholasticism in one form or another is the greatest theological power in modernity, or the greatest manifest theological power, and is so most clearly in our continual theological dissolutions of evil. But so likewise has our philosophical thinking dissolved the actuality of evil, and done so in its refusal of the very possibility of a real and actual nothingness. If this refusal is reversed in the advent of German Idealism, this occurs only by way of an apprehension of an absolute abyss or nothingness in Godhead itself, a nothingness which is a divine nothingness, indeed, and hence an ultimate or absolute nothingness. No greater assault upon scholasticism has ever occurred than that which is realized in German Idealism, and above all so in Hegel. Already in Kierkegaard, Hegelian thinking is apprehended as the most profound assault upon faith, and such an apprehension becomes truly universal in twentieth-century theological thinking.

Perhaps the question of evil or nothingness is the deepest threat to all theological thinking, or surely so in the West, if not in the East. Here there truly lies a gulf between Occidental and Oriental thinking, and most clearly so in the radical differences between Eastern and Western apprehensions of nothingness itself. While it is true that our deeper Western mystical theologies have known an absolute nothingness, these have inevitably posed deep threats to the orthodoxies of their worlds, and this is true not only in Christianity but also in Judaism and Islam, for the very apprehension of a pure and absolute nothingness appears to be inseparable from "pantheism," which the West has ever known as the deepest threat of the East. Nevertheless a genuine paradox is present here, as can be seen in the decisive role of a radical Neoplatonism in all of the classical expressions of Jewish, Christian, and Islamic scholasticism. This Neoplatonism is at the very least implicitly pantheistic, but it nevertheless dominated even such an orthodox thinker as Augustine. Medieval Aristotilianism, as initially born in Islam, and then carried into Judaism and Catholicism, is truly revolutionary at this point. For it recognizes an actuality of the world that is not simply a dim and shadowy reflection of an absolutely transcendent Godhead, but rather an actuality that is purely and actually real. This dissolves the Neoplatonic gulf between the Creator and the creation, and Aquinas can even know God as that pure Act-of-Being who is the very actuality of being as being. Now God or Being itself or *esse* is identified as the very core of being, it is that "act-of-being" lying at the very root or ground of the real as such, with the consequence that here and for the first time in Christian scholastic thinking there can be no ontological chasm between God and the world.

This is just why Luther could know an Aristotilian scholastic thinking as a Satanic thinking, as could Barth himself in the twentieth century, but the truth remains that medieval Aristotilianism deeply transformed scholastic philosophy in Judaism, Catholicism, and Islam. One such transformation was its far deeper dissolution of any possible nothingness, for now the very ubiquity of the actuality of being as being dissolves any possibility of a nothingness that is actually "other" than being. Seventeenth-century rationalism was itself a consequence of this transformation, and even Descartes' radical doubt cannot doubt the reality of the doubter. Only in Pascal is a truly radical doubt first released in thinking itself, and this inevitably led to an assault upon all theoretical thinking. Pascal could know an actual nothing, and know it as sin itself, a sin which is ubiquitous in consciousness, hence Pascal could call forth an absolute chasm between God and the world, and one that could be crossed only in the Crucifixion itself. The Pascalian God is the God who hides Himself, and everything bears the mark of this hiddenness, so that in Pascal there is a radical move from God the Creator to God the Suffering Savior. Here lies a gulf between Pascal and Descartes, and one reflecting a deep dichotomy in early modernity.

Now it cannot be denied that there is an epiphany of nothingness in full modernity which is unique in history, unless it is paralleled in ancient Gnosticism. Unlike a Buddhist nothingness, which is absolutely positive and absolutely negative at once, this is a purely negative nothingness, one calling forth visions of an absolute darkness, and an absolute darkness that is an absolute evil. Never before had evil been so absolutely central in our imaginative enactments. This evil is a pure *and* actual nothingness, hence one that is absolutely opposed to every scholastic understanding of evil, and just thereby opposed to every scholastic understanding of God. It is not "atheism," which is most deeply opposed to an established faith in full modernity, but rather a uniquely modern apprehension of Godhead itself, a Godhead torn asunder by an absolute opposition between its positive and negative poles. With the realization of that opposition, every positive polarity of Godhead finally withers away and disappears, and Godhead can then appear and be real only as an awesome and total abyss, and as an absolutely negative abyss.

This is the abyss against which Barth's theology is most deeply directed, and the very power of Barth's theology is inseparable from its ultimate conflict with this abyss. Thereby Barth's theology is ultimately directed against modernity itself, and if only in this perspective Barth is a reborn Pascal. Yet Pascal could know an actual nothingness as Barth cannot, or all too significantly, Barth can only know it in a world or actuality uneffected by the Crucifixion and the Resurrection. For Barth, it is simply inconceivable that faith could apprehend an actual nothingness. Barth is not only in full continuity with all scholasticisms, but it was his very turn to Anselm, the purest of all medieval Neoplatonists, which made possible the "science" of his *Church Dogmatics*, and it is at this very point that the greatest distance lies between the *Church Dogmatics* and his earlier *Goettingen Dogmatics*. And just as he now breaks away from his initial discipleship to Kierkegaard, he likewise distances himself from every theoretical thinker and establishes Christian theology for the first time as a purely church dogmatics, thereby aligning himself with those medieval Islamic and Jewish thinkers who repudiated every philosophical theology in the name of the community of faith.

Is a deeply and uniquely modern alienation of faith from the world and history an inevitable consequence of faith's absolute affirmation of the nothingness of nothingness, or its absolute affirmation of that God who is an absolute No to the nothingness of nothingness? And if a pure nothingness is absolutely unreal, is the No of God itself finally unreal, so that the No of God ultimately is and only is the Yes of God? Is this precisely the meaning of the affirmation that God *is* God? Are all of our theologies finally coalescing at this crucial point? Not only our Christian theologies but our Islamic and Jewish theologies as well, so that hereby we are truly promised a genuinely ecumenical theology? How odd that Barth's radically Christocentric theology can thereby appear as an ecumenical theology, and one not only therein open to the theologies of Judaism and Islam, but at least implicitly open to the metaphysical traditions of the West, or open to them insofar as they effect ontological dissolutions of nothingness. Oddest of all, such theology would appear to be in continuity with both common language and common sense, a language which can only know the nothingness of nothingness, at least in its manifest if not in its latent meaning. Can it possibly be said that to know the nothingness of nothingness is to know that God *is* God?

Perhaps theology itself has now become our purest "atheism," or that thinking most distant from everything in our world which could possibly be an epiphany or manifestation of God, and if traditionally it was the question of evil that was the deepest challenge to faith, are we now being given a theology in which this question cannot possibly be asked? Theologically, the only evil we have known is one identified with nothingness, so that if nothingness is finally quite simply nothing, then so, too, is evil quite simply nothing, even if it is so as a consequence of God's redemptive act. But how is the nothingness of nothingness that faith knows decisively different from the nothingness of nothingness that common sense and common language know? Is the language of faith simply a purer form of our common language? And is this a language finally known by all, so that every genuine theology could only be an ecumenical or universal theology, a theology implicit in all genuine language whatsoever? If so, how is it that theology appears to be so alien to our world?

Historically, nothing is more distinctive of Christianity than its calling forth of the ultimacy of sin, death, and evil. If Augustine is the most deeply Neoplatonic of all our Western theological thinkers, he is also that thinker whose thinking is most deeply centered upon sin and damnation, so that there is a deep contradiction or opposition at the very center of Augustinian thinking. This is at least implicitly true of all of our Western theological thinkers, with the possible exceptions of Aquinas and Barth. Is this a major reason why

Barth and Aquinas are the most influential theological thinkers in our time, and are they most deeply united in their understanding of evil or nothingness? Is this a union far more significant than are their manifest theological differences? Can theology truly be liberated by finally knowing the nothingness of nothingness, and thereby be liberated by knowing that God *is* God? Can we truly know that God *is* God only by knowing the nothingness of nothingness, and is that finally what the very word "God" most truly and most actually means? Is the very question of nothingness the deepest question posed by theology, a question to which everyone is called, so that if only at this point everyone is a theologian? Nevertheless, the truth is that only relatively small sections of either the *Summa Theologica* or the *Church Dogmatics* are given to the question of nothingness. Even if this question is always implicit throughout this vast writing, it seldom explicitly appears, and just as one could think of the question of evil as the most deeply forbidden theological question, and as that question that most deeply threatens every theology, it is precisely thereby the question of nothingness that may well be the most ultimate theological question.

Now if the question of evil is ultimately the question of nothingness, then the question of the actuality of evil is inescapable, for if nothingness is ultimately quite simply nothingness, then evil likewise is finally nothing at all, and the actuality of evil is finally an illusion. Philosophers as radically diverse as Plotinus and Spinoza have finally reached this conclusion, a conclusion or a premise which is at the very center of all scholastic philosophy, just as it is at the center of all established Christian dogmatics. Yet this center is in profound conflict with itself, and is so if only because Christianity above all other traditions has placed an ultimate emphasis upon fall. This is just the point at which anti-philosophical dogmatics have been most powerful, as witness the whole world of Protestant dogmatics, and it is just the charge that philosophical thinking cannot apprehend the actuality of evil that has most resonated within our religious worlds, and not only within our religious worlds, but within our imaginative worlds as well. Is pure thinking closed to the actuality of evil, and therefore closed to the actuality of nothingness itself? This would appear to be true of the whole realm of our established Western philosophical thinking, and it is just at this point that the deepest conflicts have occurred between philosophical and theological thinking, as above all manifest in Augustine himself. And if Augustine is the true founder of a uniquely Western theological thinking, he is thereby the founder of a deep dichotomy in that thinking, and one not only between its philosophical and its theological poles, but also and even thereby between its human and its divine poles.

Although seldom recognized, Augustine is of overwhelming importance in Western philosophical thinking, for he was the first thinker to draw forth and to understand the subject of consciousness, or to understand the subject of consciousness as a true center and ground. Not until Augustine is the "I" or the center of consciousness actually thought in the ancient world. One could even regard his discovery of this subject or "I" as being inseparable from his conversion to Christianity, as so forcefully recorded in his *Confessions*. Augustine's *Confessions* is the first full and genuine autobiography, and the very creation of this new literary genre was a revolutionary event, one recording his revolutionary breakthrough to the subject of consciousness, and one inaugurating a uniquely Western centering upon self-consciousness. Nowhere else in his vast corpus of writing are philosophical and theological thinking more fully united than they are in the *Confessions*, but so, too, nowhere else in that corpus is there such a deep dichotomy between philosophical and theological thinking, one inseparable from both an ultimate union and an ultimate discord between the "I" of self-consciousness and the "I" of God.

Few thinkers are open to Augustine's purely theological thinking, as can be seen in an almost universal revulsion against his understanding of predestination and damnation. Yet the truth is that this thinking is inseparable from his deeper philosophical thinking, for that subject of consciousness that he draws forth is positive and negative at once. Here our "I" is simultaneously the creation of God and in deep and ultimate rebellion against God, just as our uniquely human freedom, a freedom which Augustine philosophically discovered, is inseparable for us from a deep and ultimate impotence and bondage, and just as we can know the actuality of nothingness in the bondage of our will, we can know the actuality of God in the actuality of our freedom. This is certainly a dichotomous actualization, as fully manifest in the actuality of our will. Our will is free and enslaved at once; its freedom is inseparable from its bondage, a dichotomy of the will that can only be resolved by the free and total grace of God. Augustine can justly be said to be the creator of the full dogma of original sin, just as he was the creator of the dogma of predestination. Theologically these dogmas are inseparable, for it is precisely the totality of fall which necessitates the totality of predestination, just as it is the totality of predestination which necessitates the totality of fall. At no other point did Augustine more decisively break from his Neoplatonic ground, just at no other point was he a more original Biblical theologian.

Lesser theologians are alienated from Augustine at this crucial point, but this is certainly not true of Barth, who is our one full theologian of predestination since the Reformation. Paradoxically, Barth shares this deep motif with both Hegel and Nietzsche, who are our only modern philosophers of predestination. Yet Hegel and Nietzsche, are those philosophers who have most deeply thought the death of God, a death of God which is at the very center of their mature thinking, and even if these are radically different real-

izations of the death of God, each could understand the death of God as a
consequence of predestination, just as each of them were more deeply Augustinian thinkers than any other modern philosophers. If only through Hegel
and Nietzsche, we can understand that the thinking of predestination is the
consequence of a deeply dialectical thinking, or a deeply Western dialectical
thinking. Just as Augustine is our most fully dialectical pre-modern theologian, as most fully manifest in the dialectical dichotomy that he establishes
between sin and grace, this is the very dichotomy that eventually draws forth
in his thinking a full and total affirmation of predestination, and a predestination apart from which freedom itself would be unthinkable.

Augustine knows freedom, and only knows freedom, as a consequence
of grace, first the grace of creation, and then the grace of redemption, for an
original freedom is predestined to fall, and predestined to a total fall. This is
the totally fallen condition in which redemption is realized, and only that
redemption can draw forth freedom from the totally impotent and totally
fallen will. At no point is Augustine more dialectical than in drawing forth the
essential relationship between freedom and impotence in the fallen will. It is
precisely in our deepest moments of freedom that we are most deeply aware
of our impotence, just as it is our deepest moments of impotence that most
fully actualize the call of freedom, and only a full realization of that ultimate
impotence makes possible an opening to grace. That is a grace which is only
possible by way of predestination, for the pure and actual impotence of our
will is a pure and actual nothingness, but it is that nothingness alone which
can be an avenue of grace for us, a grace which is wholly and only the grace
of God, and which is enacted in that predestination which is the one eternal
act of God. And predestination is a double predestination, even if not so
explicitly formulated by Augustine himself, for it is a predestination to eternal
life and to eternal death, each is not only inseparable from the other, but
finally each is identical with the other, and identical in the one eternal act of
God. This is why Augustine is our first true theologian of the providence of
God, for everything that actually occurs is willed by God, and willed in the
one eternal act of God. Even if Augustine will not say that God wills evil, he
again and again affirms God's permission of evil (*The Enchiridion,* XCVI),
a permission apart from which providence could not be real, and a permission
which is enacted in predestination, and even enacted in the predestination of
the great mass of humanity to an eternal death.

Now it is not insignificant that predestination was accepted after Augustine by every known Western theologian until the full advent of the modern
world. This is true of Aquinas himself, who gives far more attention to predestination than to evil and nothingness in the *Summa Theologica,* where he
can affirm that God wills everything that goes to the perfection and beauty
of the universe, and therefore evils are divinely willed (*Summa Theologica,*

I, 19, 9). Now even if this affirmation occurs in his presentation of a position that he is opposing, Aquinas then goes on to affirm that God neither wills evils to be nor wills evils not to be, but "wills" to allow them to happen, thereby bringing a truly new meaning to an Augustinian permission of evil. These very words, *ergo Deus vult mala*, were a deep subterranean ground of Christianity until the end of Christendom, and thereafter they are only realized philosophically rather than theologically, as is above all true in Hegel and Nietzsche. Yet Hegelian and Nietzschean thinking can be understood as a theological thinking, and as the only thinking in which philosophical and theological thinking are truly integrated in the modern world. This is perhaps most decisively manifest in the very role of predestination in their thinking, a predestination that Nietzsche knows as Eternal Recurrence, and Hegel knows as the absolute *kenosis* or self-emptying of absolute Spirit.

Inevitably, it is Hegel and Nietzsche who have thought most deeply about evil and nothingness in the modern world, and they have deeply thought evil and nothingness by thinking predestination. If this is the most radical thinking about predestination that has ever occurred, it is also the most comprehensive such thinking, for both Nietzsche and Hegel can call forth predestination in every dimension of thinking, and can do so by thinking totality itself. Yet, here, the thinking of totality is the thinking of a radically new totality, a thinking which is the thinking of apocalypse itself, and if this never occurred in our theological traditions, or occurred only as a thinking of the primordial movement of eternal return, now it occurs as an ultimate thinking of ending itself. This is a predestined ending, and predestined if only because of the ultimate actuality of evil and nothingness, an actuality so ultimate that it can only be enacted by an eternal predestination. Just as Augustine could so purely know the actual nothingness of the fallen will, this is the nothingness that could only be the consequence of an eternal predestination, and this is the very nothingness that Nietzsche in his most Augustinian moments can know as the "I" of self-consciousness, an "I" that is the consequence of an original repression or ressentiment, but an "I" that is reversed in an absolute Yes-saying, or in an absolute affirmation of Eternal Recurrence. Nietzsche's vision of Eternal Recurrence is an absolute reversal of what Augustine most deeply knew as redemption, therefore it is a reversal of an Augustinian predestination, but precisely thereby it is a deep and ultimate affirmation of predestination itself.

Of course, an Hegelian predestination is much clearer than a Nietzschean predestination, as most clearly manifest in his lectures on the philosophy of history, but which is far more deeply enacted in the *Phenomenology of Spirit* and the *Science of Logic*, both of which enact an absolute negation which is an absolute affirmation, and both of which draw forth an actual nothingness, and an actual nothingness which is absolutely self-negated or self-emptied in absolute Spirit or the absolute Idea. Not until the *Phenomenology of Spirit* is evil or nothingness systematically or fully comprehended in Western philosophy. Indeed, it is not until the *Phenomenology of Spirit* that evil is fully thought in Western thinking. Even Augustine was prevented from fully thinking about evil by his Neoplatonic ground, and while Augustine could know that God permits evil, he could not or would not know that God wills evil, even if this is an inevitable consequence of the dogma of predestination, and one that Aquinas himself recognized. Yet it is Hegel who first fully conjoins evil and predestination, a conjunction made necessary by Hegel's full acceptance of the very actuality of the world as world. Evil certainly abounds in this world, and therefore evil necessarily abounds, for no one has known more deeply than Hegel that "isness" and necessity are not only inseparable but finally indistinguishable. Even if at this crucial point Hegel was deeply inspired by Spinoza, Hegel understood this necessity more comprehensively than any other thinker, hence he was inevitably a thinker of predestination, and the first thinker to think the totality of predestination.

Now just as it was Augustine who first fully thought freedom in the ancient world, and his early understanding of freedom is finally inseparable from his mature understanding of predestination, it was German Idealism that first fully thought freedom in the modern world. While Schelling, Fichte, and Hegel were all philosophers of freedom, it was only Hegel in that world who fully thought predestination, and this is the inevitable consequence of the fact that Hegel is our only fully and comprehensively systematic philosopher. This alone brings a radically new meaning to predestination, for now predestination is inseparable from totality itself, and just as this totality comprehends everything whatsoever, so, too, does predestination comprehend all and everything. If it was Augustine who initiated this truly new understanding, it is only consummated in Hegel and Nietzsche, and then consummated by a genuine inversion or reversal of Augustinian thinking. This reversal is decisively manifest in the deep and ultimate enactment of the death of God in Hegelian and Nietzschean thinking, but all too paradoxically this reversal calls forth a genuine renewal of Augustinian thinking, as is all too manifest in the deep role of evil and nothingness in this radically new thinking.

Indeed, it is precisely Hegel's and Nietzsche's philosophical realization of the death of God that calls forth the ultimacy of nothingness and evil. Only as a consequence of that death does an absolute abyss consume consciousness, an abyss which is a sheer nothingness, and yet a totally actual nothingness, and a nothingness whose full advent is finally undeniable and inescapable. And just as Hegel can understand this abyss as the necessary and inevitable consequence of the absolute *kenosis* or self-emptying of absolute Spirit or the Godhead, Nietzsche can understand it as the necessary and inevitable consequence of the death of God. Each can know this abyss as being absolutely new, so far from being a renewal or resurrection of a primordial chaos (a chaos which deeply tempted the young Nietzsche), it is a chaos comprehending everything whatsoever, and only by passing through the totality of this absolute chaos or abyss is a true or actual consciousness or life now possible. Here, Hegel's deep choice of the symbols of crucifixion and resurrection in his thinking is of genuine significance. Only a resurrection from an ultimate death can now make possible a new life. This is the very death that is an absolute abyss of nothingness, an abyss ending everything that is namable as either God or Being, and, as Nietzsche realized, ending everything that is possible or real as the "I" or the center of consciousness. But this very ending is an absolute advent, and is so for Hegel and Nietzsche alike, for it is the advent and the absolutely new advent of an absolute actuality, and an absolute actuality that is the intrinsic "other" of either God or Being. Nietzsche, as the first philosopher of Eternal Recurrence, absolutely inverted the primordial movement of eternal return. That inversion is possible only as a consequence of the death of God, and if this is an ultimate transformation of an absolute transcendence into an absolute immanence, this uniquely modern transformation is already abstractly embodied in the *Science of Logic*. But in each case this is only possible by way of the full and final advent of an absolute nothingness, an absolute nothingness which is the consequence of the death of God, and that death makes possible the actual advent of absolute immanence itself.

Both Hegel and Nietzsche could know an absolute nothingness as being at the very center of Godhead itself. This alone makes possible what Hegel knows as an absolute *kenosis* or an absolute self-emptying, and while the late Nietzsche, unlike Hegel, could know an absolute nothingness as being fully identical with Godhead itself, which is just why the death of God is far more total in Nietzsche's thinking, each could know that nothingness as the ultimate source of every evil, and it is only thereby that evil itself for the first time passes into a full and actual thinking. So it is that this thinking is a pure reversal of the thinking of Christian orthodoxy, now an evil that Christian scholasticism could know as a pure nothingness is called forth in thinking as a pure actuality, and this is possible only by way of the negation or self-negation of Godhead itself. It is this negation and this negation alone which makes possible an epiphany or a realization of the actuality of nothingness, as the dissolution or self-emptying of that God whose "isness" is the very annihilation of nothingness inevitably and necessarily calls forth an absolute nothingness, an absolute nothingness which truly is the absolute "other" of Godhead itself. Yet Hegelian and Nietzschean thinking can know the absolute "other" of the Godhead to be either wholly within or wholly identical with Godhead itself, and if this is the deepest theological difference between Nietzsche and Hegel, this is an historical difference between full modernity and postmodernity, or between the twilight of modernity and the advent of the age of nihilism.

Now this is just the age in which Barth's dogmatics was constructed, so that this dogmatics can know a nothingness that is far beyond the horizon of any previous dogmatics. This and this alone makes possible a theological understanding of the totality of the redemption of Christ, one inevitably issuing in a "Christomonism," and a Christomonism only possible in response to a deeply nihilistic age. Barth thereby stands forth as the greatest dogmatic theologian in the history of Protestantism, but if this is a theology only made possible by nihilism itself, only made possible by the uniquely modern epiphany of an absolute Nothing, then there is an essential and necessary relation between this theology and nihilism, and one that is echoed in every genuine theology in the twentieth century. Surely there are echoes here of that deep medieval theological conflict that arose in response to the advent of Aristotilianism, one occurring in the Islamic, Jewish, and Christian worlds, and one profoundly reacting against what here could be known as a theological "atheism"—an atheism in that context inseparable from an apprehension of the essential reality of the world itself, one which was clearly either an assault upon or a deep transformation of all Neoplatonisms, and therefore an ultimate challenge to the deeply established theological ground of more than a millennium of Christian history. What we know as the High Middle Ages is a deep consequence of that struggle, for an Aquinas or a Dante or a Giotto would be simply inconceivable in a Neoplatonic theological world, and if the high Middle ages ultimately gave birth to modernity, that is a modernity which is itself consummated in a Hegel or a Nietzsche. While such an understanding of history would have been impossible in the medieval world, it is inescapable in the modern world, and not least because of the radical historical thinking of both Nietzsche and Hegel.

Hegel and Nietzsche are alone among our truly major modern thinkers in being philosophical and historical thinkers at once. If it was Augustine who created such a thinking, and did so in the *City of God*, this is a truly new thinking only made possible by a deep understanding of predestination, and of a double predestination, an eternal predestination of the City of God and the City of Man. Here it is the City of God which is the genuine mystery, for Augustine very rarely identifies the City of God with the Catholic Church, and perhaps clearly so only once (XIII, 16). A comparable mystery is present in the radically new understanding of predestination in Hegel and Nietzsche, and certainly so if we look upon the *Phenomenology of Spirit* rather than his university lectures as the real enactment of Hegel's understanding of predestination. Only one thing here is clear in Hegel, and that is a radically and comprehensively forward movement from absolute beginning to absolute ending, a movement that is seemingly reversed in Nietzsche. Yet that reversal certainly is not the primordial movement of eternal return, but rather its very opposite, and thereby it is in deep continuity with Hegelian thinking, for Nietzsche and Hegel alike transformed an absolute transcendence into an absolute immanence.

Now an apprehension of the truly forward movement of history does not appear until the advent of Christianity, a movement of history which Augustine could understand as a preparation for Christianity, and he can go so far as to maintain that the Roman Empire was ordained by God, for the providence of God governs all history (V, 21). The *City of God* culminates with an apocalyptic theology that had an enormous impact upon subsequent Western history, but the same could be said of the conclusions of the *Phenomenology of Spirit* and the *Science of Logic*, and even of Nietzsche's work as a whole. A genuine understanding of predestination is inevitably apocalyptic, and is so because it is only in an apocalyptic context that it is possible to apprehend a dynamic or self-transforming or self-transcending totality or whole. So it is that it is only in the context of an apocalyptic ending that it is possible to apprehend an absolute beginning that is truly other than that ending. This alone makes possible an apprehension of historical actuality, or an apprehension of historical difference or uniqueness, a difference that is simply impossible in visions of eternal return, but that is inevitably called forth in genuinely apocalyptic vision.

One of the ironies of the *City of God* is that it so deeply maintains the nothingness of evil, insisting that nothing causes an evil will, and that our evil choice takes its origin from our having been created from nothing (XII, 6), whereas vast portions of the book are given to depictions of evil in the City of Man, a world wholly consumed by evil, and one predestined for Hell. Nevertheless, there is a forward movement in this book, and one culminating in either an eternal Heaven or an eternal Hell. This is precisely the apocalyptic ending which ultimately gives meaning to history, a history not only resolved in this ending, but apart from which history itself would finally be meaningless. Nietzsche seemingly renews such a meaninglessness, but this is not true, for Nietzsche absolutely affirms history, and even affirms the actuality of history, even if this is possible only in the context of the end of history. Yet this is largely true of Augustine himself, and far more comprehensively true of Hegel. Here we have a deep clue to the meaning of predestination, and to the meaning of the predestination of history, which can only appear as such in the context of an apocalyptic ending, an ending which is absolutely fundamental in the understanding of predestination in Augustine, Hegel, and Nietzsche alike.

Indeed, it is precisely an apocalyptic ending that calls forth the deepest abyss, a truly absolute abyss effecting not only the end of history but the end of the world itself. Only that ending makes possible the advent of a new aeon or a new creation or a new world, an absolutely new world which is the ultimate goal of predestination itself, and one which can only be realized through the full and final actualization of absolute abyss. So it is that all genuine understandings of predestination have been understandings of absolute abyss, an absolute abyss apart from which predestination is impossible. Hence the inevitability of a predestination to eternal death, and while Barth can maintain that it is Christ alone who suffers that death, which is the one source of our salvation (*Church Dogmatics,* II, 2, 346–52), the absolute necessity of eternal death is inescapable in predestination, an eternal death apart from which eternal life is illusory. But so, too, is history itself meaningless or illusory apart from such an absolute abyss, and while it is Nietzsche who knows this most deeply, it is Hegel who knows it most comprehensively. For Hegel, every true movement of consciousness or of history is a movement of deep self-emptying or self-negation, an *Aufgehoben* which can transcend only by negating, and it is only an absolute perishing or loss which can ultimately advance the movement of Spirit, so that Hegel can conclude the *Phenomenology of Spirit* by affirming that history is ultimately the Calvary of absolute Spirit, apart from whose actuality Spirit would be lifeless and alone.

Now it is truly remarkable that the great body of modern theology could be so indifferent to the challenge of predestination. At no other point is there a greater distance between modern theology and ancient and medieval Western theology. But we might also observe that modern theology is far more distant from the challenge of evil and nothingness than are medieval and ancient theology, and at this point, too, Barth's theology is truly unique. Despite his repudiation of systematic theology, Barth's theology is far more systematic than is any other modern theology, and at no point is this more true than in his understanding of redemption as the annihilation of evil, for that is the consequence of God's election or predestination, a predestination that is simply impossible apart from this ultimate goal. Therefore to think redemption is to think that annihilation, an annihilation which is the annihilation of nothingness or the Nothing, hence that Nihil is absolutely essential to redemption, and thus absolutely essential to predestination. If Eastern Christianity far more than Western Christianity is ultimately directed to the goal of an eternal return to primordial Godhead, this alone could account for the absence of predestination in Eastern Christianity, for predestination is ultimately directed forward and not backward, and predestination can only be realized through the actuality of history itself. Accordingly, Western and not Eastern Christianity places a deep emphasis upon history, and Western and not Eastern Christianity has been deeply transformed by the movement of history itself.

Just as Protestantism would be inconceivable in Eastern Christianity, so, too, would be inconceivable there any deep or profound transformation of

Christianity, such as occurs not only in Hegel but in the whole body of Western Christian imaginative vision from Dante through Milton and Blake and even into our own time. Certainly a great body of this vision is apocalyptic, but it is even more clearly centered upon an absolute evil or abyss, an abyss of nothingness unknown to our theologians until Barth, but not unknown to a Hegel or a Nietzsche, and not unknown to our deepest mystical thinkers. Hegel and Schelling were deeply inspired by Eckhart and Boehme, and all too indirectly we can call forth such an impact upon Nietzsche. Nietzsche can go far beyond Hegel in apprehending Being itself as an abyss of nothingness. This recalls Eckhart's apprehension of Godhead itself as the Nothing, but in Nietzsche, unlike Eckhart, this abyss is realized in the actuality of history, and realized in such a way as to call for an absolute transformation of history and the world. That transformation is clearly an apocalyptic transformation, hence it can be realized only through the most ultimate abyss, and just as that abyss is absolutely necessary to an apocalyptic transformation, it is absolutely necessary to predestination itself.

Nietzsche scandalizes everyone by calling for an absolute affirmation of everything that has occurred, and of everything that has occurred in the actuality of history, certainly including everything whatsoever that is manifest as evil, and Nietzsche far more than any thinker who preceded him understood the full actuality of evil. Yet, at this point, too, he is a reborn Augustine, for Augustine's understanding of the providence of God, a providence in which God wills everything that occurs, surely has the consequence of sanctioning everything that has happened in history. Yet Augustine, unlike Nietzsche, deeply loathed everything that he could understand as profane history, which is to say virtually everything that the historian can understand as history. While the word is foreign to him, it was Augustine who created what much later was known as theodicy. This is a theodicy which is profoundly renewed by Hegel, who not only embraced it more than any other thinker, but who created a philosophy and a theology of history which embodies it, thereby moving far beyond Augustine in understanding history as predestination. Nevertheless, he is in full continuity with Augustine, and now the providence of God truly does embody the totality of history. And if this can occur only through the "cunning of reason," that is a cunning which is the cunning of providence or predestination, and just as it can occur only through an ultimate suffering and violence, that violence is absolutely necessary to predestination itself.

In our time, theology has become an extraordinarily "soft" discipline, seemingly practiced only by those whom William James knew as the tenderhearted, but truly classical theology is extraordinarily "hard," as fully embodied in both Augustine and Aquinas, and as renewed in the twentieth century by Barth, and perhaps by Barth alone. And a "hard" theology is inevitably a theology of predestination. If Barth is our only modern theologian of predestination, he is also the only modern theologian who is actually open to nihilism, the only one who has not tamed it so as to make it into an avenue to faith, the only one who can understand an actual nothingness as pure evil. Yet surely Barth is a "soft" theologian in denying the reality of damnation and Hell, at no other point is he more distant from classical theology, or more distant from a "church dogmatics" which he seemingly so totally embraced. An older Hegel was also distant from the language of damnation and Hell, and at no other point is he more distant from Nietzsche, for while Nietzsche loathed virtually all theological words, including these, he envisioned damnation and Hell as has no other real thinker, and could unveil a truly new Hell, a Hell which is the consequence of the death of God, a Hell which his Madman proclaims as an "infinite nothing," thereby recapturing the long lost language of classical theology.

That language is essential to the theology of predestination, and always until Barth accompanied it. But Barth's theology of election does know that Christ suffered damnation, for in totally revising the dogma of predestination, Barth understood Jesus Christ rather than the eternal decree of predestination as the real basis of election. Christ is here simultaneously the electing God and the elected man; he is the man abandoned to damnation and Hell, a Hell which is the inevitable destiny of us all, but that judgment is diverted to Christ alone, and consequently damnation is impossible for all others (*Church Dogmatics*, II, 2, 346). Of course, for Barth there is no genuine or true humanity outside of the humanity of Jesus Christ, which perhaps leaves open the possibility of the damnation of the great mass of humanity, a damnation which every classical theologian accepted. If that is a bitter truth that virtually every modern theologian resists, it simply cannot be denied that Christianity far more than any other religious tradition proclaims the ultimacy and finality of Hell, and does so not in its periphery, but rather in its very center, as witness the New Testament itself.

Nietzsche knew this more deeply than any other thinker, and this is a deep reason why the late Nietzsche came to know the Christian God as the deification of nothingness, the will to nothingness pronounced holy, and yet this is a profoundly ironic identification, for it was Nietzsche far more than any other thinker who called forth an absolute nothingness, and an absolute nothingness that now is absolutely real. Hence the late Nietzsche's deepest struggle was with nihilism, a nihilism now incarnate in the world itself, or in the totality of our history, and yet a nihilism that is our inevitable destiny, and an inevitable destiny that truly can be named as predestination. Nor is that nihilism truly distant from what Augustine knew as the world of the City of Man, or what classical Western theology knows as that great body of humanity which is eternally predestined to damnation. The great difference is that

Nietzsche knows this nihilism as the eternal destiny of all humanity, but just as Nietzsche calls for an absolute Yes-saying which is the one possibility of transcending this destiny, and which can occur only in the ultimate depths of nihilism itself, classical Christianity in both East and West knows that all humanity has been damned by the fall, and redemption is redemption from that damnation. Now this is just what modern theology has lost, and lost it in "forgetting" damnation, but Nietzsche recovered damnation as has no modern theologian, and recovered it in realizing the totality of predestination. Is it Nietzsche who is our one truly modern theologian?

༺༻

CHAPTER 5

Evil and the Godhead

Now just as the question of evil is our most deeply forbidden and our most deeply challenging theological question, it can finally only be posed in relation to Godhead or absolute totality itself. If our purest orthodoxies know a totality or a Godhead that is absolutely other than evil, our deepest heresies know a Godhead or a totality that is absolutely inseparable from evil. Finally, in true orthodoxy evil itself is absolutely unreal, whereas in true heresy evil is absolutely real, and most real insofar as it is finally inseparable from absolute totality or Godhead itself. Therefore evil is finally namable only in such heresy, and if our deepest heresy is our deepest naming of evil, that is a naming which is the consequence of an ultimate rebellion, and a rebellion against a Godhead that is absolutely other than evil. We can see this rebellion most clearly in the modern world, and above all so in Blake, Hegel, and Nietzsche, those primal figures of the deepest modern heresy, a heresy which is finally a pure and total reversal and inversion of orthodoxy, and precisely thereby a profound drawing forth of the ultimacy of evil, and of the ultimacy of evil in totality or Godhead itself. Yet this ultimate heresy is an intended transfiguration of evil, a transfiguration impossible if evil is purely dissolved, and impossible in a totality or Godhead in which evil is wholly and totally absent, which is to say impossible in everything that orthodoxy has known as Godhead or totality.

Why is there any being at all? Why far rather not nothing? This deep question of Leibnitz was profoundly renewed in the twentieth century, and asked as it never could have been asked in the seventeenth century. This becomes perhaps the most ultimate question of Heidegger, and is just as profoundly asked by Kafka or Beckett, and if this question is now unanswerable, then so, too, is every ultimate question. Of course, predestination can answer this question, but if predestination has now become unthinkable, then so likewise have Godhead and evil become unthinkable, and above all unthinkable if they cannot be thought simultaneously and at once. Is it because we cannot now think Godhead or totality without thinking evil that we so resolutely refuse to think about God? As Kafka and Joyce knew so profoundly, is it now impossible to name God without speaking blasphemously, impossible to utter the very word "God" without calling forth a curse, and a curse which is inevitably and most deeply the curse of damnation? Is damnation the necessarily unspoken answer to our question as to why is there any being at all? And if predestination knows the necessity of damnation, and the absolute necessity of damnation, is that a damnation truly and finally inseparable from the only redemption that predestination can know? Here, if "being" is embodied in redemption, must "being" be embodied in damnation as well?

Of course, it has now become impossible for us truly or actually to speak of "being," but we have no less lost the capacity to speak of either damnation or redemption. While this is certainly not true of full modernity, it is apparently true of a new postmodernity, and certainly true of a language in which the "I" or the center of consciousness is silent and unspeakable. Nietzsche could know that "I" as a pure negativity, an "I" that is the consequence of ressentiment, but that knowledge is a dialectical knowledge, for it is the consequence of the full advent of an absolute Yes-saying, a Yes-saying which Nietzsche knew as redemption. Just as this "I" is a truly evil "I," one that is the consequence of a pure No-saying, it is this very "I" that is transfigured in an absolute Yes-saying, and transfigured by undergoing an ultimate and final reversal, a reversal in which it becomes the very opposite of itself. Blake, Hegel, and Nietzsche all envision an absolute transfiguration, and an absolutely dialectical transfiguration, a transfiguration which is apocalypse, and an apocalypse which can be spoken because it has actually dawned. Only now does a final age of the Spirit fully dawn in vision and thinking, for even if it was fully at hand in the eschatological proclamation and the parabolic enactment of Jesus, this is just the apocalyptic enactment which is truly reversed in the advent of Christian orthodoxy. Only the most radical heresy can reverse that reversal, a heresy which is fully enacted in full modernity, but only by way of a profound enactment of the depths of evil itself.

Only with the advent of modernity is Satan fully named in our history, not even Dante was capable of that, and if this initially occurs in *Paradise Lost*, it is consummated in Blake's *Milton* and *Jerusalem*, but only by way of a naming of God Himself as Satan. Now it is extraordinarily important that this naming deeply occurs in full modernity, and neither Hegelian nor Nietzschean thinking is truly conceivable apart from it. Perhaps nothing else has brought forth such a bitter opposition to this thinking, just as nothing else could make possible such an ultimate heresy, but this heresy is inseparable from a radical and total thinking of the transfiguration of evil. Such thinking is impossible if evil is known as a pure nothingness, just as it is impossible if Godhead itself is known as the pure and total opposite of a pure nothingness. Not only does such thinking finally make dialectical thinking and vision impossible, but it precludes all possibility of understanding the actuality of evil, and therefore is ultimately a profound turning away from actuality itself. But to know Satan is to know actuality itself, or to know the actuality of evil, and not only the actuality of evil but the absolute actuality of evil. If it was Jesus who first fully and actually named Satan, only Christianity has known the depths of Satan, even if these are the very depths that Christianity has most dissolved in its very knowledge of God.

Not until the advent of Christianity is Godhead itself known as that absolute totality which is absolutely "other." A profound other-worldliness possessed the world itself at this moment of history, issuing in deep disruptions of the higher civilizations of both East and West. This was a time when a deep transformation of history occurred throughout the world, but it occurred most violently in the very birth of Christianity, a birth which Nietzsche could know as the most catastrophic event in history. Of course, Hegel could know this birth as the full and final advent of absolute Spirit, but Hegel knows absolute Spirit as an absolutely dichotomous Spirit, and one manifest and actual as such in Christianity alone. This is precisely why Hegel could know Christianity as the absolute religion, and if here the absolute religion embodies the absolute destiny of the world itself, that world is an absolutely dichotomous world, hence it is inseparable from the totality of an absolute negation. If such a totality is unique to Christianity, as both Hegel and Nietzsche so deeply believed, then Christianity itself is inseparable from absolute evil, an absolute evil apart from which no absolute negation could occur. Is this, then, a deep and ultimate ground of a uniquely Christian apprehension of the Godhead, a Godhead which truly is absolutely "other," and finally and ultimately absolutely other than itself?

We need not wonder that Christianity released a comprehensive other-worldliness that had not existed in the West until the advent of Christianity. If this is an other-worldliness that eventually and perhaps necessarily passed into its very opposite, that would be a genuinely and fully dialectical ground of Christianity, one releasing an absolute Yes-saying that *is* an absolute No-saying, or releasing a Godhead that is an absolute No and an absolute Yes at once. If the Christian God is the absolute No to the "nothing," the very absoluteness of that No is inseparable from the absoluteness of that "nothing" which it absolutely negates, so that inevitably such absoluteness must be known as being within Godhead itself. Perhaps this finally occurs in every genuinely Christian theology. This alone could account for a uniquely Christian apprehension of the absolute otherness of the Godhead, an otherness that Christianity alone can know as being within the Godhead, and surely only such an otherness could make possible and real what the Christian alone knows as the Crucified God. While only a uniquely modern Christianity fully knows and realizes the Crucified God, this very realization calls forth a truly new "otherness" of the Godhead. Now it can only be an otherness most deeply and most profoundly directed against itself, so that now Godhead itself can be known as being in absolute opposition to itself.

Now language itself, or our deeper language, becomes possessed by an absolute evil. This language impels a deep flight of all of our theological languages, each of which is a flight from actuality itself, or from a deeply modern actuality, and most clearly a flight from an ultimate evil or nothingness, and nothing more manifestly unites all of our modern theologies than a final refusal to speak that evil itself. At no other point has modern theology more decisively been reduced to silence, just as at no other point is theology so deeply alienated from our world. If here our imaginative languages wholly and finally transcend our theological languages, that very condition embodies a deep theological call, and a call for a theological understanding of absolute evil itself. Let us recall that our first mythical novel, and our only full epic in America, *Moby Dick*, centers upon absolute evil, and the absolute evil of the Godhead. Here history itself is called forth as an ultimate struggle with this evil, which is just why *Moby Dick* is a genuine epic. Yet it is a tragic epic, and tragic not only in the self-destruction of Captain Ahab, but far more deeply tragic in the self-destruction of Moby Dick. This is the first American vision of the death of God, and this is a truly tragic death. Only Melville among our modern novelists is truly Shakespearean, and Melville created a tragedy of God, an inevitable tragedy proceeding from that absolute evil which is the center of the Godhead, and this is the very tragedy which is the ultimate source of tragedy itself.

Every genuine tragedy is a tragedy of absolute evil. Both Shakespeare and the Greek tragedians shared a deep apprehension of absolute evil, and when tragedy is reborn in the modern world, this rebirth is inseparable from a deep ground in absolute evil, for only absolute evil makes possible what we know as tragedy, an absolute evil apart from which a true catharsis is impossible. The tragic hero or heroine is a mask of God, and most clearly of the darkness of God. That darkness is essential to genuine tragedy, and if the tragic plot is an anamnesis or renewal of primordial sacrifice, it, too, is a repetition of the sacrifice of God, and ultimately a sacrifice of the absolute darkness of the Godhead. Therefore this sacrifice is a transfiguration of darkness, and thus a transfiguration of evil. This is a transfiguration realizing an ultimate catharsis, an ultimate catharsis which deep tragedy enacts, and a catharsis inseparable from an absolute sacrifice, and finally an absolute sacrifice of the absolute evil of the Godhead. Christianity has always known this sacrifice in knowing the absolute event of the Crucifixion, and the absolutely redemptive event of the Crucifixion, a redemptive event that is absolute death itself, and therefore a redemptive event inseparable from absolute evil. For it is enacted by the enactment of absolute evil, but that enactment is an absolute self-negation of evil, and thus an absolute self-negation or self-emptying of Godhead itself.

Classical Christian theology does not and cannot know that absolute self-negation, because that theology can only know the absolute negativity of the Godhead as an absolute affirmation, hence it is closed to the actuality of both evil and nothingness. In its Augustinian mode, it can only know the actuality of evil as a wholly fallen humanity, and a fallen humanity that is absolutely other than the absolute goodness of the Godhead. All too significantly such an absolute goodness disappears both in a uniquely modern thinking and in an uniquely modern imagination, and now absolute evil for the first time is called forth in the depths of both the imagination and thinking, and called forth in the depths of Godhead itself. Perhaps it is virtually impossible to bring absolute goodness and absolute evil integrally together in either thinking or the imagination. Here Dante stands virtually alone, but Dante cannot know either the Crucified Christ or the Crucified God, for he can know Christ only as an absolute transcendence, one demanding the mediation of the Mother of God if redemption is either possible or real, so that Dante could only know the incarnate Christ in Beatrice. The beatification of the epic hero in the *Paradiso* ends every possible evil, or ends the actuality of every possible evil, but the rebirth of absolute evil in *Paradise Lost*, one going far beyond the *Inferno*, dramatically and tragically enacts the final loss of an original or primordial paradise, one inseparable from the first full poetic and epic vision of Satan.

While it is true that Gnosticism can know the Biblical God or the Creator as Satan, it can do so only by knowing an absolutely undifferentiated totality as the Godhead, an undifferentiated totality that is the very opposite of the world, so that matter itself is an absolute evil, an evil whose only possible source could be a Satanic Creator. At this crucial point Blake is the very opposite of any possible Gnosticism, and so, too, are Hegel and Nietzsche, and so far from being a rebirth of ancient Gnosticism, a uniquely modern "atheism" is an apprehension of totality itself as an absolute life and energy. True, this energy is an absolutely dichotomous energy. Hence it is inseparable from an absolute evil or an absolute nothingness, but this is the very "contradiction" that makes possible an ultimate life, an ultimate life which is an ultimate transfiguration. Yes, such transfiguration is a tragic transfiguration. It is impossible apart from the full realization of absolute evil, just as all tragedy is impossible from some such realization, and if it is tragedy which has given us our clearest imaginative enactment of evil, tragedy itself is a model or paradigm of the transfiguration of evil, a transfiguration here occurring only by way of the very enactment of evil.

For the first time epic poetry passes into tragic poetry in *Paradise Lost*, and the poetic weakness of its concluding books envisioning redemption is a decisive witness to the finality of a new tragic destiny. This destiny renews the destiny of Greek tragedy, but now tragedy is finally the tragedy of Godhead itself, even if Milton cannot and will not accept the deity of Christ as being equal to the full deity of the Godhead. Only in full modernity is the tragedy of the Godhead openly enacted and envisioned, and just as this fully occurs in both Blake and Hegel, it ushers in a new universal destiny, and one that can be realized only in the depths of an absolute evil. Yet this occurs through an absolute transfiguration of evil, one which is here known and envisioned as occurring in the Crucifixion itself, and thereby the very destiny of Godhead itself can be known as a tragic destiny, and now and only now tragedy truly becomes all in all. Now ancient and classical tragedy is truly transformed, and for the first time it is realized in thinking itself. Just as for the first time tragedy is actually understood, it is understood in the thinking of a truly new totality, a totality inseparable from absolute evil, as for the first time a totality is known which is absolutely inseparable from absolute evil.

Now, and for the first time in the West, an absolute Nothing is fully realized in thinking and in the imagination, and unlike every Eastern vision of an absolute nothingness, this is a Nihil which is actually and historically real, manifest and real not only in the depths of interiority but in the depths of history itself, depths calling forth a truly new Godhead, and a Godhead for the first time manifest as absolute evil. Never before had the depths of Godhead itself been manifest as evil, an evil which is an absolute nothingness, and deeply unlike all apophatic mysticisms throughout the world, this is an absolute nothingness that is an absolute energy or activity, an absolute negativity now for the first time called forth as absolute origin itself. Only now can creation *ex nihilo* be known and manifest as creation out of an absolute nothingness, a nothingness that is the very opposite of any possible void or emptiness, or of any nothingness that is simply and only nothing, as a primordial chaos is now truly renewed. If this is that chaos that was negated by the birth of Yahwism in Israel, and absolutely negated by the prophetic revolution, which shattered all archaic or primordial worlds, now such a chaos is truly resurrected, and resurrected as it had never been resurrected before. Now a chaos appears and is real which is "cosmos" itself, or which is inseparable from any possible totality. Each of our primal modern poets have resurrected that chaos, thereby they are in deep continuity with Dante, but now an *inferno* appears which is finally indistinguishable from *paradiso*, as not only Blake but each of our greatest fully modern poets has called forth a union or marriage of Heaven and Hell.

Already a primordial shamanism enacts a way up which is the way down, and if such a way is truly resurrected in modernity, this, too, occurs by way of a descent into Hell. But now Hell is a totality as it could never be in any possible archaic world, a totality decisively appearing in an absolutely new naming of Satan, as Satan now and for the first time can be employed as a primal name of Godhead itself. Yet this occurs only as an apocalyptic naming, a naming occurring in response to the death of God. Only the dead body of God can truly be named as Satan, and even if that dead body is now resurrected as it had never been so before, and resurrected in a "chaos" which is totality itself, that very body of death, and total body of death, is actual and real only as the absolute otherness of a new Jerusalem, a new aeon or new creation which is apocalypse itself. So it is that a truly new joy is released in the world, a joy which *is* apocalypse, but now a joy which is certainly not the joy of any possible Heaven, or any possible beyond, but the joy of absolute immanence, an absolutely new immanence, and one only possible as the consequence of an absolute negation of absolute transcendence. This is the negation that is shared by Hegelian and Nietzschean thinking, but it is born in the very birth of the modern world, as fully manifest in the scientific revolution of the seventeenth century, which in its very discovery of an infinite universe brought to an end every real distinction between the heavens and the earth.

The very discovery of the infinity of the universe is inevitably a profound challenge to every apprehension of absolute transcendence, and if this discovery is inseparable from that new science that then was born, that science plays a decisive role in the uniquely modern transformation of an absolute transcendence into an absolute immanence. While Spinoza was the first to purely think that immanence, it is not comprehensively understood until the nineteenth century, that very century which first understands and enacts the death of God. Modern science itself can be understood as being apocalyptic insofar as it actually effects the ending of an old world, but also apocalyptic in calling forth a truly new world. Here the very dissolution of all possible teleology is a dissolution of everything that theology had known as the Creator, but that dissolution is essential to modern science, just as it is finally essential to modern thinking itself. Thus the thinking of the death of God in Hegel and Nietzsche can be understood as a true resolution of the whole movement of a uniquely modern thinking, and just as both Nietzsche and Hegel can understand that death as apocalypse itself, now apocalypse is resurrected as it had never been so before, and resurrected as a total apocalypse.

One of the deep paradoxes of this new vision is the full union which it establishes between an absolute evil and an absolute joy. At no other point are Blake and Nietzsche more deeply united, and just as each of them could know the Christian God as that Satan who is an absolute nothingness, each of them could know this absolute No-saying as the deepest source of repression or "evil," and it is the very reversal of this absolute evil which calls forth an absolute joy. Again, Nietzsche and Blake are united in transforming every possible innocence into the depths of "experience." Not only is this a response to the ultimacy of history itself, it is also a response to the absolute sovereignty of repression or ressentiment in everything that we can know as history, which is to say a response to the uniquely Christian God, who can now appear and be real only as an absolute No-saying. This, too, is a consequence of the death of God. Only as a consequence of that death does God undergo a metamorphosis into Satan, an absolutely alien Satan who is a pure and total No-saying, but that No-saying is absolutely real. No one knew this more deeply than Blake and Nietzsche, and it is absolutely necessary for either a Blakean or a Nietzschean joy. That joy is an absolute reversal of an absolute No-saying, hence it is impossible for any kind of innocence, and is only possible as a consequence of the deepest descent into Hell.

Hence the naming of God as Satan is absolutely essential for both Blake and Nietzsche. Only when Godhead itself is known and realized as absolute nothingness is such an absolute reversal possible, and not only an absolute nothingness but an absolutely actual absolute nothingness, an actuality inseparable from everything that we can now actually know as either history or consciousness, but that is the very consciousness and history now called to an absolute reversal, and that calling is the deepest vocation of both Nietzsche and Blake. So it is that an apocalyptic Yes-saying is absolutely inseparable from an apocalyptic No-saying, and it is precisely the advent of an apocalyptic Yes-saying which necessarily calls forth an absolute No-saying. Just as Blake created a cosmic epic or epics centering upon the warring polarities of the Godhead, Nietzsche created a new history of Eternal Recurrence, and an Eternal Recurrence of Yes-saying and No-saying, or an Eternal Recurrence of an absolute totality or Godhead itself. While Blake could not or would not break away from all visions of innocence, this is just what occurs in Nietzsche's thinking and vision, and Nietzsche is our only thinker who is finally absolutely free of innocence, and therefore free of any possible primordial ground. So far from being a rebirth or renewal of a primordial eternal return, Nietzsche's Eternal Recurrence is its absolute reversal, for not only is all transcendence here transformed into an absolute immanence, but every possible innocence is transformed into the depths of experience, depths which are an absolute abyss, and only a passage through that abyss makes possible an ultimate joy.

Yes, that ultimate abyss is Godhead itself, and the only Godhead that can be known in a moment of apocalyptic joy, for an apocalyptic joy is the consequence of an absolute transfiguration, and of an absolute transfiguration of the depths of evil itself. Indeed, Christianity has always known that genuine redemption is redemption from the depths of evil. Such depths of evil were not even manifest in the world until the advent of Christianity, although they have a clear parallel in a Buddhist calling forth of the ultimate depths of samsara. If it is Buddhism and Christianity that promise the most total redemption, this is a redemption inseparable from a realization of the depths of evil or nothingness, depths here comprehending everything whatsoever that is manifest or real in either history or consciousness. Yet, in the Western world, it is not until the advent of modernity that a genuine totality of evil or nothingness is truly called forth in consciousness, not until then that an abyss can appear which is a total abyss, one comprehending Godhead itself, and comprehending the deepest depths of the Godhead, as for the first time these appear and are real as a totally negative abyss, and an abyss apart from which Godhead itself can no longer be known or envisioned.

Spinoza stands alone in early modern philosophy in intending to think the depths of Godhead itself, and Spinoza is the purest thinker in all of Western philosophy. Here substance or God is totality itself, and a totality inevitably called forth in what he created as thinking itself. All of the truly major modern philosophers until the twentieth century were theological thinkers, but Spinoza was alone among them until the nineteenth century in daring to think the depths of the Godhead. If only thereby, we can see how such thinking was so deeply forbidden in early modernity, and Spinoza could only dissolve every possible abyss or negativity in the Godhead by the most radical thinking that had thus far occurred in modernity. While Spinoza was reborn in German Idealism, he was reborn only through a reversal of his thinking at this crucial point, for now it has simply become impossible to know Godhead apart from abyss, and apart from an absolute abyss, an abyss that far earlier had been called forth by the Western imagination. If only for this reason, thinking and the imagination had been deeply dissociated or discordant throughout early modernity. Kant, in his third critique, was the first philosopher to cross this chasm, but he did so only by thinking abyss in his understanding of the sublime, thereby inaugurating a fundamental philosophical thinking which could only culminate in a thinking of total abyss, and a total abyss inevitably inseparable from Godhead itself.

Already Kant could call forth the joy of the sublime, a joy then bursting forth in the very advent of the romantic imagination, but this joy almost immediately reversed itself in this imagination, as visions of an absolute abyss gradually but decisively either numbed or inverted all full and active imagination. This led to yet another deep chasm between thinking and the imagination, one only crossed by Hegel, Nietzsche, and Heidegger. To refuse the deep negativity of these thinkers is to refuse the imagination itself, and therewith to refuse every possibility of joy. If the joy of innocence has wholly disappeared in our world, and joy itself is now inseparable from the deepest abyss, that abyss is certainly an abyss of evil, even if evil itself is now seemingly impenetrable to all thinking. At no other point is thinking itself now so distant from the imagination, and most clearly so our theological thinking, one closed to the very possibility of apprehending evil in the Godhead, and thus closed to the possibility of understanding an ultimate transfiguration of evil, or a transfiguration of evil occurring in the Godhead itself. Already Boehme deeply envisioned such a transfiguration, hence the fundamental importance of Boehme for both Schelling and Hegel, but that transfiguration is impossible apart from an evil or negative pole in the Godhead, and a pole which is not simply a dark abyss but far rather pure evil itself.

Is it possible to think pure evil itself, and to think of it not as a pure nothingness but rather as a purely actual nothingness? Yes, the Augustinian thinker does this in thinking of the actuality of sin, and all too significantly this thinking inevitably thinks the totality of sin, or the totality of sin in everything that we can actually know as consciousness, or know as consciousness apart from grace. We know from the *Confessions* that such thinking was essential to Augustine's conversion, and essential to his understanding of redemption, a redemption from the deepest depths of sin, which is to say from the deepest depths of evil, so that here redemption is clearly a transfiguration of evil. Yet in orthodox theology this transfiguration can have no possible corollary in the Godhead. Luther, in his most Augustinian mode, could know the forgiveness of sin or justification as a creation from nothing, but in our deepest Western theology, justification or redemption is not simply a restoration of our original or unfallen condition, it is far rather a truly new creation. This and this alone makes possible theodicy, which is certainly a justification of evil, one knowing the necessity of evil for genuine redemption, hence the necessity of God's willing of evil, as so decisively called forth in the uniquely Western dogma of predestination.

The dogma of predestination is ultimately a dogma of the transfiguration of evil, as luminously brought forth in Barth's doctrine of election or predestination, and it is a transfiguration of evil precisely as a dogma of double predestination, so that Barth can understand the damnation of Christ as the redemption of humanity. This is that double predestination which Barth can know as the gospel itself, and it is the consequence of God's eternal election. Here, Barth profoundly challenges our deepest theological tradition, and does so by so fully correlating the transfiguration of evil in redemption with the transfiguration of evil in God's ultimate act of election. Thereby the thinking of double predestination can only awaken a pure joy in us, but that joy is inseparable from God's act of making His only Son "to be sin" (*Church Dogmatics*, II, 2, 352). This affirmation is based not only upon Paul's affirmation that Christ redeemed us from the "curse" of the Law by becoming a curse for us (*Gal.* 3:13), but also upon Paul's declaration that for our sake God made Christ, who knew no sin, to be sin (II *Cor.* 5:21). Perhaps there are no more challenging words in scripture, but Barth met this challenge, although he only does so in his doctrine of election, and if this gave us

Barth's deepest theology, it is inevitably a theology of the transfiguration of evil in the Godhead itself.

⟿

Classical Christian theology can know creation and redemption as the one eternal act of God, but Western theology, in knowing that act as the act of predestination, can know the necessity of the transfiguration of evil in that very act, and thus finally cannot know either redemption or creation apart from the enactment of an absolute evil. Only Barth among our theologians has recognized this consequence, but he can do so only by maintaining that evil or nothingness has been annihilated by the crucifixion and the resurrection of Christ, so that genuine faith can finally know nothing of either evil or nothingness, and this is the very condition that the Christian most deeply knows as freedom itself. Adolph Harnack, our greatest historian of Christian dogma, and also our greatest historian of Marcionism, could respond to the early Barth as a rebirth of Marcion. Surely the early Barth did call forth a deep dichotomy between Law and Gospel, or "religion" and faith, or the God of this world and the Biblical God. Is that dichotomy truly transcended in the *Church Dogmatics*? Or is it inevitably preserved in a dual affirmation of the reality of nothingness and the annihilation of nothingness? If each is known in faith, is it faith in God's election or predestination which most deeply dissolves any possibility of the apprehension of nothingness? Yet that election is the election of God in Christ to an eternal perdition or damnation, a damnation which faith knows in knowing predestination, a damnation which is certainly an enactment of an absolute nothingness, even if that enactment annihilates nothingness itself.

Here, we can observe a genuine parallel to a Buddhist apprehension of an absolutely negative nothingness which is an absolutely positive nothingness. In each, an actual freedom is impossible apart from this nothingness, a nothingness which is a genuine *coincidentia oppositorum* between its negative and positive poles, and apart from a realization of that *coincidentia* we are condemned to an absolute bondage, or to damnation itself. Barth is alone among our truly modern theologians in being able to speak of damnation, but he can know damnation only as the damnation of Christ. Therein we are inevitably reminded of the Buddhist Bodhisattva, just as we are reminded of a Buddhism that can know nirvana as being all in all. Yet Buddhism has given us a vast body of symbolism, ritual, meditation, and thinking that incorporates this realization, whereas every such Christian realization is wholly alien to the dogma of the Church, and has only fully appeared in the deepest Christian heresy. Future historians of dogma may well recognize Karl Barth as the deepest heretic of the twentieth century. Is he a true "heretic" by so deeply affirming predestination? That would be a genuine irony, for is there any dogma more truly distinctive of Western Christianity than the dogma of predestination?

Western theologians almost invariably know every deep Eastern vision as an enactment of creation as fall, but is not the dogma of predestination such an enactment, and inevitably so if the eternal act of creation is identical with the eternal act of predestination? This is a deep Western dogma, for even if it was created by Augustine, it was deeply affirmed by every truly major Western theologian, and would appear to be inescapable for any genuine affirmation of either theodicy or the providence of God. Christian theology has ever responded to the question of why is there any being at all, why not far rather nothing, with the answer of redemption, and an eternal redemption which is even the glorification of God, a final glorification which is insepa-rable from the original creation, and which is an ultimate transfiguration of everything that is truly "other" than the Godhead. So that, even if only im-plicitly, Christian theology knows that "evil" is transfigured in redemption, is absolutely transformed, and even if it is thereby reduced to a pure and final nothingness, such a transformation is a genuine act, and is the eternal act of redemption. But that act is finally the original act of creation, a creation that must necessarily establish a genuine potency of evil, but a potency that must become actuality if a genuine redemption is to occur, for Christian redemp-tion can only be a redemption from the depths of evil.

Now if the eternal act of creation is identical with the eternal act of predestination, then creation is finally the creation of evil, and of the deepest depths of evil, apart from which nothing that Christianity truly knows as redemption could be actual or real. Profoundly alien as this realization is to every classical or orthodox theology, it would appear to be an inevitable consequence of that theology, even if that consequence is not called forth until the full advent of modernity. Blake and Nietzsche deeply knew this, which is precisely why they could know an established or orthodox Christian redemption as a realization of nothingness, and of an actual nothingness, or a total condition of repression or ressentiment. So it is that Nietzsche can know the Christian gospel as *dysangel*, or a call to an absolute nothingness, just as Blake could know the orthodox Christian God as Satan, a Satan whom Nietzsche could know as an absolute No-saying, and an absolute No-saying only truly or purely embodied in the Christian God. Yet it is just this thinking and vision that called forth the clearest vision of redemption in full moder-nity, a vision that has had an overwhelming impact upon our subsequent history, and above all so upon the deeper imaginative enactments of the twentieth century, enactments that are inconceivable apart from such a ground.

Nothing more distinguishes Christianity from all the religions of the world than its profound and ultimate affirmation of an original fall. While

Christian orthodoxy radically distinguishes creation and fall, it nevertheless cannot know a creation independent of fall, just as it cannot know a fall that is independent of the creation. Nevertheless, Milton profoundly enacted a primordial fall in *Paradise Lost*, a fall not only prior to the creation, but which itself necessitates the creation, as revealed to Adam by the archangel Raphael in its seventh book, so that here and elsewhere in deep Christian heresy it is a primordial fall which is a deep ground of creation, and one inseparable from the final apocalyptic goal of the creation. Although Milton resolutely refused any possibility of fall in the Godhead, this was yet another deep ground of his revolutionary creation of Satan, and if Milton's Satan is the pure evil of darkness incarnate, that is the absolute evil which is absolutely necessary for the epic drama of *Paradise Lost*. And this drama is a dialectical drama, impelled by the absolute opposites of Satan and the Messiah. Satan and the Son of God are not only dialectical opposites but dialectical polarities, each of whose deepest actions dialectically inverts and reverses the actions of the other, but in that very dialectical polarity each is absolutely necessary to the other. Nor is this imaginative drama simply and only an imaginative drama, for it was destined to be resurrected in a purely conceptual expression in Hegel's *Phenomenology of Spirit*, and Hegel's *Phenomenology* was the first philosophical work to be deeply grounded in the primal expressions of our imagination.

Deeply heretical as Hegel and Milton certainly are, the deep Christian ground of their work cannot be denied. Just as Hegel created a dialectical philosophical thinking deeply grounded in the ultimate movements of creation, fall, incarnation, crucifixion, and resurrection, Milton created a dialectical epic poetry not only deeply grounded in creation and fall, but equally grounded in incarnation and crucifixion, and just as Hegel was the first philosopher of the death of God, Milton was the first poet to envision a divine death in the crucifixion. Of course, for Milton this is not the death of Godhead itself, as it is for Hegel, but that deep difference between Hegel and Milton is also a difference between full modernity and early modernity, and even as Milton was profoundly reborn in Blake, it was Blake who first envisioned the death of God in the conclusion of *America*, engraved in 1793. Blake's purest vision of the death of God is all too significantly given us in his *Milton*, where Milton or a personified Christ goes to "Eternal Death," an eternal death in which "I in my Selfhood am that Satan" (14: 30), for now it is revealed that the self-annihilation of God in Christ is the self-annihilation of Satan. For the atoning death of Christ is the sacrifice of the fallen and empty body of the Godhead, the very Godhead that is the repressive ruler of a wholly fallen world, and this is that final sacrifice which is apocalypse itself.

This very motif can be discovered in the concluding movement of the *Phenomenology of Spirit*, in the section entitled "The Revealed Religion."

Here Hegel most deeply calls forth the self-emptying movement of *kenosis*. Absolute Being is demonstrated as attaining its highest essence in its own *coming down*; here the lowest is at the same time the highest, and God is *revealed as He is* (760–61). Yet this revelation cannot occur apart from a deep realization of the self-alienation of the Divine Being, a self-alienation which is "Being-in-itself" or absolute transcendence. This is that alienated Godhead that yields to death, and thereby is first manifest as "Spirit" (779). For this ultimate death of the Divine Being is its resurrection as Spirit. Here Hegel absolutely reverses the orthodox dogma of the Trinity, and if this is only possible by calling forth the absolute self-alienation of the Creator, only that self-alienation can undergo an ultimate death, but this is that absolute sacrifice issuing in an apocalyptic resurrection, and an apocalyptic resurrection which is the final destiny of an absolutely self-alienated Godhead. "Spirit" is the Hegelian name of resurrected Godhead, but Spirit is possible and real only by way of an absolute death, and the actual and ultimate death of a purely abstract or purely self-alienated Godhead.

CHAPTER 6

∽

The Genesis of Evil

The deepest and most universal of all mythical motifs is origin, and above all so an absolute origin or an absolute genesis, an origin which is also enacted in our deepest rituals, rituals whose anamnesis is a renewal of that origin. Every genuine ritual is ultimately a ritual of origin, and insofar as such ritual enacts or embodies a primordial sacrifice, that is the very sacrifice which is herein recalled, and recalled as an ultimate origin, an origin which deep ritual repeats and renews. Yet that is a renewal of a violent disruption, a primordial disruption which is enacted or renewed in primordial sacrifice. This disruption embodies what Hegel could know as an original self-negation or self-emptying, and a disruption apart from which there could only finally be an original or primordial calm that Buddhism can know as nirvana or sunyata. Buddhism knows evil as a pure illusion, which is perfectly consistent with the deep ground of Buddhism. Even if illusion is here known as being virtually universal, being truly transcended only by the arhat or the Bodhisattva, illusion is nevertheless truly and finally and only illusion, which is precisely why Mahayana Buddhism can know sunyata as an absolute void or nothingness. Just as a deep logic was not born until the advent of Mahayana Buddhism, it was Buddhism which first evolved a truly universal or comprehensive philosophy, but one in which thinking itself is finally an illusion, although it is the depths of thinking which realizes this illusion, and realizes it in the very purity of its thinking of ultimate or absolute origin.

Origin as origin disappears in all such thinking, and most clearly disappears as an origin that is an actual origin or beginning. No such origin can be possible in anything that ancient thinking can know, which is why Catholic theology can maintain that genesis can be known or manifest only through revelation. No thinking knows origin more deeply or more purely than does Buddhist thinking, and yet here origin as origin vanishes more decisively and more finally than in any other thinking. Even if Mahayana Buddhism has

79

given us comprehensive mythologies and rituals enacting origin, these rituals and mythologies themselves disappear in the depths of Buddhist meditation and praxis, and disappear with the ultimate disappearance of origin itself. There are genuine parallels to this disappearance in Neoplatonism, and above all so in the depths of Neoplatonism, and the mystery of origin has been an ultimate mystery in the West, as it has surely not been in the East. Origin or ultimate origin has become a deeply forbidden or deeply threatening question in the West, and one only truly broached by our most radical heresies. At no point do Marxism and Freudianism more fully coincide than in their centering upon the question of origin. Here such thinking is truly an ultimate assault and an ultimate offense, and all too significantly it disappears in both neo-Marxism and neo-Freudianism, just as it disappears in all our theological neo-orthodoxies.

Theologically, absolute origin is both absolutely orthodox and absolutely heretical, a simultaneity unveiling the deep ambivalence of the very category of origin. Nothing is more forbidden theologically than the question of absolute origin, or the question of the origin of God or the Godhead, and yet theology is simply unthinkable apart from the question of origin, and ultimately the question of absolute origin. If only for this reason, deep theology has always been a profound threat to our Western traditions. Precisely the opposite has been true in the East, where the deepest thinking has overwhelmingly been a religious or sacred thinking. Even the "atheisms" of the East have been deeply incorporated within Eastern religious traditions, and secularism in the Western sense was unknown in the East until the advent of Western imperialism. Therefore the question of origin has always been a sacred question in the East, and, all too significantly, Chinese tradition, which the West can know as the most secular of all Eastern traditions, is virtually bereft of myths of origin. Buddhist thinking begins with the question of origin, the origin of pain and suffering, which is here the question of the origin of selfhood or the ego, and if that very thinking necessarily leads to the dissolution of any possible selfhood, that is a dissolution of any possible origin, and just thereby a dissolution of anything whatsoever that the West can know as either God or the Godhead.

If only in this perspective, we can see how the question of absolute origin is necessarily essential to what the West knows as theology. If this question is purely orthodox and purely heretical at once, it does unveil a deep ground of Western orthodoxy, and that is its essential and necessary relation to heresy, and just as the deepest orthodoxy has called forth the deepest heresy in the West, at no point have our heresies been so overwhelming as they have been in calling forth a truly and finally subversive origin, and one most subversive of our deepest orthodoxies. All of these heresies have centered upon the origin of an absolute evil, an absolute evil which is here manifest as beginning or genesis itself, a beginning that is the beginning of actuality itself, and therewith the beginning of a full actualization of a pure negativity. Eastern vision can know every such beginning as the beginning of illusion, but our deeper Western heresies know this beginning as the beginning of a pure actuality, although a wholly fallen or negative actuality. Just as a purely actual fall is wholly unknown in the East, it is primal in Western heresy and orthodoxy alike, but in our deeper heresies creation itself is fall, and a totally actual fall. The calling forth of that fall deeply subverts everything that orthodoxy can know as creation, and if thereby origin becomes a wholly and finally negative origin, it does unveil the deeply negative potentiality of the very category of origin, and brings a revealing light to Buddhism's pure dissolution of origin.

Violence is a primal motif in innumerable myths and rituals of origin, and these comprehend both primordial and historical worlds, and just as a primordial New Year festival, a festival reenacting the creation, can pass into the Christian Holy Week, that week is centered in the violence of the crucifixion rather than in the joy of resurrection. The very violence of this celebration is the deep center of a uniquely modern epic, which not only knows creation as fall, as in Milton, Blake, and Joyce alike, but also calls forth the pure violence of genesis or origin itself. Not only is this a pure violence, it is also an absolute violence, as most comprehensively enacted in *Finnegans Wake*, and the *Wake* is not only our most comprehensive realization of creation as fall, it is also and even thereby a deep celebration of violence, a celebration fully embodied in the very language of this epic text. Now cosmos and chaos are fully united, and fully united in this new epic language, but that language is a renewal of a primordial language, and a primordial language celebrating absolute origin, an absolute origin which is an absolute fall. True, the *Wake* culminates in resurrection, the apocalyptic resurrection of Anna Livia Plurabelle, but that ending is simultaneously the beginning of this apocalyptic epic, and the apocalyptic beginning of an absolute negativity.

Nothing more fully illuminates an absolute evil than does the very question of its origin. If this question is comprehensively and overwhelmingly posed in our deepest modern heresy, it is only possible in reaction against a deep theological orthodoxy, an orthodoxy knowing only the goodness of the Creator, and therefore an orthodoxy refusing the very actuality of evil. Spinoza is our first purely heretical modern thinker, and his very thinking of "God" or "substance" dissolves any possibility of knowing a transcendent Creator. For the first time, belief in such a Creator is known as the consequence of a pure passivity, and if it is passivity alone which Spinoza can know as a true evil, this is the very passivity which is the origin of our deepest illusion, so that even Spinoza can know a genesis of evil, and even know it in knowing the impossibility of the actuality of evil. If only at this point, Spinoza is a deeply orthodox thinker, so that if deep orthodoxy and deep heresy are inseparable even in Spinoza, the very thinking of evil calls forth such an inseparability, and inevitably such thinking has ever been deeply forbidden in the West. For it is impossible for the Western thinker to think about evil without thinking of the origin of evil, and even if that origin lies in a pure passivity, this is just the passivity that Spinoza can know as the origin of violence, a passivity that Nietzsche can know as repression or ressentiment, and if it is repression alone which can now be known as the origin of evil, that is nevertheless an actual origin, and the actual origin of an actual evil.

While Spinoza seemingly refused the very possibility of thinking of evil, he nevertheless thought of evil in thinking of passivity, thereby calling forth a genuine origin of evil. Spinoza knows the great mass of humanity to be enclosed within passivity, and even knows our most advanced thinkers to have been enclosed in such a passivity, a passivity that they call forth in thinking teleology or final causation, or in thinking of any possible transcendence of God or Being. So it is that Spinoza transforms every final cause into an efficient cause (*Ethics,* I, 31), and even the creation itself negates or excludes all causes except the efficient cause, an efficient cause which is the absolute power of God. That is the power which is an absolute necessity, but an absolutely immanent necessity, and Spinoza knows all things whatsoever not as contingent but as necessary, for only the imagination looks upon anything as being contingent (*Ethics,* II, 44). All imagination or fantasy is here a consequence of passivity, and it is impossible when the mind is fully active, such activity of the mind is fully harmonious with the body, and in it no genuine illusion or evil is possible. Yet the historical truth is that no such mind existed until Spinoza, and inevitably Spinoza was condemned as our deepest and purest heretic, just as he was the first heretic to be condemned as a purely philosophical or purely rational thinker.

Surely Spinoza knew an evil or passivity which comprehended everything that our Western traditions have known as God, and if Hegel was the first thinker after Spinoza fully to incorporate Spinoza's thinking, he did so only by transforming Spinoza's absolute substance into an absolute negativity. In each thinker an absolute transcendence is transformed into an absolute immanence, and negation is the primary method of both Spinoza and Hegel. Now the genesis of evil can be known as the genesis of transcendent Godhead, and while this is only implicit in Spinoza, it is nevertheless inseparable from his understanding of passivity. Spinoza could not publish apart from a deep censorship, so that the *Ethics* could only be published after his death; he has ever remained our purest heretic, and our purest heretic as our purest thinker. Not even Nietzsche can truly challenge Spinoza at this point, and surely not that Hegel who could never openly or decisively distinguish himself from Christian orthodoxy. If Spinoza can now be unveiled as a forerunner of Marx, he is also a hidden ground of our most radical modern poets, and perhaps a ground of a uniquely twentieth-century physics, as Einstein himself acknowledged.

When evil is known as an illusion, a deep thinking can call forth the origin of that illusion. This certainly occurs in Buddhist thinking, and occurs more comprehensively here than anywhere else, but it also occurs in thinkers as diverse as Spinoza and Plotinus, just as it occurs in Augustine and Aquinas, so that a deep thinking about evil has occurred throughout the world, even if it is wholly absent today. Is it possible that a genuine thinking about evil is more deeply forbidden today than it ever previously has been? And if the ubiquity of evil is more fully manifest in our world than in any previous world, is that a ubiquity foreclosing the question of origin, and foreclosed if only because a genuine absence of evil or innocence of evil is simply inconceivable in our world, and thus the question of the origin of evil cannot even arise? Yes, we know repression as the origin of evil, but we can only know repression as a ubiquitous repression, and therefore cannot be open to the question of the origin of repression, and this despite the fact that this was an absolutely crucial question for both Nietzsche and Freud, and a question apart from which no genuine understanding of repression is possible. And if the origin of repression is unknowable and unthinkable, how is it possible to know the very actuality of repression, an actuality inevitably invisible and unheard if nothing whatsoever is truly manifest which is other than repression?

Hence truly to know the actuality of repression is to know the origin of repression, and truly to know the actuality of evil is to know the origin or genesis of evil, or, at least, to be open to the actuality of that origin, and above all to be open to the actuality of that origin within ourselves. Both Buddhism and Augustinianism overwhelmingly demonstrate that a genuine openness to our own interior is an openness to the deep negativity of that interior. A fully comparable negativity is deeply called forth in the modern world by both Nietzsche and Freud, just as it is in the deepest modern imaginative voyages into our interior. Have all such voyages now ended, and ended by the disappearance of an interior that is truly distinguishable from the exterior? This disappearance was already occurring in Spinoza, so that once again our world would appear to be a resurrection of Spinoza, even if it can only know a "substance" which could have no possible association with "God." Evil surely disappears in such a "substance," but does it wholly disappear, and disappear without any traces whatsoever? Or do such traces remain as deep ciphers or surds, surds both voiceless and imageless, but nonetheless inescapable, and inescapable in the brute actuality of our world? One such surd is the very vacuity of a new interior, one perhaps no longer namable as a desert or an abyss, but nevertheless namable as a deep cipher or knot, and a knot unhearable apart from a calling forth of its origin, or an opening to the actuality of genesis itself.

While our new cosmologies center upon a genesis or an absolute beginning, such a genesis is truly opaque to us as an interior genesis. Here everything that we could know as a truly actual genesis is fully silent or invisible, and while a deep and ultimate disjuncture between the interior and the exterior was established with the very birth of modernity, this made possible deep voyages into both exterior and interior worlds. Our interior voyages have now seemingly ended, and with them have apparently ended all traces of an interior genesis, which perhaps has made possible the depth of our new voyages into a purely exterior genesis. Yet if the interior and the exterior are now truly united, or no trace remains of any true division between them, are we being initiated into a new harmony between body and mind, or matter and spirit? Spinoza already knew this harmony, but perhaps only prophetically. Surely it has never been actually realized before, but is it now perhaps upon our horizon? This could well be the actual advent of what Blake could envision as an apocalyptic marriage of Heaven and Hell, and the very vacuity of our new interior could be a decisive sign of such an advent, and if that vacuity is only actually namable as darkness, that darkness could be an apocalyptic darkness, and one whose genesis is apocalypse itself.

Now an apocalyptic darkness is a universal darkness, and even if it is a darkness before the dawn, an apocalyptic dawning is inseparable from an absolute darkness. Only in that dawning is darkness fully or actually manifest as a universal darkness, so that a genuine ubiquity of darkness is a consequence of an actual beginning or genesis of apocalypse. Here, genesis is the consequence of the advent of apocalypse, a new genesis that is nevertheless a repetition of an original genesis, and repetition in the Kierkegaardian sense as opposed to what Kierkegaard could know as a pagan recollection, for this repetition is a forward rather than a backward movement of eternity, and thus it is the very reversal of the archaic movement of eternal return. This is the reversal that is the movement of apocalypse, and if a new genesis is the center of apocalypse, that is clearly a genesis of an absolute darkness, and an apocalyptic darkness inseparable from an apocalyptic light. Now darkness is truly universal, and is necessarily universal as a consequence of this new genesis. If an original creation is a creation *ex nihilo*, then so, too, is an apocalyptic creation, but an apocalyptic nothingness embodies a totality truly transcending an original nothingness, and a totality which is the consequence of the forward movement of apocalypse.

Evil, and an absolute evil, is certainly embodied in the totality of an apocalyptic nothingness; just as this is an evil which is named by every apocalyptic seer, it is an evil fully actual in an absolute darkness, but now evil is just as ubiquitous as is this new darkness, and therefore within that realm it cannot stand forth or be manifest as evil itself. Every genuine apocalyptic prophet enacts an ending of everything that has previously stood forth as light. Here no previous epiphany of light could possibly illuminate a new darkness, and thus darkness is now unnamable from every previous horizon, and the evil of that darkness is unnamable as well, and if now darkness is truly incarnate, then so, too, is now incarnate a truly new and apocalyptic evil. This is why it is only apocalypticism which has actually named Satan, a Satan unknown to revelation itself until the advent of apocalypticism, hence a Satan unknown to the Torah, and unknown to all wisdom traditions until the advent of Gnosticism. For Gnosticism and apocalypticism are dialectical twins. Each played a decisive role in the genesis of Christianity, and each was negated in the triumph of orthodox Christianity. Now darkness ceases to be manifest as that totality which both apocalypticism and Gnosticism could know, and with that dissolution darkness once again becomes open to the horizons of primordial traditions, and evil ceases to be manifest as a totality and becomes once again an evil that is the opposite of the good.

But with the ending of Christendom, an ending already germinated in the late Middle Ages, darkness is once again resurrected as a totality, and evil is once again fully namable as it had not been since the advent of apocalypticism and Gnosticism. Now a new ubiquity of evil is at hand, and one inseparable from a new apocalypticism, if not a new Gnosticism, and this new apocalypticism is inseparable from the death of the Christian God. Even Spinoza could be understood as an apocalyptic thinker in this perspective, for Spinoza was the first thinker fully to think the dissolution or ending of the transcendent God, just as he was also the first thinker actually to think an absolute immanence, thereby transcendence itself can only be manifest as an alien transcendence, and an alien transcendence whose ground could only be that deep and universal passivity which Spinoza could know as evil. Such a passivity is truly invisible and unheard of in thinking itself until Spinoza, and even if Spinoza is that thinker who is most innocent of evil, and whose thinking makes impossible every actual naming of evil, this is a thinking inseparable from that new world born in early modernity, and thus inseparable from truly new epiphanies of darkness and evil. And now evil and darkness are actual as they never were in the ancient world, or actual in thinking and the imagination as they never were in previous worlds. With the culmination of modernity, evil is once again truly ubiquitous, but now ubiquitous in a new totality, and in a new apocalyptic totality.

If the advent of that totality can be known as the genesis of a new ubiquity of evil, then such evil is not truly nameless, not simply a cipher or a surd, but far rather an evil inseparable from that new apocalypse. Apocalyptic thinkers and visionaries truly abound in late modernity, their deep naming of evil might well be recognized as a genuine naming, and one whose resonance could surely have issued in a postmodern anonymity or namelessness. For if an apocalyptic genesis is a universal genesis, and the evil which

is a consequence of that genesis a universal evil and darkness, then even if
it is seemingly nameless, a universal namelessness could be known as an
embodiment of that universal darkness. Such namelessness could indeed be
naming itself, just as the deep anonymity of our late modern imaginative
enactments is not a simple anonymity, but a truly new anonymity, and if it is
truly paralleled in a Buddhist selflessness, it embodies a truly alien ground
wholly unknown to Buddhism, just as it embodies an alien or negative nothingness that is truly the opposite of any possible Buddhist nothingness, or any
possible Buddhist calm.

So it is that the very violence that is so manifest in primordial myths of
creation has truly been reborn, and reborn not only in our imagination but in
a uniquely violent twentieth-century history as well, a history seemingly ending
modernity itself, but if that ending is the inevitable consequence of a new
apocalypse, it is the consequence of an absolute genesis, and a new genesis
which is the origin of a truly new evil. Theologies that can only know evil
as an ancient or primordial evil are truly closed to this new evil, and just as
our philosophies have become silent about evil in response to this new condition and this new world, everything that we have known as philosophical
and theological thinking might well have come to an end. If so, this, too, is
a decisive sign of a new world. Are we confronted with a truly new
unspeakability of evil, or do we speak evil in that very unspeakability? Do we
speak it not simply in a voicelessness of speech, but in a new vacuity of
speech, a vacuity echoing this new evil, and echoing it most deeply within?
Empty as our psychologies have surely become, is this emptiness a consequence of a truly new understanding of a truly new human condition? This
new psychology strangely echoes Buddhist and Augustinian psychologies in
drawing forth the emptiness or the negativity of consciousness, and surely
parallels Augustinianism and Buddhism in knowing the ultimate emptiness of
the human condition apart from grace or enlightenment.

Just as Buddhism and Augustinianism can know illusion or sin as being
most deeply our own, it is this very ownness that is our deepest bondage, a
bondage that is a full and genuine impotence, and it is the very realization of
this impotence that opens us to the possibility of freedom. That freedom is
a freedom from impotence, and a freedom from an impotence that is truly our
own, so far from being an impotence that is simply a natural or a given
condition, it is an impotence that is a consequence of our own acts, and most
deeply of our own interior acts, interior acts which only become manifest as
such with the realization of our own role in creating that very impotence.
Hence both Augustinianism and Buddhism realize a profound responsibility.
We ourselves are truly and fully responsible for our every act, and even if
Buddhism can know our ultimately painful and negative condition as the
consequence of a false or illusory selfhood, its *paticca-sammuppada* or chain

of causation or dependent origination created the first comprehensive realization of the depths of our interior. These depths are simultaneously physical and psychical chains; each is integrally related to the other, and each the consequence of an ultimate *tanha* or craving, which is present nowhere but within ourselves. Truly to know that craving is to be delivered from our bondage, for truly to know it is to dissolve it in that very knowledge, a profoundly interior knowledge, even if it is only possible as a consequence of the dissolution of our selfhood. And the Augustinian, in knowing the depths of our sin, knows these depths as profoundly interior depths, depths which are the very opposite of any possible exterior necessity. Truly to know these depths is to be liberated from their bondage, a liberation which is quite simply a total responsibility for our fallen condition, and even if it is possible only by grace, that is a grace through which we are first confronted with our totally fallen condition.

In both Buddhism and Augustinianism, truly to know evil is to know that evil which is most deeply within. Every association of evil with an exterior cause or necessity is to evade or dissolve true evil, an evil which is only deeply within, and which can be realized as such only by grace or enlightenment. Does this mean that when the within becomes invisible or unheard that evil, too, is then unheard and invisible, or manifest only as purely exterior condition or necessity? Is our refusal of evil, and of our own interior evil, itself a refusal of grace or enlightenment? This is the very condition that both Buddhism and Augustinianism can know to be characteristic of the great mass of humanity, indeed, of all humanity apart from grace or enlightenment, and surely such a humanity has never been so manifest as it is today. Now even if Mahayana Buddhism knows a humanity in which all are enlightened, and thus knows a grace transcending everything that Christianity has manifestly known as grace, it does so only by knowing the totality of Buddha or nirvana, that is a totality which Christianity knows as an apocalyptic totality, and a totality only possible as the consequence of the deepest and most final ending.

Yet that very ending is inseparable from the realization of the most absolute evil, an evil embodied in a final apocalyptic darkness. Only the full and final advent of that darkness makes possible a truly apocalyptic ending, and the totality of that darkness fully parallels a Buddhist void or nothingness, if only because it is absolutely inseparable from the totality of an apocalyptic "light." Just as the Mahayana Buddhist can know the dialectical identity of nirvana and samsara, the apocalyptic Christian can know the dialectical identity of darkness and light. Yes, apocalyptic prophets are prophets of an ultimate darkness, but precisely thereby they are prophets of an ultimate light, a light that "shines" only in that darkness, is visible only within the horizon of an ultimate and final night, or is actual only in the actuality of an absolute and final darkness. And just as it was not until the advent of Buddhism that a deep interiority was called forth, and an interiority that is a wholly negative or empty interiority, it is not until the advent of apocalypticism that an absolute guilt or "bad conscience" becomes manifest and real, a totally guilty "I" that is the bad conscience or a purely negative consciousness, and one inseparable from the full advent of an absolute grace and forgiveness. For it is impossible to know this grace and forgiveness apart from the depths of an absolute guilt, just as it is impossible to know enlightenment or nirvana apart from a full realization of the ultimate depths of the absolute bondage of samsara. Paul is the deepest and purest thinker of ancient apocalypticism, and nothing is so central in his genuine letters than the *coincidentia oppositorum* that he draws forth between guilt and grace, a grace that can be real only in the depths of guilt, and a guilt that is invisible and unheard apart from the advent of an apocalyptic redemption. A fully parallel *coincidentia* can be discovered in Siddhartha Gotama, who called forth an absolutely new freedom from the depths of an ultimate bondage or illusion which he was the first to unveil, so that the discovery of this freedom is inseparable from the discovery of this bondage, and even as guilt and grace are inseparable in Christianity, nirvana and samsara are inseparable in Buddhism.

Thus the genesis of evil, and the genesis of an absolute evil or darkness, is absolutely necessary for a total or totally actual redemption; if it is only through that redemption that an absolute darkness or evil can be known and realized as an absolute nothingness, that nothingness is absolutely essential for an ultimate freedom or grace, or for an ultimate joy and peace. Again and again, and most clearly so by Nietzsche, Paul and Gotama have been identified as the purest ancient nihilists, but if only thereby they are prophets of our world, the most nihilistic world in history, and ours is a nihilism realized in our deepest depths. If only in this perspective, we can know Christianity and Buddhism as the most nihilistic of all religions, thereby becoming open to Nietzsche's identification of the Christian God as the deification of nothingness or the will to nothingness pronounced holy (*The Antichrist,* 18). Nietzsche knows nihilism and nothingness more deeply than does any other modern thinker, and this does establish a genuine continuity between Nietzsche and both Paul and Gotama, but this is a continuity between our nihilism and an ancient nihilism, or between a profane nihilism and a sacred nihilism. Each, in this perspective, is an ultimate nihilism, and each ultimately calls forth an absolute Yes-saying or an absolute joy. But that joy is inseparable from absolute judgment, or what Nietzsche could know as an absolute No-saying, a No-saying which he could know as the Christian God, and if that God is the deification of nothingness, that is a "deification" absolutely essential for an absolute joy, or absolutely essential for an ultimate act of Yes-saying. Hence the genesis of an absolute darkness is absolutely necessary for the genesis of an absolute "light," or the genesis of an absolute evil is absolutely necessary for the genesis of an absolute grace. Here an ultimate genesis is necessarily a *coincidentia oppositorum*, so that an absolute nihilism is essential for the depths of Christianity and Buddhism alike.

Now a *coincidentia oppositorum* is certainly not confined to a mythical or religious realm. It can and does appear in our deepest thinking and imaginative vision, and most clearly so in full or late modernity. If such a *coincidentia* even now is real, then the ubiquity of our darkness cannot finally be distinguished from the ubiquity of a new light, and the ubiquity of our evil cannot finally be distinguished from the ubiquity of a new grace. The very namelessness of our evil could be a sign of such a grace, and if never before has evil been so deeply nameless or anonymous, this could be a veil for a new transfiguration, a transfiguration that could only be a wholly anonymous transfiguration, hence one both invisible and unheard, or one which is most deeply "nothing." Yet if our nothing is a reflection of an absolute nothingness, and is so if only because of its very universality, and a universality from which there is clearly no exit, or no exit which does not entail an impossible voyage to an irrecoverable past, then the very advent of such a nothingness cannot be unrelated to that "nothingness" which both Buddhism and an apocalyptic Christianity know, a nothingness voiding the deepest ground of the worlds from which they evolved, just as our nothingness has deeply voided the ground of the world from which we evolved.

A movement of ultimate and universal negation is deeply fundamental to both apocalypticism and Buddhism, and in each a deep negation is finally a pure affirmation. This movement is essential to dialectical thinking, vision, and faith, hence it is primal in the prophetic revolution, where faith is born as a truly individual faith, but only by knowing the totality of a judgment that alone makes possible a new redemption, a new redemption inseparable from the ending of every established ground of history or the world. The prophetic movement culminates in apocalypticism, or, at least, an initial apocalypticism, as in Second Isaiah, and Third Isaiah can know the near advent of a new creation and a new earth, and one in which all former things will be wholly forgotten or dissolved (65:17), a dissolution which is the inevitable consequence of a total judgment, but a total judgment that is finally a total redemption. So even as these prophets unveiled a depth of evil that had never been known or manifest before, their very unveiling of that depth is necessary and essential to the radically new hope and promise that they proclaimed and enacted, so the Christian inevitably identifies Jesus as a rebirth of these revolutionary prophets. Here, radical negation and radical affirmation are inseparable, a radical negation which is a total negation, and a radical affirmation which is a total affirmation. If that is a *coincidentia oppositorum*, such a coincidence or identity is an ultimate ground of every genuinely dialectical movement, and one even more purely present in Buddhism than in apocalypticism, but it is apocalypticism that has been the most revolutionary power in Western history, thinking, and vision.

Already in Paul an apocalyptic thinking draws forth the ultimacy of evil. This evil is at the very center of what Paul knows as *sarx* or flesh, and if *sarx* is the true opposite of *pneuma* or Spirit, it is only actually manifest with the full advent of Spirit, an advent which is an apocalyptic advent finally ushering in the end of *kosmos* or world. And this is the ending of every established ground of the world, or every genuine ground of the "old creation," an ending inseparable from the advent of the new creation, and that very ending realizes an absolute world-negation, one fully paralleling the absolute world-negation of Gnosticism. In apocalypticism, however, as opposed to Gnosticism, this negation is a truly historical negation, occurring at the very center of historical actuality. Paul could know Gnosticism, and a Christian Gnosticism, as the deepest "other" of what he knows as faith. Indeed, it was his conflict with Gnosticism that called forth Paul's deepest understanding of faith, a faith in that Christ who is absolutely other than that primordial Spirit that Gnosticism knows, and whose grace realizes an absolutely new freedom in the very actuality of the world, but only insofar as world itself is an absolutely new world. So it is that Paul knows the full advent of a new creation or a new world, that world calls forth the pure negativity of an old world, a pure negativity which certainly can be known as an absolute evil, and the very manifestation of that evil is a decisive sign of an apocalyptic ending which is an apocalyptic beginning.

Yet that ending is certainly not simply and only an interior ending, as it is in Gnosticism. Here ending is not in any sense a dualistic ending, hence its occurrence is a totally actual historical transformation, and a historical transformation ending every previous historical world. This is the very essence of a full apocalypticism, and it occurs again and again thereafter, with every new apocalypticism unveiling a truly new world, but only insofar as it absolutely assaults or negates an old world. With the birth of a fully modern apocalypticism, this negation is a truly comprehensive negation, occurring not only imaginatively but conceptually and politically as well, thereby realizing a universal revolution, and a universal revolution which truly transforms the world. Apocalypticism has ever been the deepest threat upon our Western horizon, the one most purely and most ruthlessly opposed by all orthodoxies, and the one that has generated our deepest and most powerful heresies. But also, and precisely thereby, it has called forth our most powerful counterrevolutions, and even if these seemingly dominate the world today, they are nevertheless a deep witness to the revolutionary power of apocalypticism.

Deep conservatives can know apocalypticism as an ultimate evil, even as an absolute evil, as it surely apparently is in its movement of absolute negation. If that negation is an assault, and perhaps the deepest possible assault, it is an interior and an exterior assault at once, and an assault making possible not only an absolute naming of evil, but also an absolute realization of evil, one inevitably occurring if only to make possible its assault, and one apart from which its assault or negation would be wholly unreal. But apocalyptic negation certainly is fully actual and real, not only did it occur in the very birth of Christianity, but it has occurred in our deeper thinking and deeper imagination, too, just as it has occurred in our political revolutions. All of these are united in drawing forth an absolute evil, and even if this evil is unrealizable apart from an apocalyptic negation, it surely is embodied in that negation, an embodiment apart from which no genuine apocalyptic movement is possible. So, too, a truly apocalyptic negation is impossible apart from an ultimate ground, a ground which Hegel can know as Absolute Spirit, or Nietzsche as Eternal Recurrence, each of these are uniquely modern expressions of an apocalyptic Godhead, and a Godhead that is an absolute No and an absolute Yes at once.

Spinoza, Hegel, and Nietzsche are united in knowing an absolute transcendence as an absolute immanence, and in each that immanence can be realized only by a negation of absolute transcendence. Moreover, the very emptiness of that negated transcendence is necessary and essential to the realization of an absolute immanence. Only when that emptiness is a fully actual emptiness is an absolute immanence possible, hence it is possible only by way of the dissolution of an absolutely transcendent Godhead. And each of these thinkers can know that dissolution as the absolute act of Godhead itself, indeed, a dissolution inseparable from that absolute act, and while this is far clearer in Spinoza and Hegel than it is in Nietzsche, only Nietzsche knows the death of God as an ultimately and finally apocalyptic event, and as that event which is the realization of an absolutely new creation. Is it thereby the repetition, and an apocalyptic or forward moving repetition, of an original creation? Just as Spinoza can know the Creator as an absolutely immanent Creator, is Nietzsche's naming of Eternal Recurrence a naming of such a Creator, but now a naming far more apocalyptic than was possible for Spinoza? And is it precisely because it can far more deeply know the absolute evil of an original or primordial Creator? If so, such a realization is essential for a fully and finally apocalyptic naming, just as it is for a finally apocalyptic negation, a realization apart from which no final apocalyptic negation could occur.

Just as a new creation is an absolute genesis, it is an absolute genesis of God or the Godhead. This genesis inevitably transcends both an original creation and an original Creator, so that now not only can an original creation be known as an "old creation," but an original Creator can be known as a truly negative or wholly alien Creator. Although this occurs as early as the Book of Job, it is only a uniquely modern apocalypticism that knows the death of that Creator, and knows it in knowing the very advent of a new creation. Consequently, the genesis of apocalyptic Godhead is inseparable from the absolute negation of primordial Godhead, and that negation can occur only through a realization of the absolute negativity of that primordial Godhead. Even if this is an absolutely new realization, and hence an absolutely new realization of the negativity of Godhead itself, that realization is necessary and essential for anything that could be a finally actual apocalypse of God. Do Spinoza, Hegel, and Nietzsche all know such an apocalypse, even if in radically different ways? Is such an apocalypse present in our great modern epics, and again in radically different ways? If so, is such an apocalypse an inevitable consequence of what a pure apocalypticism must inevitably know as an original or primordial Creator?

Both Hegel and Nietzsche can know the genesis of a primordial Creator as the genesis of an absolute evil, and this is true of Blake and Joyce as well. That genesis is absolutely essential to the very actuality of world as world, an actuality finally unreal if the creation is simply and only "good," or if the fall is not the fall of the creation itself, and a fall inseparable from the original act of creation. Neither Buddhism, Islam, nor Eastern Christianity can know such a fall, but both Paul and Augustine implicitly know it, and know it in knowing the totality of sin, or the totality of a wholly fallen world or "old creation." This totality is under the absolute sovereignty of the primordial Creator, and a totality whose very evil is "permitted" by that Creator. This permission becomes a full and absolute will in modernity, and this as early as nominalism, that "new philosophy" that so deeply affected the early Luther. Nominalism was itself the expression of a truly new Augustintianism, an Augustintianism that can now know an absolute predestination, and therefore know an absolute predestination of an absolute and eternal evil. This is a theology against which both Milton and Spinoza deeply reacted, but they nevertheless deepened it in knowing a new absolute Creator, and a new absolute necessity, for even if that necessity is here inseparable from freedom, that freedom itself is inseparable from a new absolute sovereignty, and the absolute sovereignty of a Godhead or "substance" that is purely and only itself. This is the very sovereignty which both Hegel and Nietzsche can know as being absolutely alien or "other," and now, and for the first time, a pure transcendence can only be known as a purely alien transcendence. Yet it is this very realization that makes possible the absolute negation of that transcendence, and the negation of that transcendence in every genuinely transcending moment or movement.

Here, the genesis of evil is finally the genesis of an absolute transfiguration of that evil, but a transfiguration impossible apart from such an original or primordial genesis. Therefore that primordial genesis is absolutely essential for a truly and finally apocalyptic transfiguration. Now just as predestination finally knows the necessity of evil and the fall, and knows it as being necessary for salvation itself, a full or fully modern apocalypticism knows the necessity of an absolute evil, an absolute evil inseparable from all full actuality, as most purely manifest within the depths of our own interior. If these depths are truly negative depths, as manifest in every calling forth of those depths, these negatives depths are absolutely essential for every deep transfiguration, just as a predestination to an eternal damnation is absolutely necessary for a predestination to an eternal salvation. This is a truth that is known by every deep and genuine Christian theology, or by every such Western theology. So, too, is it known by all fully modern apocalyptic thinking and vision, and this as early as Dante, and as late as Joyce, even if it is clearest in Blake's apocalyptic vision and Nietzsche's apocalyptic thinking, a thinking and vision for which an absolute No-saying and an absolute Yes-saying are not only inseparable, but finally identical, an identity which is finally the identity of "Heaven" and "Hell."

If it is Buddhism that most purely realizes a *coincidentia oppositorum*, it is in apocalypticism that this identity most actually occurs. In this actualization, interior and exterior realization are inseparable, hence it occurs historically as well as inwardly. If here interior realization never approaches the purity of its Buddhist counterpart, an exterior or historical realization is overwhelming, as is so fully manifest in that apocalyptic ending that is now consuming the world. And just as Buddhism is most deeply grounded in the absolutely primordial, apocalypticism is most deeply grounded in an absolutely new creation, and a new creation in which the absolute ending of evil is simultaneously the absolute ending of the "good." Such an ending is inevitable in any true apocalyptic transfiguration or transformation, one which Paul could already know, and if this inevitably called forth an antinomian apocalypticism, that is an apocalypticism that is purely called forth by both Blake and Nietzsche, who are thereby not only genuinely Pauline visionaries, but truly consistently or comprehensively apocalyptic visionaries, a consistency or comprehensiveness impossible for Paul, but inevitable in any genuine rebirth or renewal of an original and only initial apocalypticism. What Newman could discover as an organic and evolutionary development of Christian doctrine can now be understood as a far deeper evolution of apocalypticism, but it proceeds by far deeper breaks and transformations than does the development of Christian orthodoxy, and unlike that orthodoxy it truly recovers its original ground, yet it recovers it only by totalizing it, only by totalizing apocalypticism itself.

Of course, there are multiple forms of a uniquely modern apocalyptic totality, and these are deeply inconsistent with each other, but they are not inconsistent with their original ground, not inconsistent with an original apocalypticism. They are not even truly inconsistent with the earliest expressions of that apocalypticism, in which an absolute negation and an absolute affirmation are inseparable, and in which an absolute evil and an absolute good are likewise inseparable, or inseparable in every genuinely apocalyptic movement. So it is that the genesis of an apocalyptic light is inseparable from the genesis of an apocalyptic darkness, and the realization of an absolute joy is inseparable from the realization of an absolute guilt or impotence, and the advent of a new creation is inseparable from the ending of an old creation. All of these apocalyptic realizations are ancient and modern simultaneously, and while ancient apocalypticisms differed considerably from each other, such a difference is profoundly deepened in modernity. This difference is seemingly infinite between Marx and Nietzsche, and seemingly unbridgeable between Hegel and Nietzsche. Yet no such deep difference is manifest in modern imaginative apocalyptic vision, or, insofar as it exists, it can be understood as being transcended in the very evolution of that vision, as is most clearly manifest in the deep continuity between Dante and Joyce, or between Milton and Blake. And that is a continuity calling forth absolute evil, but some such continuity also exists in our modern apocalyptic thinking, which is perhaps nowhere more manifestly continuous than in its deep thinking of an absolute evil or an absolute negativity, or in its deep calling forth of an absolute ground, even if an absolutely empty ground, of a deep passivity, or a deep otherness, or a deep ressentiment. Indeed, this occurs imaginatively and conceptually at once, a simultaneity truly alien to the ancient world, yet truly present in the modern world, and perhaps most present in a uniquely modern negativity, yet a uniquely modern negativity inseparable from a uniquely modern apocalypse.

CHAPTER 7

⌒

The Transfiguration of Evil

Nothing is more central or more primal in the praxis of Jesus than the forgiveness of sin, and if at this point Jesus is unique among our prophets, no
greater mystery is here at hand, and all too significantly, both Blake and
Nietzsche could know the forgiveness of sin as the very center or essence of
the praxis of Jesus. Yet, here, the forgiveness of sin is an apocalyptic forgiveness, one only possible and real in an absolutely new world, and if that world
is the consequence of an absolute ending, it is thereby the ending of everything that is humanly or interiorly knowable as forgiveness. Perhaps the Old
Testament words most clearly preparing the way for Jesus' enactment of the
forgiveness of sin are contained in a post-exilic prophecy recorded in the
Book of Jeremiah, a joyous prophecy embodying the initial promise of a new
covenant, one wherein everyone will fully "Know the Lord," and "I will
remember their sin no more" (Jer. 31: 34). Indeed, Kierkegaard underwent his
second conversion or "metamorphosis" only when he finally came to realize
that God had *forgotten* his sin, and then wrote *The Sickness Unto Death*,
whose dialectical thesis is that sin is the opposite not of virtue but of faith.
So it is that the apocalyptic Blake can finally pray: "Come, O thou Lamb of
God, and take away the remembrance of Sin" (*Jerusalem* 50: 24), and Jerusalem in everyone is a "Tabernacle of Mutual Forgiveness" (*Jerusalem* 54: 4),
but only as an absolutely new Jerusalem or an absolutely new apocalypse. No
one knew sin more deeply than did Blake and Kierkegaard, but they knew it
most deeply only as a consequence of the forgiveness of sin, and such a
dialectical understanding of the forgiveness of sin is already primal in Augustine and Paul.

Recognizing that here the meaning of forgiveness is wholly other than
every given or manifest meaning of forgiveness, and is so if only because it
is truly apocalyptic, and as such is absolutely new, we can recognize that this
is a truly revolutionary forgiveness, and is so in its very abolition of sin. But

95

the abolition of sin is not simply and only the dissolution of sin, it is far rather its ultimate transformation, a transformation which is a transfiguration, as here sin is transfigured not into an original innocence but rather into an apocalyptic grace, so that Jesus can recognize the forgiven sinner as wholly transcending any possible innocence, a transcendence only possible by way of the full and immediate advent of the Kingdom of God. Now the 'Kingdom of God' in the language of Jesus, as recorded in the synoptic gospels, is clearly an apocalyptic name or title, one unspoken or unrecorded until Jesus. So despite our ecclesiastical and conservative traditions, it cannot truly be understood as the "reign" or "rule" of God, cannot be understood as a re-newal of Israelitic priestly or Deuteronomic traditions, but rather as an apoca-lyptic kingdom, or an absolutely new creation, or absolutely new reality. So it is that Luther could understand the forgiveness of sin as a creation out of nothing, yet as such an absolutely new creation. Hence it is wholly alien to all historical and religious traditions, and just as nothing aroused a deeper rejection of Jesus than did his forgiveness of sin, nothing is or could be more inherently offensive, or more profoundly blasphemous, and most blasphe-mous and most offensive to those who are most deeply bound to the "rule" of God.

The very act of the forgiveness of sin is profoundly antinomian; perhaps no other act could so deeply challenge the "rule" of God, and if this act is a truly and purely apocalyptic act, it thereby reverses an "old creation," and such an act is clearly not a dissolution of an old creation but far rather its absolute transfiguration. At no point does the New Testament more clearly differ from the Old Testament than in its calling forth of the ultimate depths of sin, but, here, and above all so in the words and acts of Jesus, sin is actually evoked or named only in calling forth its forgiveness. Here, only the forgiveness of sin makes possible a realization of sin; only the actual forgive-ness of sin makes possible a calling forth of the ultimate depths of sin, depths unknown and unmanifest until this forgiveness. While there is a full parallel to this dialectical realization in the prophetic oracles of the Old Testament, never therein does either sin or forgiveness become so total as it is in the New Testament. Yet this is fully consistent with an apocalyptic enactment. Only the advent of the deepest darkness makes possible the advent of the deepest light; only the "end" of the old creation makes possible the triumph of the new creation, or only a total realization of sin makes possible a total realiza-tion of grace.

Hence the forgiveness of sin is the forgiveness of the deepest depths of sin, depths truly hidden or veiled until this forgiveness, and just as in the synoptic gospels it is only the demons who immediately recognize Jesus, demons truly alien to the Old Testament, it is only the depths of darkness which are here the arena for the realization of the depths of "light" or grace, only the depths of sin which are the arena for the forgiveness of sin. While we can understand such a realization as a genuine *coincidentia oppositorum*, it is a coincidence of real opposites, opposites not called forth or purely called forth until this realization, and opposites apart from which such a realization would be impossible. So it is that grace is truly meaningful here only through sin, just as sin is truly or fully meaningful only through grace. Each is impossible apart from the other, or each is realized only through the other, and if it is only Christianity that calls forth the ultimate depths of sin, death, and Satan, it is only Christianity that gives witness to an ultimate apocalypse of grace. Yet just as Christianity almost immediately transformed itself in its historical development, and did so most clearly in its dissolution or transformation of its original apocalyptic ground, it is Christianity which has most deeply known sin apart from grace, or known grace itself apart from sin. For Christianity not only gave birth to Gnosticism, but gave birth to an imperial Church that could establish a dualistic dichotomy between sin and grace, or between the City of Man and the City of God.

Dualism has dominated Christianity as it has no other major historical or religious tradition, a dualism truly alien to its original ground, one certainly absent in the Old Testament, and even in the great body of the New Testament, but it's already overwhelming in a post-Pauline Christianity, and then truly comprehensive in an imperial or post-Constantinian Christianity. Now it is true that dualism has again and again been challenged in Christianity, and profoundly challenged, each of the great imaginative and theological breakthroughs of Christianity can be understood as such a challenge, but the mere fact that these have again and again occurred gives witness to a deep polar ground in historical Christianity. This can be understood as an ultimate opposition between a dualistic and a dialectical Christianity, but it is so deep and so comprehensive that neither a purely dualistic nor a purely dialectical Christianity has ever existed as such. Each has always embodied the other, as is most clear theologically, for Christianity is clearly bereft of either a purely dualistic or a purely dialectical theology.

Nowhere else is this so clear as it is in our theological understandings of the forgiveness of sin. Even if these can deeply differ from each other, a truly dualistic understanding of the forgiveness of sin is impossible, or impossible apart from a purely Gnostic ground, but so likewise is a purely dialectical understanding of the forgiveness of sin seemingly impossible, or, at least, it has never been embodied communally or ecclesiastically. Clearly no such understanding is possible unless both sin and grace are apprehended and realized as being in a fully continuous or dialectical relationship to each other. Moreover, the forgiveness of sin must here be understood as the transformation or transfiguration of sin, so that so far from being only a dissolution of sin, here sin itself is radically transfigured or radically reversed, and reversed so as to realize the full actualization of its very opposite. But that actualization is impossible apart from the full realization of the deepest depths of sin, depths which themselves are here transfigured or reversed, for only the actualization of those depths make possible a forgiveness of sin which is the transfiguration of sin. Yet, most difficult of all to grasp, is that these opposites, even while being full and actual opposites, can and do pass into each other. Only that *coincidentia oppositorum* makes possible the forgiveness or the transfiguration of sin, a transfiguration impossible apart from the simultaneous movement of the depths of grace into the depths of sin and of the depths of sin into the depths of grace.

Of course, a genuine understanding of the forgiveness of sin is an understanding of redemption, but nothing has been more elusive in Christian theological understanding than an understanding of redemption, and when it has been actually understood, it has been understood as an eternal return to a primordial beginning or a primordial innocence. This understanding is a true reversal of any possible apocalyptic understanding, and finally entails a total negation or dissolution of all cosmic, historical, or interior actuality, as most purely embodied in Gnosticism itself. Gnosticism has ever been the deepest Christian theological temptation, but just as Paul created Christian theology by way of his conflict with a primitive Christian Gnosticism, our greatest theologians have been profoundly anti-Gnostic theologians, and above all so in Western Christianity, as witness not only Irenaeus and Augustine, but perhaps most purely Aquinas himself. Yet none of our Western theologians have been able fully to understand redemption, except insofar as they understand it by way of a movement of eternal return, thus once again renewing a Gnostic or primordial ground, and certainly an anti-apocalyptic ground, one therein dissolving the full actuality of the forgiveness of sin, and doing so if only by way of a full dissolution of the actuality of evil.

Now there simply is no way to an understanding of the forgiveness of sin apart from an understanding of evil, and an understanding of the full and total actuality of evil. This actuality is inseparable from an actual forgiveness of sin, but so likewise it is inseparable from a fully actual realization of grace. It is this full conjunction which our theologies have inevitably dissolved, and done so if only by way of their final refusal of the actuality of evil. But to refuse that actuality is inevitably to refuse everything that is actually understandable as grace, thereby understanding grace as a spirit which is spirit alone, or a purely Gnostic or primordial "spirit." This spirit is not only invisible and unheard, but wholly other than any possible bodily, historical, or interior actuality, as though only an absolutely bodiless spirit could possibly be the actuality of grace, or only an absolutely disincarnate spirit could possibly effect the forgiveness of sin. While such an understanding is clearly anti-Christian, and hence has never appeared as such in a genuinely Christian theology, it nevertheless is deeply echoed in our theologies, is deeply implicit if not explicit in our theological understanding, and has certainly dominated our common or public theological language, and so much so that a genuinely Christian language inevitably evokes a profound offense. Now if that offense begins with Jesus, it is ever present in a calling forth of the forgiveness of sin, so that to know that forgiveness apart from a radical offense is to unknow or to dissolve that forgiveness itself.

Although nothing appears to be clearer in Christianity than its understanding of sin, this is finally an illusion, and clearly so if our theologies inevitably dissolve the actuality of evil, thereby foreclosing all possibility of an understanding of the transfiguration of evil, or even all possibility of understanding evil itself. The truth is that there can be no actual possibility of understanding evil apart from understanding its positive or actual ground. Here theological and Biblical languages are surely at a deep distance from each other, and this is above all true of the dominant language of the New Testament, which is unique as a scriptural language in calling forth an absolute evil or an absolute darkness, and a darkness that is here finally inseparable from an absolute light. It is precisely that darkness which is transfigured by the actualization of an absolute "light," but such light cannot possibly be a dualistic opposite of darkness, cannot possibly be simply and only absolutely other than darkness. If this is a light that shines in the darkness, or a Word that became "flesh," then it is finally inseparable from darkness itself, finally inseparable from its own act of transfiguration, a transfiguration impossible apart from the full actuality of darkness or evil itself. Accordingly, a deep Gnostic or primordial call is virtually inevitable within this horizon of language, a call to a pure and absolute transcendence, an absolute transcendence absolutely other than any possible darkness, and absolutely other than any possible body or "flesh."

We need not wonder that Christianity has generated the deepest and most comprehensive "heresies" in history, and perhaps most so in Christian "orthodoxy" itself, and above all in our dominant Christian understanding of God. Even if this understanding has undergone deep transformations in our history, it has released a uniquely modern Christian orthodoxy, one not only centered in the absolute transcendence of God, but in a transcendence which is pure transcendence and transcendence alone, seemingly renewing an ancient Gnosticism, and surely foreclosing any possibility of an actual forgiveness of sin. So it is that it is a uniquely modern Christianity which is a full embodiment of an absolute guilt, a guilt without any possibility of forgiveness, as so deeply known by both Luther and Kierkegaard. If this made possible a deeply dialectical understanding of guilt, as it also did in both Augustine and Paul, it made possible a realization of pure guilt and pure guilt alone, and one which becomes overwhelming in full modernity. This is the guilt that made possible the absolute reversals of a Blake or a Nietzsche, but it also ushered in a new and wholly vacuous humanity, as so deeply known by Blake, Nietzsche, and Kierkegaard, and a vacuous and empty humanity that is truly a reverse image of a pure and absolute transcendence.

Both Blake and Nietzsche could know this very condition as the consequence of an original Christianity, but an original Christianity that is a reversal of Jesus, and most clearly a reversal of the forgiveness of sin. Both Nietzsche and Blake could know the advent of Christianity as the advent of an absolute guilt, a guilt that is a wholly inverted body or "flesh" itself, and even if original Christianity proclaimed the resurrection of the dead, it could only actually know resurrection as the resurrection of spirit and of spirit alone, a spirit that is wholly other than body or "flesh," and one whose resurrection for both Blake and Nietzsche is the resurrection of an eternal death or nothingness. Clearly both Blake and Nietzsche were profoundly reacting against a uniquely modern Christianity, but both could unveil a revolutionary Jesus unknown to either Biblical scholarship or modern theology. Both could know Jesus by way of the forgiveness of sin, but now a forgiveness of sin inseparable from the death of God, or inseparable from the death or "Self-Annihilation" of that God whom Nietzsche could know as an absolute No-saying, or whom Blake could name as Satan. Nowhere else in modernity have we been given such a profound understanding of the forgiveness of sin, but nowhere else in modernity have we been given such purely and totally negative images of God. If these are inseparable in both Nietzsche and Blake, they may well prove to be inseparable in any possible contemporary understanding of the forgiveness of sin.

Certainly the Christian can only understand the forgiveness of sin as a consequence of the Incarnation, but it is precisely the Incarnation, or the Incarnation and the Crucifixion, which has most defied theological understanding, and defied it if only because of our profound resistance to the very possibility of a full and final union between "flesh" and Spirit or "darkness" and light. Nothing is more elusive in our theological understanding than an understanding of either "flesh" or "darkness," and above all so in our understanding of the Incarnation. Here Gnosticism is once again a profound threat to our theological understanding, and just as Docetic Christologies, whether directly or indirectly, abound in our theological understanding—so much so that it is possible to ask if there has ever been a Christology that is not at least implicitly Docetic—the question inevitably arises as to whether a theological understanding of the Incarnation is actually possible. But if this is impossible, it is surely impossible to understand the forgiveness of sin, and if the forgiveness of sin must inevitably be a deep mystery to us, then its actual possibility for us is profoundly called into question. Even if that is the condition making possible the forgiveness of sin, if a full and actual forgiveness of sin has indeed occurred, then our humanity has truly been transformed, and if in this new covenant we fully "know the Lord," then all deep mystery will finally have been shattered.

Yet that is precisely the mystery which we most deeply embrace, even if in embracing it we refuse the Incarnation, and we do refuse the Incarnation in refusing the sanctification of "flesh" and darkness, for that is a refusal of the forgiveness of sin, and one thereby calling forth an ultimately new and infinitely deep darkening of consciousness, an absolute guilt known by Christianity alone, or an *Angst* which truly is an encounter with the Nothing. Now if that very *Angst* is unique to Christianity, just as is absolute guilt itself, it can be understood as a reversal of the forgiveness of sin, a reversal giving birth to this very *Angst*. This is the birth of a full and actual Nothing, one known to Christianity alone, and one which is the consequence of an inversion or reversal of the forgiveness of sin. For if the forgiveness of sin calls forth the deepest depths of sin, when that forgiveness is reversed, these depths do not simply dissipate or disappear, they far rather become overwhelming as pure guilt and pure guilt alone, a guilt that is an echo or reflection of a new emptiness or a new nothingness, one that is itself a fully actual Nothing, and an actuality that is itself a consequence of the Incarnation.

While Christianity has again and again refused the very possibility of the absolutely new, its innermost faith is inseparable from an absolute apocalypse, or from the absolutely new. If the Incarnation itself is absolutely new, it inevitably releases absolutely new worlds or horizons, and one of these that we can historically understand is the advent of a truly new guilt, one apparently first known by Paul, but which has been renewed again and again in Christian history, and which both Blake and Nietzsche could know as the very body of a wholly repressed humanity. This is the body that Nietzsche could know as a purely nihilistic body, a body that is the full embodiment of ressentiment, and while therein it is an absolutely empty body, that is precisely the body which is a body of nothingness, and of a full and actual nothingness. Hence it is the very reversal of a Buddhist Sunyata or pure emptiness, and is so in the very actuality of its nothingness. This actual nothingness is known in the Christian and Western world alone, and as such it truly is absolutely new, and thereby the embodiment of a pure and actual Nothing that is equally new. True, there are intimations of such a nothingness in Greek tragedy and in the prophetic revolution of Israel, just as there are in the Book of Job, but never therein is such a nothingness fully incarnate, never therein is it manifest or actual as pure nothingness itself, a nothingness which dawns only with the advent of Christianity.

Yet the advent of an actual nothingness is just what one would expect with the occurrence of an apocalyptic forgiveness of sin, or with the actual occurrence of incarnation itself. This is an incarnation into the depths of

"darkness," and one therein calling forth those very depths, depths invisible
and unheard apart from such an incarnation, but depths now speakable and
hearable as darkness itself, or as a full and actual nothingness. Now even if
these are the very depths that are transfigured in the forgiveness of sin, when
that forgiveness is now refused or reversed, these depths are seeable or hearable
only as pure darkness alone, a darkness which is not only an actual nothingness, but an overwhelming nothingness, and one truly calling forth an absolutely new *Angst*. That is the *Angst* releasing a new and absolute guilt, but
that guilt is a witness to the Incarnation, or to a pure reversal of the Incarnation, one made possible by the Incarnation alone, and one which is perhaps
an inevitable consequence of the Incarnation. Just as Hegel could profoundly
understand a "cunning of reason" which is a reversal of every actual intention
and goal, a "cunning of reason" which is theodicy itself, it is possible to
understand *Angst* itself as the most open or actually understandable consequence of the forgiveness of sin.

If only at this point, we truly can understand the forgiveness of sin, and
even as Luther, Kierkegaard, and Heidegger could all know *Angst* as effecting
the deepest possible call or summons to us, this is a call only possible as the
consequence of the advent of a full and actual Nothing, a nothingness released by the reversal of the forgiveness of sin, and only actual as such in that
very reversal, an actuality indubitably present in a uniquely Christian and
Western history, just as it is in a uniquely Western and Christian imagination.
So it is that only this imagination has given us full and actual visions of Hell,
but all such naming of Hell can be understood as a consequence of the
Incarnation, or of the forgiveness of sin. Only that forgiveness calls forth the
ultimacy of damnation itself, or the ultimacy of darkness itself, a darkness
which is an incarnate darkness, and an incarnation of darkness only possible
as a consequence of the Incarnation itself. All too significantly, no primal
imagery is more minimal in historical Christianity than is the Descent into
Hell, or the Harrowing of Hell. Just as the Harrowing of Hell or the Descent
into Hell are equally minimal in all Christian theology, this is surely a deeply
forbidden subject in Christianity, and one therefore deserving the deepest
attention. Indeed, the New Testament itself is virtually silent on this crucial
front, and this despite the fact that the New Testament is more centered upon
damnation and Hell than is any scripture in the world.

Why this silence? True, this silence is broken in our deeper theological
thinking and in our deeper imaginative visions, but even then it has circum-
vented an actual calling forth of Christ's Harrowing of Hell, for even if this
is an inescapable consequence of the Incarnation, or of the forgiveness of sin,
it is as though we are absolutely forbidden to name or to envision it. Is this
a mystery that will finally end only with the full and final epiphany of apocalypse itself? Or has it already ended, but only in the depths of the uncon-

scious, an unconscious which is truly unnamable, but nevertheless indubitably real? Or is it truly ended in any actual naming of the Incarnation, or any actual calling forth of the forgiveness of sin, a forgiveness of sin which is finally not only a transfiguration of sin, but a transfiguration which is a sanctification, or a harrowing of sin itself? Paul could deeply affirm, and do so in the very context of his purest apocalyptic thinking, that for our sake God made Christ who knew no sin "to be sin" (II Cor. 5: 21), but this statement is unique in the New Testament, and it has apparently never called forth an actual Christian imagery. But how else is it possible actually to understand the fullness of the Incarnation, or to understand a forgiveness of sin which could actually occur, or which could be actual and real for us?

Once we understand that the forgiveness of sin embodies a true dialectical movement, a movement of opposites into each other, so that the depths of sin pass into the depths of grace, even as the depths of grace pass into the depths of sin, then we can understand that not only are the depths of sin and grace inseparable, or the full actualization of their depths inseparable, but that this very actualization, a truly apocalyptic actualization, embodies an ultimate *coincidentia oppositorum*. Already Paul affirms that God made Christ to be sin so that in him we might become the "righteousness of God" (II Cor. 5: 21), a righteousness of God that Paul knows as the very opposite of our self-righteousness, but once we are free from sin we become "slaves to righteousness for sanctification" (Rom. 6: 19). And we are freed from sin only by Christ having become a "curse for us" (Gal. 3: 13), a "curse" that is damnation itself, for even if Paul does not affirm that the Crucifixion is a descent into Hell, it necessarily follows from this affirmation. Just as a genuinely Pauline language is the clearest dialectical language in the New Testament, it inevitably calls forth a genuine *coincidentia oppositorum*, but here an apocalyptic *coincidentia oppositorum*, a new creation, and a new creation in which "everything has become new" (II Cor. 5: 17). That "everything" certainly comprehends sin, a sin that has not simply passed away, but has become "new," and if this is an apocalyptic sanctification, it is a sanctification of the deepest depths of sin.

Nothing has more profoundly obscured or even reversed Pauline language than those non-apocalyptic interpretations that have overwhelmingly dominated our understanding of Paul. The truth is that these include every major theologian in the Christian tradition, so that, if only at this point, a genuinely Pauline language is truly an alien language in Christianity itself, or certainly in the dominant forms of Christianity, and this is clearly true of virtually every Christian understanding of "sanctification." Perhaps nowhere else has "paganism" so dominated Christianity, and a paganism which in its Christian expressions has been truly dualistic, establishing a dualistic and not a dialectical dichotomy between sin and grace, so that the sacred and the profane are simply and only opposites of each other, and sanctification is the realization of a truly dualistic "holiness," a holiness that is wholly other than body and world and time. Now it is true that such a dualism is often present in Paul's own language, but Pauline language, unlike Johannine language, is seldom truly consistent. Again and again it regresses to a pre-Pauline ground, and this is most clearly true of the Corinthian correspondence whose language is so contradictory that it has simply been impossible to understand it as a coherent whole. But here we may discover Paul's most purely apocalyptic language, and perhaps because this is a truly new language it inevitably evokes continual reversals of itself.

Such a movement is itself deeply revealing of a new apocalyptic language. It is as though its very newness provokes a reversal of itself, and if so, this unveils a deep ground of that profound reversal which Christianity underwent in the first three generations of its existence. If it was Paul who most deeply discovered a uniquely Christian identity of grace, this is a grace that soon loses its uniquely Christian ground in the post-Pauline Hellenistic churches, and it is discovered again in Christian history only in the deepest Christian revolutionary movements. Apparently nothing like this is present elsewhere in the history of religions, but nowhere else does there occur an apocalyptic forgiveness of sin, one so revolutionary that it is inevitably reversed, and most clearly reversed in that radically new realization of sin which so rapidly overwhelmed the Christian world. Now a truly new Church comes into existence, one having no real precedents in the pre-Christian world, and one revolving about a truly non-apocalyptic Eucharist and priesthood, one truly reversing the earliest Christian communities, and certainly reversing Paul. And now there evolves an absolute religious authority going far beyond anything which had previously existed, one not only expressing itself in an imperial episcopacy, which itself was a consequence of the Roman Empire, but even thereby realizing itself in an absolute conflict with heresy, a heresy wholly within Christianity itself, and a heresy whose dismemberment established the contours of the established Christian world.

Certainly the apocalyptic Paul could only be known as a deep and ultimate heretic within this world, and above all so in his truly dialectical understanding of sin, and while Augustine effected a theological revolution in recovering a Pauline understanding of sin and grace, he could do so only by deeply transforming both the apocalyptic and the radical Paul, and while such a transformation is perhaps inevitable in every deep interpretation, no other scriptural transformation has ever been more historically powerful than this one. Augustine can know the forgiveness of sin, and know it deeply. It is just this forgiveness which draws forth Augustine's revolutionary discovery of the subject of consciousness, or a uniquely human self-consciousness, one dichotomously polarized between sin and grace or freedom and impotence, and it is just this radically new apprehension and realization of the subject of consciousness that was destined to be the deep center of a new Western world. While Augustine's own understanding is dualistic and dialectical at once, which even could be said of Paul, and has indeed been true of every truly Western theologian, it is this understanding which draws forth the interior depths of consciousness, and while these are indeed dichotomous depths, as they never are in Eastern voyages into such depths, they inevitably therein give witness to an ultimate *coincidentia oppositorum.*

These are the dichotomous depths in which there has occurred a uniquely Western transfiguration of evil, one inseparable from a drawing forth of the ultimate depths of evil, depths lying far beyond any possible exterior evil, but depths now inevitably called forth, and called forth if only to make possible such a profoundly interior voyage. Hence that voyage is necessarily a voyage into darkness, and into the deepest darkness, a darkness invisible and unheard apart from such a voyage, but a darkness essential and necessary to an apocalyptic realization of light. While apocalypticism is profoundly transformed in these voyages, it nevertheless ever remains at least implicitly a profound ground of such voyages, and most clearly so in its ultimate movement from darkness to light. So long as this movement remains at hand, there can be no darkness or no actual darkness which is simply and only darkness, just as there can be no actual light which is simply and only light. Each is dialectically related to the other, and it is precisely the transmutation of a dialectical realization into a dualistic realization which inverts and reverses every such voyage. Then darkness and light are wholly isolated from each other, inevitably leading to a purely alien darkness and a finally empty light.

Now if it is in full modernity that a purely alien darkness is most manifest and real, this can be understood as a genuine and necessary consequence of our interior voyage, and if, as opposed to Dante's *inferno*, this is an *inferno* offering no way into a *purgatorio* or a *paradiso*, it is nevertheless in genuine continuity with that radically new sin and new darkness called forth by the New Testament. Even if our darkness seemingly offers no way into light, it does embody an ultimacy and a finality which clearly echo these radical New Testament categories, one which can be understood to be genuinely apocalyptic, and certainly so if such an ultimate condition embodies an ultimate call. Perhaps it is a total isolation of light and darkness that embodies the deepest call, and above all so if such an isolation is dialectical and not dualistic, one foreclosing the possibility of either light or darkness having any resonances whatsoever beyond themselves. A decisive sign of this is that our darkness is truly namable; it is certainly not a pure surd, as witness its profound imaginative embodiments in late modernity. And if we can name our darkness, and name darkness as it has never been named before, that very naming is an embodiment of light, and if this is truly a light shining in the darkness, and shining in the deepest possible darkness, it is certainly in continuity with that absolutely new light and darkness enacted in the New Testament.

But that naming is most deeply an apocalyptic naming. It is a new creation which is the consequence of an absolute darkening of an old creation, a new creation which certainly cannot be identified with the Church, an ultimate blasphemy which Augustine himself perhaps commits only once (*City of God*, XIII, 16). And if the new creation is an absolutely new world, it must ever repel every naming grounded in an old creation. If that repulsion is more actual in our world than in any previous world, it could be a decisive sign of an apocalyptic transfiguration occurring even now, even if it can now occur only with no signs whatsoever of the actual presence of an apocalyptic light. But the very abatement of all such signs could be the very condition making possible a truly new transfiguration of darkness, and therefore a transfiguration of the deepest depths of evil; if that very transfiguration is inaugurated by what the Christian knows as the Incarnation, it could be occurring universally today, but only insofar as it effects a dissolution of every manifest source of light. Clearly New Testament language is a dialectical conjunction of both light and darkness, but if this is a language recording only the inauguration of the forgiveness of sin, only the dawning of the Kingdom of God, it will inevitably bear the imprint and the echo of a pre-apocalyptic light and darkness, of that old creation which even now is coming to an end, but with the consummation of this apocalyptic dawning all such language comes to an end.

Certainly it has come to an end in our world, or in our deepest imaginative realizations. If we can know a new evil which is truly and fully unthinkable, one wholly transcending everything that was once manifest and actual as evil, and transcending it in a truly new universality of evil, one so universal that its very presence is virtually unseeable and unheard, then this can be understood as an apocalyptic epiphany of evil, but now an apocalypse of evil occurring only by way of an eclipse of an apocalypse of light. Yet such light is not simply and only invisible and unheard, and cannot be if we have any openness whatsoever to our new darkness, any awareness whatsoever of its dark ground, or any opening to a darkness that is namable as darkness. For if we can name our new darkness, we are inevitably therein open to an apocalyptic light, and even if that light is now unnamable as such, it is evoked in our naming of our darkness, and that very naming is a decisive sign of the actual presence of a transfiguration of evil. Imaginative naming, and deep imaginative naming, is necessarily such a transfiguration, and is so if only in calling forth the deepest speech, the deepest naming, out of the deepest silence or the deepest abyss, an abyss apart from which deep naming can never occur, and an abyss which is truly transfigured in that very naming.

If twentieth-century philosophical thinking is unique in Western philosophical thinking in its virtual dissolution of all actual thinking about God, this goes hand in hand with its dissolution of all thinking about evil itself. At no point is our conceptual thinking more withdrawn from the brute actuality of our world, and yet this very philosophical void, and virtually universal philosophical void, has perhaps made possible the preservation of philosophical thinking itself, for apart from such a void, thinking in our time and world would surely have passed into a pure nihilism. If Nietzsche's deepest thinking was an ultimate conflict with a pure nihilism, a nihilism only released by that ultimate event which Nietzsche proclaimed as the death of God, this is a nihilism that can only be transcended by profoundly knowing and affirming that death, thus by deeply naming God and an absolute darkness at once. When such naming becomes silent and unheard, a new nihilism becomes a truly universal nihilism, and a new darkness becomes so dark that it is unnamable as darkness. This is a deep and ultimate condition demanding a truly new void, one making both God and an ultimate evil unspeakable, and if that is a comprehensive void in our new conceptual thinking, and one truly unique in our history, it surely is a deep witness to that ultimate darkness which is universally incarnate in our world.

Masters of silence would teach us to be most attentive to that which is not said, and if the genuine philosophers of our world do not speak of either God or evil, they do speak in that silence, for in making them truly unspeakable they nevertheless thereby evoke their presence. The truly unspeakable is certainly not simply the unsaid. Deep discipline is demanded to embody the truly unspeakable, as demonstrated in radically different ways by both Wittgenstein and Heidegger in our world. Here such unspeakability clearly speaks, and in so speaking reverses that silence which otherwise is so totally present. Hence such speaking is a deep witness to the presence of such a transfiguration for us, and if this is a transfiguration of evil, even if unnamable as such, it can occur even if its occurrence is silent and invisible, and perhaps most invisible and silent in the deepest depths of its occurrence. Could it be that only such silence makes possible the ultimate depths of our imaginative voyages into darkness? We have long since learned that both Dante and Milton were deeply blocked by their bondage to the theological languages of their day, and each of their voyages finally transcended and even reversed those languages. But if our deeper modern artists are free of all bondage to either a philosophical or a theological language, is it possible that this is an essential condition for either a truly modern or a truly contemporary voyage, and one made possible by our century's philosophical thinking itself?

Certainly we must be free of every idea and image of God that we have been given if we are to become open to an ultimate transfiguration of evil, but so likewise must we be free of every image and idea of evil in our traditions if we are to become so open. If the anonymity of God and the anonymity of evil are overwhelming in our century, this could be absolutely necessary to such a transfiguration of evil, one apart from which such a transfiguration could never occur. Of course, our truly new anonymity is inseparable from the advent of a new and universal nihilism, one which both Nietzsche and Heidegger could know as the culmination of the history of Being in the West. If that nihilism is a uniquely Western nihilism, it has nevertheless become truly universal in our new world, so that an *Angst* which was once the consequence of deeply individual and interior encounter with the Nothing is now a universal *Angst*, and a universal *Angst* inseparable from our new anonymity, and certainly a deep ground of that anonymity itself.

Yet a new universal anonymity could only be a reflection and indeed an embodiment of a truly new Nothing, a Nothing as universal as is that anonymity itself. If that Nothing is a universalization of an original Christian Nothing, or a Nothing that is the consequence of the Incarnation itself, it is an Incarnation whose ultimate impact inevitably draws forth the deepest depths of nothingness itself. But the universalization of these depths of nothingness could be the site of an ultimate but now universal transfiguration of evil, a transfiguration occurring in this very Nothing. Now we can see another deep ground of a Christian refusal of or flight from the Descent into Hell, for if that is the descent which releases an actual nothingness, and releases it so as to make possible its transfiguration, that transfiguration is the Harrowing of Hell, and one occurring only in that body or Body which is a truly new body of nothingness. Yes, Christianity knows the resurrection of the body, but only a resurrection of that body which has descended into Hell, or passed into an ultimate nothingness. It is a resurrected body, yes, but here a resurrection that could only be the resurrection and therefore the transfiguration of a full and actual nothingness. Just as Blake and Nietzsche could fully grasp this nothingness, and know it as a truly new nothingness, even if it is a uniquely Christian and uniquely apocalyptic nothingness, it is also, and even thereby, as Nietzsche and Blake knew so deeply, an actually universal nothingness, but one which dawns as such, or is actually manifest as such, only with the death or "Self-Annihilation" of the uniquely Christian God.

Now the truth is that a fully modern or late modern imagination has been a voyage into a transfiguration of an ultimate body of nothingness. This already occurs in the conclusion of the second part of Goethe's *Faust*, just as it occurs in Blake's full apocalyptic epics. It even can be understood as a universal enactment in the deepest expressions of a late Western imagination, so that even if alien to our theology, or to the great body of our theology, it is known by everyone who is open to our deeper imaginative vision, and can be understood as being actually embodied in a new anonymous but absolutely empty humanity, an empty and universal humanity which could indeed be a site for such a universal transfiguration. Yet such a transfiguration could only be possible by way of the full and actual union of the Body of Christ and the body of a new humanity, and if that new humanity is indeed a body of nothingness, and one only released or actualized by the Body of Christ, that Body is the body which is the consequence of the Descent into Hell, or the consequence of an ultimate movement of Incarnation and Crucifixion, a consequence which is that Descent into Hell which is the Harrowing of Hell. All too inevitably, historical Christianity has been a flight from that harrowing, but a flight nevertheless engendering a new and ultimate *Angst*, an *Angst* which truly is an encounter with the Nothing, and with that full and actual Nothing released by the Incarnation itself, or released by what the Christian alone knows as the forgiveness of sin.

Inevitably, we have known evil as a true nothingness, even if thereby we have refused it as an actual nothingness. While this refusal is belied by our actual history and consciousness, and is manifest for all to see in that consciousness and history, that consciousness and history has been profoundly transfiguring in its actual effect, and most clearly so upon and within our consciousness itself. Already Gnosticism is a refusal of an interior consciousness, or an interior consciousness that is a truly and purely negative consciousness. This consciousness is historically born with the advent of Christianity, and born as a profoundly divided and self-alienated consciousness, a truly doubled consciousness releasing an ultimate self-negation, and a self-negation inseparable from what the Christian knows as the forgiveness of sin. But that forgiveness is possible only by way of what the Christian knows as the Incarnation and the Crucifixion, and even if this is that absolute event calling forth an absolute joy, that joy itself is inseparable from an absolute darkness or an absolute guilt, a guilt inseparable from this forgiveness, for here forgiveness could only be forgiveness of such guilt. Here, that guilt truly is evil itself, and a truly actual evil, and even if it is fully actualized only in this forgiveness, thereby and therein it is actually real, even if it is actually real only in its own transfiguration.

Yet this is the very transfiguration which we refuse in refusing the actuality of evil, for tempting as it is to think that the forgiveness of sin is the obliteration of sin, the very opposite of this is true in a uniquely Christian history. Even if sin and evil are absent in the depths of faith, they are absent as an unforgiven sin or as an untransfigured evil, therefore they are certainly not simply absent or gone, certainly not simply and only dissolved, but therein and thereby are truly transfigured, and precisely thereby absolutely real. This is the reality that is refused by a refusal or evasion of the forgiveness of sin, and if this reality could only be an apocalyptic or absolutely new reality, an actual transfiguration of evil is inseparable from that apocalypse, and inseparable in the very actuality of its occurrence. Yet this transfiguration could occur only in the full actuality of evil, and even if that actuality is a consequence of this transfiguration, so that apart from this transfiguration the full actuality of evil would be invisible and unheard, the pure actuality of evil is absolutely necessary for this transfiguration, and its very sounding could be a decisive sign of that transfiguration, a sounding apart from which a genuine forgiveness of sin would be illusory and unreal.

How is it that our modern theologians can be so indifferent to the simple historical fact that Jesus called forth damnation, Satan, and Hell more fully and more comprehensively than had any previous prophet? And why is it that it is inconceivable that this is truly necessary for his forgiveness of sin? Does that forgiveness release an absolutely new dialectical realization, one inseparable from an ultimate *coincidentia oppositorum,* and hence inseparable from an absolute conjunction or coincidence of sin and grace or darkness and light, a conjunction alone making possible an absolute transfiguration of evil? Of course, a truly dialectical way is almost immediately transformed or reversed in historical Christianity, but it is nevertheless reborn again and again in Christian history, and at just those moments of an ultimate or absolute crisis. Certainly our time is such a moment, and if ours is a time of ultimate darkness, it could also be a time of a transfiguration of that very darkness, a transfiguration impossible apart from the very advent of such darkness, and from the advent of that darkness both in and as our deepest ground.

CHAPTER 8

⌒

The Self-Saving of God

Perhaps Heidegger's greatest treatise is "Nihilism as Determined by the History of Being," the conclusion of his primal study of Nietzsche, which was written at a time of great crisis for himself, 1944–45. Here, Heidegger speaks with unusual force of "the default" (*das Ausbleiben*) of Being, a default that is the very destiny of Being, and yet Being saves itself in its default. This is the treatise in which Heidegger, in response to Nietzsche, gives us his deepest understanding of nihilism, a nihilism which he can now identify as the history of Being, and this is the very history in which Being saves itself. For Heidegger, this history is the history of metaphysics, one which determines the history of the Western era, but metaphysics thinks Being only in the sense of "the Being" as such, therefore Being itself is necessarily unthought in metaphysics, and as such metaphysics is nihilism proper. This is the history that comes to an end in Nietzsche's thinking, even if Nietzsche is the last metaphysical thinker, and it comes to an end in the "self-withdrawal" of Being. Yet this self-withdrawal is the very advent of Being, and the abode of this event is "*das Sein gibt.*" That giving is finally the self-saving of Being, one proceeding from the withdrawal or self-concealing of Being, and the advent of the default of Being is the advent of the unconcealment of Being, one which is an essential occurrence of Being itself. This occurs in the final or apocalyptic age of the destitution of Being itself, wherein a closure of the holy occurs, and while Being itself now fails to appear, the disclosure of its default is an ultimate sign and seal of its own "self-saving."

Now the very symbol of the self-saving of God or Being is extraordinarily rare until the full advent of the modern world. Perhaps it can be found in the ancient world only in Gnosticism, and above all so if a truly Gnostic redemption is the "self-saving" of the Godhead. Alone in the ancient world, Gnosticism could know a primordial fall in Godhead itself, wherein a devolution of deity occurs. This is an ultimately inner divine devolution, one

111

embodying an ultimate tragedy within the Godhead, a tragedy wholly unknown in the pre-Gnostic world. This is the very devolution that is reversed
by a redemption effecting the reintegration of the impaired Godhead, and if
that is effected for Valentinian Gnostics by the Incarnation itself, this is an
incarnation transforming everything whatsoever, and thereby Godhead itself
becomes "all in all." Conservative critics have long known Heidegger's "Being" as a Gnostic Godhead, but the truth is that Heidegger knows the finitude
of Being more deeply than any other thinker, an absolutely anti-Gnostic motif,
and Heidegger could finally know redemption as the absolute event of *Ereignis*,
and all too significantly, *Ereignis* is the very word that Goethe employs in
envisioning the final redemption of Faust in the conclusion of the second part
of *Faust*, that very Faust who embodies a uniquely Western damnation, or a
uniquely Western "soul."

The absolute hatred of the world that was born in ancient Gnosticism
can be understood as the advent of a true nihilism, which is yet another
reason why Gnosticism has been so deeply reborn in our world, and even as
the Hellenistic world becomes ever more gradually a nihilistic world, Gnostic
theologians were deeply influential in that world, as witness their impact not
only upon Plotinus but indirectly upon Augustine himself. While we still lack
a history of Gnosticism in the post-ancient world, it would be difficult to deny
that the symbol, if not the actuality, of the self-saving of God is at least
potentially deeply present in that world, as it is in the depths of a truly new
Jewish, Islamic, and Christian mysticism, then bursting into the open in the
circles surrounding Meister Eckhart and Jakob Boehme. This is a genuinely
dialectical mysticism which is reborn in German Idealism, and the self-saving
of God is at the very center of the thinking of Fichte, Schelling, and Hegel, just
as it is in the visionary depths of Hölderlin, Goethe, and Blake. At no other
point has such a deep modernity been a more profound threat to theology, and
if Christian theology was born in Paul in response to a primitive Christian
Gnosticism, a uniquely modern Christian theology could be understood as
having been born in response to a uniquely modern self-saving of God.

Yet God can be saved only from God's own darkness, a darkness which
truly is the "alien" God. This is that God who is purely and fully an absolute
No-saying, as so deeply known by Luther, Kierkegaard, and Nietzsche. This
absolutely alien darkness is ultimately a divine darkness, as first unveiled in
the Book of Job, and then as fully released in the world in the very advent
of Christianity. If it is Christianity that first embodies an absolute world-
negation, hence the Christian origin of Gnosticism, that world-negation itself
is inseparable from a new and ultimate redemption, a redemption that can be
known, and has been known, as the self-saving of God. This and this alone
makes possible what the Gnostic knows as the perfection of the elect. This
perfection is an absolute deification, one surely echoed in deeply Christian

quests for deification or Godmanhood, a quest already present in the earliest expressions of Christianity. But if that quest is truly new, or truly new in the Mediterranean world, it could be understood as a response to an absolutely new self-saving of God, and one not only absent from the Hellenistic and Classical worlds, but from the Oriental world as well. Nowhere there can we discover the image or the symbol of the self-saving of God, just as nowhere there can we discover a symbol or image of an actual or ultimate death of deity, a death that is an absolutely redemptive death, and a death transforming everything whatsoever.

While Gnosticism could know the Crucifixion, it could only know it as resurrection, a deeply Gnostic motif which soon overwhelms the great body of Christianity. While this is a pre-Christian motif, and is truly present in the Hellenistic mystery cults, never therein is it so absolute as it is in Gnosticism, never there calling forth a total union with the depths of Godhead itself. But it is possible to understand this very union as being possible only as a consequence of the fall of the Godhead, for that fall could make possible a profound transfiguration of Godhead itself, and if it is Gnosticism that first knows such a transfiguration, it is Gnosticism that first knows the fall of Godhead. So it is that if a Gnostic deification is truly new, and new as an absolute deification, it could be understood as a reflection or embodiment of an ultimate transfiguration of the Godhead, a transfiguration wherein the depths of darkness pass into the depths of light, and now the Godhead is fully all in all, and even all in all in the "perfect" or the elect. Thereby matter itself wholly passes into nothingness. Just as *The Gospel of Truth* can know a cosmic "forgetfulness" as the very creation of the world, the material universe passes into nothingness when the "Father" is truly known, but the Father's secret is His Son, and the name of the Father is the Son (38:6), that Son by whom alone the Father can be known, a gnosis that is an absolute return from forgetfulness to that Father who is all in all.

A knowledge of this very forgetfulness is essential to a Gnostic redemption, for even if that forgetfulness is reversed in this redemption, it is precisely thereby essential to it, and only thereby can a profoundly divided Pleroma be restored to its original or primordial condition. Here, Gnosticism profoundly differs from Buddhism, and from every Oriental and ancient way; it does so most clearly in knowing an ultimate self-division or self-alienation of the original Pleroma, a self-alienation that is an ultimate fall, and a self-alienation that is reversed in a uniquely Gnostic redemption. This is just the point at which an original or nascent Christian orthodoxy most deeply struggled with Gnosticism, ever more fully refusing any possible transfiguration of the Godhead, and just thereby coming to understand the absolute immutability of the Godhead, an immutability becoming the very core of the orthodox Christian doctrine of God. Now that we know that there were deeply Gnostic expressions of primitive Christianity, as in the Gospel of Thomas and quite possibly in the earliest strata of Q, a profound struggle was clearly therein at hand, and one creating ultimate divisions in the Pauline and Johannine communities. These divisions become overwhelming in the second century of the Christian era, and even if the Great Church is the victor in that conflict, a true Gnosticism returns again and again in Christian history, just as a muted or transformed Gnosticism is seemingly deeply embedded in Christian orthodoxy itself.

It continues to remain impossible fully to understand the depths of the transformation of an original Christianity, and even if the earliest Christianity which we can know was a deeply divided Christianity, as can most clearly be seen in the deep polarity between its Gnostic and its apocalyptic poles, these poles did not simply disappear in the triumph of orthodox Christianity, they were profoundly transformed, and transformed within a new orthodox Christianity. Now a truly new Godhead is manifest and real. This Godhead is absolutely immutable, but absolute immutability is impossible within the horizons of a Biblical Godhead. It is likewise impossible within the horizons of apocalypticism and Gnosticism, both of which could know profound transformations of the Godhead that make possible what both Gnosticism and apocalypticism know as an absolutely new redemption or an absolutely new totality. The very word "totality" is illuminating here, for just as a new aeon or a new Pleroma became ever more deeply alien to Christian orthodoxy, totality can here be known only as Godhead itself, an absolutely immutable totality, and one foreclosing the very possibility of an ultimate or absolute transfiguration.

With the advent of an imperial or Constantinian Christianity, not only do Gnosticism and apocalypticism seemingly disappear forever from all ecclesiastical Christianity, but Christianity itself, or orthodox Christianity, ever more fully comes to exercise a profoundly conservative role. While this very orthodoxy ever called forth new heresies, it was the profound dichotomy between orthodoxy and heresy that generated the deepest crises of Christendom, crises playing a decisive role in finally bringing Christendom to an end. Perhaps the most ultimate Christian heresy is the belief in an ultimate and total transfiguration, one inseparable from an absolute transfiguration of the Godhead, a transfiguration which here could only be a transfiguration of totality itself. While we have come to understand this transfiguration as the very core of a pure apocalypticism, it also can be understood as the core of a truly new Gnosticism, and if an ultimate and primordial fall is deeper in Gnosticism and apocalypticism than within any other horizons, such a fall is inseparable from an absolute transfiguration. Hence here an absolute transfiguration is wholly inseparable from an absolute fall. Just as it was Augustine who most fully created the Christian dogma of original sin, and did so by way of his renewal of Paul, it was also Augustine who inaugurated a profound interior transformation, one truly revolutionary in its ultimate historical impact, and one ever in profound and even explosive tension with its deep theological ground, an Augustinian God who is simultaneously immanent and transcendent, and whose absolute transcendence is inseparable from His absolute immanence.

This is an immanence that will explode in the radically new mysticism of the medieval world, but so likewise does it explode in late medieval Augustinian theology, a radically Franciscan theology which all too significantly is finally inseparable from a truly new apocalypticism, and one calling forth a truly new transfiguration. Orthodox theologians inevitably judge such a transfiguration as being either Gnostic or apocalyptic, but all too significantly with the triumph of modernity, it is ecclesiastical Christianity which becomes ever more dormant and unmoving, giving us an orthodox theology which for the first time ceases to evolve, or insofar as it evolves regresses into paganism (with, of course, the great exception of Barth's radically new understanding of election or predestination). So that a theology finally bound to the absolute immutability of God becomes immutable itself, reflecting in itself its own absolute ground, but also reflecting within itself what both Kierkegaard and Nietzsche knew all too deeply as the end of Christendom. But that ending is surely not the ending of theology. Theology is deeply reborn in a new and universal apocalyptic theology, a theology which is deeply anti-ecclesiastical, but precisely thereby deeply secular or worldly, and it inevitably calls forth an absolute transfiguration of totality itself.

At this crucial point, Hegel, Marx, and Nietzsche are united. If purely conservative critics can know all three as being deeply Gnostic and deeply apocalyptic at once, and as the very embodiment of a truly Satanic thinking— so that if here a truly new theological thinking becomes a purely anti-theological thinking, and above all so in its enactment of the death of God—it does so as a purely apocalyptic thinking, and an apocalyptic thinking thinking absolute transfiguration. If only here, the ultimate transgression of genuine apocalyptic thinking is manifest for all to see, and just as the Great Church simultaneously profoundly turned away from both a new apocalypticism and a new Gnosticism, it thereby refused not only an absolute transfiguration but an absolute transgression as well, and did so most deeply in its total affirmation of the absolute immutability of the Godhead. That is an immutability making impossible a new totality; and that impossibility makes impossible also a total transgression, or a transgression that truly and absolutely challenges a primordial totality, a totality absolutely eternal and immutable, and therefore infinitely beyond any possible challenge or questioning. The very idea of a true and absolute infinity does not dawn until the advent of Christianity, and then it dawns so as to establish an infinite distance between the creature and the Creator, and even if this releases a new ideal of Godmanhood, that is a Godmanhood calling forth an absolutely primordial humanity, and one freed of every impact of either history or the world.

This is the humanity that Augustine can know as the City of God, a humanity infinitely distant from the City of Man. Even if the Great Church before the apocalypse embodies both the City of Man and the City of God, the elect or the predestined truly exist only in the City of God, therefore they are truly unmoving in that very eternity, reflecting in their own holiness the absolute immutability of their Creator. This is a holiness simply unknown in the pre-Christian world; its nearest parallel is the absolute emptiness of Buddhism, but that is an emptiness free of any possible Godhead, and thus free of any possible actual immutability, or any possible actual necessity. Such an absolute immutability and absolute necessity are born only with the advent of Christianity. Then a pre-Christian fate or destiny is transformed into an absolute necessity, which releases a truly new and absolute authority, but now and for the first time this absolute authority comprehends everything whatsoever, as now an absolute and total obedience is truly born.

Whitehead, the one major twentieth-century philosopher who could actually think of God, could understand the new Christian Godhead as Caesar reborn, although a Constantinian empire goes beyond a pre-Christian empire in its demand for total obedience. Yet just as the Great Church ever increases its demands for total obedience, it thereby truly is a servant of this new Godhead, as now an absolute authority is born which is truly total and all-comprehending, and which in its very essence is absolutely immutable. But that absolute immutability ever more gradually and ever more decisively calls forth its true opposite, an opposite inseparable from a reversal of absolute immutability, and thus finally inseparable from an absolute reversal of the immutability of Godhead itself. Already this occurs in the medieval world, and there perhaps most deeply and most purely in Dante's *Commedia*. The *Commedia* gives us two divine empires, each embodying the authority of God, and each truly divided from the other, thereby one immutable authority and order become two authorites and orders, and time and finitude for the first time are envisioned as being fully coordinate with eternity. Dante's vision is inseparable from an ultimate assault upon the temporal authority of the papacy, thereby a new and imperial papacy can be named as Antichrist (*Inferno,* XIX). This very inversion of the authority of the Great Church is inseparable from an absolutely new recognition of the ultimate authority of the world, one fully actual in a *quia* or "thatness" which is the very heart of the real, and which even our perception can draw forth as the movement of an ultimate love (*Purgatorio,* XVIII, 22–33). Certainly that is a love unknown in the ancient world, and even deeply unknown in the ancient Christian world, but it only appears in the medieval world by way of an ultimate challenge to the deepest authority of the temporal Church. If that very challenge calls forth a new eternal Church, and a truly invisible Church, that invisibility is inseparable from a truly new visibility of the world. Further, this challenge inevitably assaults what the Great Church could know as God's absolutely immutable order and authority, as now a new world ever more gradually and comprehensively appears embodying its own absolute authority and order.

Of course, with the full dawning of modernity this new world becomes a profoundly divided or dichotomous world, one embodying an ultimate division or dichotomy between its interior and its exterior poles, and one releasing a truly new dichotomy within theology itself. Now theology becomes ultimately divided between its ecclesiastical and its philosophical and imaginative expressions, and for the first time both philosophy and the imagination become truly autonomous, and thereby truly independent of all ecclesiastical authority. While ecclesiastical spokesmen will increasingly insist that it is only an ecclesiastical theology which is a genuine theology, the truth is that both modern philosophy and the modern imagination have been profoundly theological. Even if this is a theology deeply alien to all ecclesiastical Christianity, it is nonetheless deeply theological, and even is so in its seemingly most secular expressions. This is most manifestly true in full modernity's very enactment of the death of God. So it is that Heidegger can know that the realization that "God is dead" is not atheism but rather "ontotheology," and an ontotheology in which both metaphysics and nihilism are fulfilled. Both Hegel and Heidegger, even as Plato and Aristotle, know metaphysics, or the deepest philosophical thinking, as theology, but unlike all ancient or medieval metaphysicians, Heidegger and Hegel finally know "Being" or Absolute Spirit or the Godhead as the self-saving of God, and a self-saving that occurs in the deepest darkness and abyss, a darkness only made possible by the death of God.

Indeed, both Hegel and Heidegger can know the death of God as bringing metaphysics to an end, but that ending is itself a metaphysical or "ontotheological" event, and therefore a theological event. Even if it is wholly alien to all ecclesiastical theology, it is overwhelming in the fullness of modernity itself, and not only in the imagination of that modernity, but also in its deepest and purest philosophical thinking. Accordingly, it is only in late modernity that an ecclesiastical theology arises which is vastly distant from every full cultural or social ground, but it also is not until the advent of modernity that deep theologies appear which are independent of every possible ecclesiastical ground (unless this is true of Aristotle's theology, which would be ironic, indeed, since post-medieval Catholic theology has been so dominated by neo-Aristotileanism). Milton's theology is the fullest theology ever given us by a poet, but his is a deeply anti-ecclesiastical theology, and one assaulting virtually every expression of ecclesiastical tradition. If thereby Milton's theology is a pure expression of the Radical Reformation, it is a founding expression of a uniquely modern theology, and a modern theology which truly is a radical theology, and one not confined to poets and seers, but realizing itself in pure thinking, and in that very thinking which triumphs in a full modernity. While this thinking is refused by every ecclesiastical theology, nothing else more fully makes manifest the radical isolation of modern ecclesiastical theology, an isolation which itself was only born in the modern world.

This isolation is itself a witness to the death of God, and as Nietzsche knew so deeply, everything that we can know as the Church could only be the tomb of God. Just as Nietzsche could know Christianity itself as the stone upon the grave of Jesus, everything which is publicly manifest to us as theology is such a stone, and dead and lifeless as it has become, that very death may well harbor the deep presence of its very opposite. So it is that everything that theology once knew as the absolute immutability of God has actually become its true opposite, and if nothing could be further removed from that immutability than the absolute transfiguration of the Godhead, a transfiguration which is the self-saving of God, the brute fact that this is absolutely alien to every ecclesiastical theology could be a decisive sign of its deep theological truth for us, and a theological truth not confined to a sanctuary, but is embodied in the very actuality of the world as world. Certainly, modern "secular" theologies know this truth, and the deeper the secular theology the deeper the calling forth of this truth, here our deeper thinking and our deeper imagination fully coincide. If "descent" and not "ascent" is our deeper primary image, it is the Descent into Hell and not the Ascension which is our primary symbolic ground, a Descent into Hell which is the Harrowing of Hell, or the sanctification of an ultimate abyss and darkness.

Yes, that darkness is the darkness of Godhead itself, which is precisely why it is an absolute darkness. To know and to envision that darkness is to know and to envision the darkness of God, a darkness that can be and has been known as an absolute Nothing, and an absolutely actual Nothing. This can be understood as a truly new nothingness evoking a truly new naming of damnation, Satan, and Hell, a truly original naming which has fully occurred only within a Christian horizon, but which becomes a truly comprehensive naming only within the horizon of a full and final modernity. If our deeper modern voyages have been voyages into a fully actual nothingness, a nothingness which is the very opposite of an absolutely empty or an absolutely primordial nothingness, these have been voyages into an absolutely actual Nothing, one envisioned by every deeply modern poet, and one known by every deeply modern philosopher, except for Spinoza and Husserl. It is so known even if only in calling forth a pure and absolute surd or void, a void previously unknown, unless it was known in Epicureanism, the only truly secular philosophy in the ancient world. That pure and absolute infinitude, which was born with the advent of Christianity, is at least implicitly accompanied by its very opposite, and even if this opposite is not fully born conceptually until the waning of the Middle Ages, it is ever realized in all genuinely modern Idealism, again with the exception of Husserl and Spinoza. And why is it that Husserl is the only truly or absolutely transcendental Idealist of the twentieth century? This is most purely manifest in the *Sixth Cartesian Meditation*, which intends an absolute reversal of Western philosophy, and even goes beyond Heidegger in its "deconstruction" of the Western philosophical tradition, a deconstruction now inseparable from pure philosophical thinking. Why has such a radical deconstruction now become so necessary for us? Was it inaugurated by Spinoza himself, and inaugurated if only to deconstruct a uniquely modern nothingness, and a nothingness inevitable in every post-Classical understanding of Being, or every understanding of Being within a Christian horizon of consciousness?

Spinoza's most radical thinking was not directed against Descartes but rather against the whole world of scholastic philosophy, one inaugurated by Philo and finally ended by Spinoza. Spinoza's "atheism," a truly theological atheism, is an inversion or reversal of the Western understanding of Being, although it is centered upon a reversal of a post-Classical understanding of infinity, and is so by fully calling forth a full and actual union between infinity and finitude, and one only possible by way of a pure thinking that is fully harmonious with body or world. Now this is precisely the thinking that will never appear again in our philosophy, and certainly not in the absolutely transcendental thinking of Husserl, who at this point is further from Spinoza than any modern philosopher. It is possible to think that Spinoza could know a pure harmony between mind and body that is possible only by way of a true transcendence of every possible nothingness. If it is Spinoza alone who could truly know such a transcendence, one foreclosing both the possibility and the necessity of every truly transcendental transcendence, the mere presence of any such transcendental transcendence is a decisive sign of an intended negation of an actual nothingness, and of the actual presence of that nothingness as a deep even if unacknowledged ground of every such transcending movement of thinking itself.

Is it impossible then for us to escape an actual nothingness? We surely cannot escape it by a seemingly pure empiricism, which so forcefully calls it forth, and certainly not by a pure idealism, which could only be a purely transcendental idealism and only possible (as Hegel knew so deeply) by way of a pure negation of a pure and actual nothingness. That negation does not disappear in Husserl's final transcendental idealism, and if world itself now becomes a purely and absolutely transcendental world, it does so only by way of a transcendental phenomenological reduction which is a truly "Copernican revolution." This revolution is grounded in a truly new discovery of an absolutely transcendental "I," one which can know only a transcendental cosmogony, and can realize itself only as an absolutely constituting "I," or that very "I" which all post-Classical theology has known as the "I" of the Creator. Husserl finally transcends even Hegel in his absolute Idealism, and if here the "I" of an absolutely transcendental thinking is finally the "I" of the Creator, that could only be a creation *ex nihilo*. Even if this is an absolute thinking thinking against an absolute nothingness, it is only possible by way of an absolute negation of that nothingness, and a negation here occurring only through that purely transcendental "I," or transcendental subjectivity which is the constituting source of the universe itself.

Now if only the radical Spinoza and the radical Husserl among our deeply modern philosophers are seemingly innocent of an actual nothingness, and if both had an enormous but only indirect impact upon philosophy, is that because it is simply impossible for us to be free of a fully actual nothingness, even though that may well be our deepest destiny and goal? We could understand both Husserl and Spinoza as giving us a truly and even absolutely radical thinking, that is finally directed to an absolute dissolution of nothingness, but the profound radicality of their thinking is deep evidence of the ultimate difficulty and perhaps impossibility of that goal, and even if this is a goal which would simply be meaningless in the pre-Christian world, it is certainly not meaningless in ours, as witness our deep response both to Spinoza and Husserl. And is it possible that Spinoza truly is our most God-obsessed philosopher? Just as the late Husserl clearly is that one thinker who called forth an absolutely transcendental "I" that constitutes existence itself, an "I" that could only be known theologically as the Creator? And even as both Spinoza and Husserl refuse every actual pronunciation of the name of God, is that here made possible by their purely conceptual embodiment of the very power of God, and a power of God which is finally the self-saving of God?

A uniquely modern philosophical "atheism," just as a uniquely modern imaginative "atheism," intends to embody the depths of Godhead itself in its own enactment, or to embody everything that our history and consciousness have known as Godhead, as can most clearly be seen in Spinoza, Hegel, and Husserl, but no less so in Nietzsche and Heidegger. Thereby Godhead itself can be realized only by a pure reversal of its own absolute immutability, and with that reversal that immutability wholly disappears. Thereby every given and established distinction and division between an absolute infinitude and an absolute finitude is dissolved. While such a dissolution is impossible in the ancient or pre-Christian world, that world could know neither a true finitude nor a true infinitude. Although Christianity almost immediately comes to know an absolute infinitude or an absolute Godhead, it only very gradually comes to realize a true or fully actual finitude. This finitude is not fully called forth until the late Middle Ages, and then it dawns only by way of an ultimate chasm between finitude and infinitude, a chasm alone making possible a new *coincidentia oppositorum* between these now ultimately opposing poles. Such a *coincidentia oppositorum* certainly occurs, as can most clearly be seen in the birth of modern science, which truly not only united but identified the celestial and the terrestrial spheres, and did so with a truly apocalyptic finality. Now the universe itself can be known as an infinite universe, as infinitude and finitude are truly united, and if it is Spinoza who knows this most purely, it is the late Husserl's enactment of an absolutely transcendental "I" which most closely approximates the absolute act of creation itself. If this was possible only by way of a full reversal of philosophy, this reversal itself occurred at the very time of the triumph of Nazism. Then a new gulf between Husserl and Heidegger becomes uncrossable, and Godhead itself becomes more impenetrable than it had ever previously been, and pure thinking becomes torn asunder by the ever widening gulf between its infinite and finite poles. Finitude itself seemingly disappears in Husserl's absolutely transcendental Idealism, and if at no other point is there a deeper gulf between Husserl and Spinoza, at no other point is there a deeper gulf between early and late modernity, as now world or finitude itself either disappears as such or becomes a deep and impenetrable surd, or that very surd which Hegel could so deeply know as a pure and actual nothingness. Now a new nihilism truly becomes incarnate, and one now at least potentially present wherever either a pure thinking or a pure imagination is actual and real, and if only our deepest depths have called forth a pure nihilism, this has occurred only in the late modern world, a world which is simply inconceivable apart from such a finally incarnate nihilism.

If a truly ironic theology were now possible, it would also be possible to identify Husserl's final absolute Idealism as a Descent into Hell. It surely occurred in a world being consumed by an absolute evil, and a world inevitably affecting and perhaps even making possible this absolute "idealism." Now finitude itself can only be manifest as darkness itself, and it inevitably disappears as such in a new absolute "light." But is that "light," and the absolute "I" of that light, anything which a previous thinking could know as either subject or consciousness. Is an absolutely transcendental "I" now so absolutely pure that it can shine or appear only in an absolute light, and therefore not only be absolutely unknown but absolutely inactual in anything less than that light? Here, is a light so absolutely dazzling that it can only be known by an absolutely transcendental "I"? Therein every other "I" finally disappears in its consumption by that "I," and just as Heidegger at this very time was withdrawing from that *Dasein* which had been the center of *Being and Time*, a *Dasein* first establishing a gulf between Heidegger and Husserl, now both a Heideggerian *das Sein* and a Husserlian transcendental "I" are absolutely invisible, or visible or speakable only by this absolutely new "I" or this absolutely impenetrable *das Sein*. Each is therein and thereby inseparable from the other, and is so if only because each is an absolute transcendence that *is* an absolute immanence, as now an Augustinian Godhead is fully and finally embodied.

Of course, something very like this already occurs in Spinoza, just as it is comprehensively embodied in Hegelian thinking, and if Husserl and Heidegger are the deepest Hegelians in the twentieth century, (although perhaps being rivaled by Whitehead), they can be so only by enacting an absolute transcendence of both history and consciousness going far beyond a Spinoza or a Hegel. This transcendence is now demanded by that consciousness and history itself, a history or a consciousness that has now truly ended, as most clearly manifest in this radically new thinking itself. Now an ultimate abyss becomes truly universal, and if this now makes possible an absolutely unhearable "Being" or an absolutely invisible transcendental "I," that "I" and this "Being" are possible only by way of this abyss, or only by way of a "Descent into Hell." Our deeper theological community has long sought a truly theological way into both Husserl and Heidegger, and sought it here as they have into no other twentieth-century philosophers, with the possible exceptions of Whitehead and Wittgenstein, but this way has been profoundly blocked by the very language of Husserl and Heidegger, both of whom resolutely refused all speaking of God. They did so far more than any other major philosophers, and this despite the fact that Heidegger's background is so deeply theological, and unique as such among twentieth-century philosophers.

Yet if theirs is a truly new thinking, it will inevitably transcend everything that we have known as God, and while both an Hegelian and a Nietzschean language can be heard as a language about God, this is impossible in the language of Husserl and Heidegger, unless Husserl's "transcendental world-constitution" can be heard as the language of creation, and Heidegger's "self-saving of Being" can be heard as the language of redemption. Now the mere fact that no actual God-language is here called forth is all too significant. Indeed, its mere occurrence would dissolve the deeper language of both Husserl and Heidegger. While some theologians have been tempted to think that it is an Eckhartian Godhead that speaks here, and hence a Godhead that transcends "God," this is manifestly impossible if neither Husserl nor Heidegger are truly mystical thinkers, and equally impossible if each speaks wholly and fully within the very horizon of world itself. A truly Eckhartian language is immune to the darkness of the world, but this is certainly not true of either Husserl or Heidegger, both of whom could know an absolute "crisis" or *krisis* of the world itself, a crisis that alone makes possible their deepest thinking, and one that they certainly could not meet with a Nietzschean joy, or with anything that the Christian world has historically known as faith.

The truth is that neither Husserl nor Heidegger can know a deep light apart from darkness. This light is only called forth by an ultimate and final "crisis" of our history and consciousness, and hence is impossible not only apart from a realization of that darkness, but impossible apart from a deep descent within it, a descent that alone truly calls forth that darkness. Here, we can see the model not only of a primordial shamanic descent, but even more deeply of a uniquely Christian Descent into Hell. Here a truly Pauline dying with Christ could only be a participation in that descent, a participation which alone realizes true glory, or what the Christian most deeply knows as "resurrection." Is a reflection of that resurrection present in the ecstatic celebration of Heidegger or in the purely transcendental thinking of Husserl? And could this be a reflection of the Descent into Hell or the Self-Saving of God? For a Self-Saving of God could only be a Descent into Hell, or a descent into God's own darkness, a darkness which is an absolute nothingness, and an absolutely actual absolute nothingness, an absolutely actual nothingness which alone could effect the "death of God," or alone could effect the absolute self-negation or self-emptying of Godhead itself.

Now it is of ultimate significance that virtually all of our truly major late modern poets could evoke and enact the absolute alienness or the absolute emptiness of Godhead itself; if this naming begins with Blake, it not even yet has ended, and it surely realized its most comprehensive enactments at the very time when Husserl and Heidegger were realizing their deepest breakthroughs, breakthroughs impossible apart from the full advent of an absolute darkness, and yet breakthroughs making possible a truly new light. Is this a "light" that finally can be known as Godhead itself? Even as the absolute light of the *Paradiso* is inseparable from the ultimate voyage into absolute darkness of the *Inferno*, is a uniquely twentieth-century light inseparable from a uniquely twentieth-century absolute darkness? And if here light and darkness are pure and total opposites of each other, are they precisely thereby purely and totally bound to or essentially related to each other? In this perspective, we could understand the necessity of the new Christian dogma of the absolute immutability of God, an immutability foreclosing the possibility of an ultimate descent, or of an ultimate light only possible through such descent. This foreclosure is necessitated by the very occurrence or calling forth of an absolute Incarnation, an absolute Crucifixion, or an absolute Descent into Hell. Inevitably, it is the Descent into Hell which is the most hidden or fragile or marginal dogma in Christianity. It only barely appears in patristic Christianity, and is only actually called forth in medieval Christianity; it does not become all in all until the full advent of the modern world. But then it is truly universal, and universal as it had never previously been; then it occurs not only in the depths of the imagination but in the depths of thinking itself, and most deeply there precisely when it loses all the imagery of belief, and is present only as purely apocalyptic totality.

If Husserl is that twentieth-century philosopher most distant from all imaginative language (and here he truly is a Spinoza reborn), and Heidegger is the twentieth-century philosopher most committed to imaginative language, at least at this point they are genuine opposites in their thinking. But each is a nevertheless genuinely abstract or esoteric thinker, one who in his very thinking demands a new language, and does so as no one had done previously. Certainly Hegel's language is far closer to the Germanic language of his world than is Heidegger's, and certainly Husserl's language is far more purely abstract than is Hegel's. Both Heidegger and Husserl ever more deeply revolted against the philosophical language which they were given, with the result that they are clearly the most difficult of our twentieth-century philosophers. Yet something very like this could be said of all of our great late modern poets, and just as these poets have inspired genuine cults, so likewise has Heidegger, and perhaps Husserl as well. It is as though we have here been given a new sacred language, and a sacred language vastly distant from our common or profane language, and only meaningful to a new priesthood or a new sacred elite. So it is that both Husserl and Heidegger have been given a sacred aura by their followers, even as have our great modern artists. In Heidegger alone, however, has this sacred aura become virtually a divine aura, and this despite his Nazi period, as though, Heidegger, like a god, is truly beyond good and evil.

Indeed, it is Heidegger alone in Western philosophy who actually speaks of the gods, and speaks of the gods even while being silent about God, and just as it is only Heidegger among our philosophers who has sought an absolutely primordial ground, or only Heidegger apart from Plotinus, it is Heidegger who is seemingly our most sacred thinker. Even if this is only a mask or persona, such a mask would appear to be essential to his impact. But it is also Heidegger who is our most deeply blasphemous or theologically transgressive twentieth-century thinker. Here once again he is a reborn Nietzsche, and if it is Nietzsche who had the deepest impact upon Heidegger, or the deepest apart from Hegel, the blasphemy in Heidegger, too, is a purely theological blasphemy and the transgression a purely theological transgression. Yet it is just at this point that both Heidegger and Nietzsche are most powerful theologically, just here that they induce the deepest aura. Here a divine and ultimate voice has been heard most decisively, and heard most fully in its deepest transgression. And what could be more transgressive than to speak so powerfully of the self-saving of Being, a " Being" that here could only be heard as Godhead itself, a self-saving that soon can be named as an absolute *Ereignis*, and as an absolute event, an event that is not simply a divine event, but far rather the final actualization of Godhead itself. So it is that the late Heidegger becomes the apocalyptic Heidegger, even as the late Nietzsche becomes the apocalyptic Nietzsche, and this is the Heidegger, even as this is the Nietzsche, who can only be heard as a sacred voice. Yet this sacred voice is an ultimately transgressive voice, simultaneously deeply attracting and deeply repelling its hearer, and a voice which is finally charismatic only in its deeply repulsive or deeply demonic power. Only Nietzsche and Heidegger among our true philosophers have been capable of an actually demonic language, but only here in modern philosophy can we discover a fully actual sacred language, and now a sacred language which is inevitably a language of a full and total descent.

Of course we should not think that only Nietzsche and Heidegger assumed or were given a divine voice. This could be said of all of our great poets, and just as Nietzsche and Heidegger are truly poetic philosophers, they are thereby voices of revelation itself, and are accepted as such by their deepest followers. But it is Nietzsche and not Heidegger who writes about Jesus; he is the only philosopher who has written fully about Jesus, even if this only occurs in *The Antichrist*. Earlier Nietzsche had gone so far as to intend a recreation of the very voice of Jesus, creating an absolutely new gospel in *Thus Spake Zarathustra*, a Zarathustra who could be understood as the resurrected Jesus, but this resurrection was possible only as a consequence of the deepest descent, and it alone makes possible a freedom from all ressentiment. While Heidegger was once deeply engaged in a New Testament seminar at Marburg, and had a deep impact upon Bultmann and many other theologians, he seemingly had no interest at all in the language of Jesus. Perhaps he was Bultmannian in thinking that this can never be known, or perhaps he followed Paul in transforming Jesus' language into a truly new language. We do know of Heidegger's deep attraction to a Pauline language, even employing it in the opening of *An Introduction to Metaphysics* to insist that a "Christian philosophy" is a round square and a misunderstanding. And it is Paul's apocalyptic language which most affected Heidegger theologically. Perhaps it is only apocalyptic language which was real to Heidegger as a Biblical language, and just as he became ever more distant from his original and deeply Catholic ground, it was even thereby that he moved ever more fully into a sacred or ultimate language, a language unique to a twentieth-century philosopher.

Is it the death of God that makes possible such language? This certainly could be said of Nietzsche himself, and Heidegger was more fully drawn to the actual language of the death of God than any other twentieth-century thinker, a language surely necessary to his own project of creating an ultimate or sacred language. Just as he speaks most fully of the self-saving of Being in the context of speaking of the death of God and the destitution of the holy, he finally can speak of Being only as *Ereignis*, as Being for the first time is symbolically known through the ultimate and apocalyptic event of redemption, and if thereby Heidegger finally becomes a profoundly theological thinker, it is also thereby that he is finally freed of metaphysics, and of that nihilism which he came to know as the history of metaphysics. Yet this is possible only when "Being itself" becomes all in all, and if this is that ultimate apocalyptic event which we are awaiting, this is possible only by way of the deepest descent, and the deepest descent into the deepest darkness and abyss. Perhaps his most loyal followers can understand Heidegger's descent into Nazism as such a descent, but it is clear that Nietzsche's madness can be understood as the consequence of an ultimate descent into darkness. If that can theologically be understood as an imitation of Jesus, whether a pathological one or not, it is simply not possible for a truly twentieth-century sensibility to dissociate an actual redeemer from such a descent, and thus not possible for us to know a Self-Saving of God which is not such a descent.

It would be impossible to imagine Husserl thinking of nothingness, or thinking of an actual nothingness, and Heidegger only once fully speaks of nothingness (in his 1929 lecture, "What Is Metaphysics?"), although an actual nothingness is a profound ground of *Being and Time*, just as it is fully drawn forth in his posthumously published *Beitrage,* which all too significantly is his one work that is centered upon *Ereignis*. Indeed, it is impossible to think of either of these philosophers apart from a world which so deeply and so profoundly called forth an absolute nothingness, and one against which their thinking was most deeply directed. This is the nothingness which is the deep ground of our ultimate "crisis," and even if it is unspoken by all twentieth-century philosophers apart from Heidegger and Sartre, all genuine twentieth-century philosophers know that crisis, and embody it in their deepest thinking. Yet only in the nineteenth century does philosophy openly contend with an absolute nothingness, one deeply occurring in Schelling, Hegel, and Nietzsche, but likewise occurring in Blake, Goethe, and Mallarmé. And if it is Kafka, Joyce, and Beckett who have most clearly and most purely called forth an absolute nothingness in the twentieth century, although echoes of this occur in all deeply twentieth-century poetry, this cannot possibly be a nothingness that is alien to our real thinking, even if it inevitably is deeply disguised or muted in that thinking. But is this not precisely the arena in which we can become open to a Self-Saving of God? And while God may well be unnamable as such within that arena, this is an arena calling forth an ultimate naming, and an ultimate naming of absolute nothingness itself.

CHAPTER 9

⌒

The Absolute Abyss

A paradox immediately arises for us in our opening to the very possibility of abyss, one deriving from the simultaneous presence of its negative and positive poles, positive and negative poles which are finally inseparable from each other, and are so if only because of the ultimately positive and negative power of abyss itself. Abyss has sounded in our world with an ultimacy and a finality that is seemingly unique, or, at least, unique in its universal horizon, one comprehending all of our worlds. If any possible innocence has wholly vanished for us, that is a loss which never before has occurred so universally, and with that loss has arisen a truly new abyss, a universal abyss whose call is overwhelming and which truly transcends everything that was once manifest as abyss. Primordial traditions can know a primordial abyss, an abyss which is a deep and ultimate origin. Origin is then enacted in primordial ritual and myth, but therein abyss passes into its very contrary or opposite, and becomes the deepest possible ground of existence and life. This is the very movement that occurs in primordial sacrifice, and if primordial sacrifice is a transfiguration of a primordial abyss, one wherein a purely negative power passes into its very opposite, this is a potency present within abyss itself, and deeply within it. The actual presence of abyss at least potentially is the presence of the possibility of transfiguration, and the deeper the abyss the deeper the possibility of transfiguration that herein is at hand. Visions of transfiguration have never been more comprehensive than they are in full modernity, and if these are inseparable from visions of an absolute abyss, that is the very abyss offering the possibility of an absolute transfiguration, even if it can only be realized in the deepest depths of darkness and abyss.

Yet the darkness of true abyss is not simply and only darkness, and cannot be if the possibility of transfiguration is here at hand. The possibility of transfiguration is ever present in both a primordial and a modern abyss; it calls forth not only our deepest vision, but our deepest hearing as well. This hearing was inaugurated by the prophetic revolution of Israel, wherein a hearing of the depths of abyss is a hearing of an ultimate call to transfiguration, and those depths lie wholly and only in the very voice of Yahweh, a voice which is resaid or renewed in the prophetic oracle. The "I" of that oracle is the very "I" of Yahweh, and it is spoken out of the deepest abyss. Even if that abyss is wholly invisible, that invisibility releases the deepest possible call, a call actually spoken in the prophetic oracle, and a call to an ultimate transfiguration. Nor does this call arise in an historical vacuum. It occurs only by way of an ultimate crisis, a crisis of eschatological ending, and an ending of every historical horizon that is here at hand. Thus the prophetic oracle is an eschatological oracle; it is hence inseparable from the advent of an historical abyss, an abyss here known as the consequence of the judgment of Yahweh, but an absolute judgment embodying an absolute abyss. This abyss ends the deepest ground of every given or established horizon or world, and thereby shatters every tradition or way that is here at hand, and only as a consequence of that shattering does the prophetic oracle embody an absolutely new call to transfiguration.

This is a call to transfiguration arising out of the advent of the deepest abyss, an abyss here embodied in the very voice of Yahweh. In resaying that voice, the prophetic oracle calls forth an ultimate assault or shock, which assaults every horizon within this world, as now abyss becomes a truly embodied abyss, and only that embodiment makes possible this ultimate call to transfiguration. So it is that the prophetic oracle is negative and positive at once, and absolutely negative and absolutely positive simultaneously. This simultaneity is inseparable from this ultimately new call to transfiguration, and is embodied in the very pronunciation of the prophetic oracle. If that is a simultaneity calling forth the very voice of Yahweh, that voice is here the pure embodiment of abyss, and of an absolutely negative and an absolutely positive abyss. Only now is a total iconoclasm at hand in the world, a radical iconoclasm shattering every primordial world, and every historical world upon this horizon. Now every human world is realized as an ultimate abyss, and yet this is an abyss absolutely necessary to the realization of the prophetic promise of transfiguration, a transfiguration which is the transfiguration of the deepest abyss. Thereby a truly new horizon is called forth in the world, an eschatological horizon, yes, and therefore an horizon inseparable from an absolute abyss, and an absolute abyss calling forth a truly new hearing, which hears and only hears abyss itself.

That is a hearing inseparable from a shattering of all vision, or of all sacred or ultimate vision, and if this is the deepest uprooting which had thus far occurred in history, it will be repeated or renewed again and again in our history, for it is the prophetic revolution which is the very origin of everything that we have actually known as revolution. Nietzsche could know the prophetic revolution as the slave revolt in morality, an absolute reversal of high and low, and one only possible by way of the ending of ancient Israel. This ending is the advent of deep exile, and only the deepest exile makes possible the deepest revolution. Of course, Nietzsche's vision itself is a consequence of the prophetic revolution, and most clearly so in his vision of abyss, an abyss now incarnate historically as it never was in the ancient world, and an abyss once again absolutely negative and absolutely positive at once, but only such an abyss makes possible an ultimate call. Now just as the ancient prophets could pronounce abyss itself as the very voice of Yahweh, Nietzsche could embody our uniquely modern abyss as a consequence of the death of God. Even if he could know this death as the most ultimate event that has ever occurred in history, it is nevertheless a repetition of an ancient prophetic abyss, an abyss which both here and in Nietzsche is the very voice or echo of God.

All of our deeper Christian vision has known the presence of God as the presence of an ultimate abyss, as here total presence can only be the total presence of an absolute abyss. This is true both of mystical and of prophetic Christianity, and perhaps only here are prophetic and mystical Christianity united. Yet what we have known as the death of God certainly has not ended such an abyss. It has far rather deepened it, or, if not deepened it, it has universally embodied it, a universality of absolute abyss never previously manifest, or never previously universally actual and real. And if we know an eschatological crisis, and an ultimate eschatological crisis, that, too, is in continuity with the crisis which the ancient prophets proclaimed, and if only an eschatological crisis releases the deepest prophecy, this, too, has occurred in our world, and most clearly so in Nietzsche and Blake. Deep prophecy, just as deep mysticism, is an embodiment of absolute abyss, and that abyss is not nameless, not simply and only a deep cipher or surd, it has luminously been called forth in both ancient and modern vision, and fully spoken in our most purely actual voices. For just as a Kafka is truly in continuity with ancient prophetic oracles, and is so even in reversing every possible "I," that is a reversal only possible by way of an absolute judgment, an absolute judgment inseparable from the full embodiment of an absolute abyss.

In the prophetic oracle, that judgment is inseparable from its very opposite, as is most clearly manifest in the full realizations of post-exilic prophecy, and if this realizes the very birth of apocalypticism in Israel, that is a birth which is truly reborn in the late modern world. But now ancient apocalypticism is seemingly reversed, and reversed by the advent of a new darkness, a darkness so universal that it silences every expression of light. Of course, this is true in Amos' inauguration of the prophetic revolution, an inauguration giving birth to an absolutely new epiphany of God, and just as that epiphany is inseparable from a new and total darkness, such darkness is here the very

arena of this new epiphany of God. This epiphany realizes itself in an absolute darkness or abyss, and a darkness which is not simply a total judgment
upon Israel, but a call to an absolute transfiguration. Yes, this is a call to an
absolute reversal of high and low, one which is the very advent of a deep and
ultimate anarchism, an anarchism which is fully paralleled in Taoist prophecy,
and which is inseparable from a full assault upon every historical source of
order and authority. Here, a prophetic naming of God is a fully anarchic
naming, assaulting every name of God which it confronts, and not only assaulting but reversing it, as every given and established name of God is
transposed into its very opposite, and everything once known as "light" now
is realized as darkness itself.

That darkness is not only the arena of this ultimately new epiphany of
God, it is the very matrix or womb of this epiphany of God, and if this oracle
of Yahweh is an absolutely new voice, it is the voice of abyss itself, and of
an absolute abyss. If this is the first time in history in which absolute abyss
is fully spoken, this is the advent of a truly new voice, a voice presenting
itself as the very voice of Yahweh. It therein gives birth to a truly new
hearing, a hearing which is hearing and only hearing, therein not only
distancing itself from all vision, but opening its own depths to the depths
of abyss itself, and only the hearing of these depths is now the hearing
of Yahweh.

Not only did this hearing have a revolutionary impact upon Israel, but
it was to be reborn again and again in the future, and with comparable or
greater revolutionary consequences, for this is a hearing inseparable from
enactment. Here pure hearing embodies itself in act, and even if it is hearing
and hearing alone, it is precisely thereby enactment itself, an enactment only
made possible by this very hearing. While it is true that abyss can call forth
a virtually absolute passivity, it is equally true that abyss can call forth the
very opposite of all possible passivity. The epiphany of an absolute abyss can
violently uproot every possible order and authority, yet it is precisely in that
void or chaos that the deepest transformations can occur. This is clearly true
of the deepest modern vision, but thereby that vision is a consequence of the
prophetic revolution, for the prophetic revolution not only was but *is* truly
revolutionary, and is revolutionary in its very hearing of absolute abyss. Now
all passive hearing perishes in the full actuality of this hearing, and this very
vanishing of passivity is pure enactment itself. Nietzsche could name passivity as ressentiment, but it is only the vanishing of passivity which makes
possible a true or actual naming of passivity. If this first occurs philosophically in Spinoza, that naming, too, is a repetition of an ancient prophetic
naming of Yahweh, one that can know the very name of God as the name of
an absolute power that is an absolute negation of all passivity, and hence the
name of absolute enactment itself.

While Spinoza's thinking dissolves all possible chaos and nothingness more purely than does any other thinking, it nevertheless calls forth a pure passivity which is its very opposite. The ancient prophets could know this passivity as apostasy, a rebellion against Yahweh, but a rebellion against Yahweh which at bottom is a submission to the world, and it is the very reversal of that rebellion which is obedience to Yahweh, an obedience only possible by way of a dissolution of all submission to everything but Yahweh and Yahweh alone. Spinoza was the first thinker to understand this obedience philosophically, and he could understand this obedience as a pure activity which is the very opposite of all possible passivity, and a pure activity which is the very actualization of God. For the totality which Spinoza *knows* as God is a totality that the ancient prophets could *enact* as absolute call, and just as this absolute call is an absolute disenactment of every other call, Spinoza's thinking of the totality of God is a pure dissolution or disenactment of every previous thinking of God. Thereby Spinoza is our purest iconoclastic thinker, and therefore a truly prophetic thinker. He is most purely a prophetic thinker in his very thinking of God, and if that is the thinking of a pure and absolute act or activity which is act or activity alone, one wholly dissolving every possible teleology or final causation, it is precisely thereby a rebirth or renewal of an ancient prophetic oracle which shattered all primordial worlds, thereby shattering everything that the ancient world could know as power or cause.

Hegel could know Spinoza's God or absolute substance as a purely negative abyss, one dissolving every possible subject or subjectivity and doing so in the first philosophical thinking in history to effect a pure and actual negation of the subject or center of thinking itself. Could we not say that the ancient prophets enacted a pure negation of the "subject" upon their horizon, drawing forth that "subject" as a purely negative abyss, a purely negative abyss in absolute opposition to that absolute abyss which is now named as Yahweh? Perhaps abyss is a true name of Spinoza's "God," even as it is of that uniquely modern epiphany of God which Hegel could know as "being-in-itself" or the "Bad Infinite." If it is not until the advent of the modern world that abyss is purely and actually thought, and not until then that abyss is imaginatively fully envisioned, this, too, can be understood as a rebirth or renewal of ancient prophecy, but now a prophecy inseparable from actuality itself. Do we hear God in our abyss? Must we hear God in knowing and realizing an absolute abyss? Is an absolute abyss possible apart from a realization of God, and a realization of the very voice of God, a voice that is a pure and absolute abyss, one whose realization silences every other voice, or silences every voice that is not the voice of abyss?

Now just as both our established philosophical thinking and our established theological thinking can know a pure abyss as a pure nothingness, thereby giving us our only given or established understanding of evil itself,

within this perspective an absolute abyss could only be an absolute nothingness, one first known, and profoundly and ultimately known, by Mahayana
Buddhism. Yet Buddhism can know sunyata or an absolute emptiness as
nirvana itself, so that here an absolute abyss is an absolute transfiguration,
and is an absolute transfiguration as an absolute nothingness, even if here
"isness" itself wholly disappears, or becomes indistinguishable from "is-
notness." But as the late Nietzsche came to know so deeply, a "new Buddhism" is now overwhelming the West. This is a purely nihilistic Buddhism,
one strangely parallel with that pure nihilism which *The Antichrist* unveils as
the deepest ground of Christianity, and now and only now a nihilism fully
incarnate in the world. Certainly it is possible to know an absolute abyss as
an absolute nothingness, but now, and for the first time, it is impossible to
know, or actually to know, an absolute abyss as an absolutely inactual nothingness, or a nothingness that is quite simply nothingness alone. Our uniquely
modern nihilism is a decisive sign of this condition, and just as it has not yet
been unthought by any of our thinkers, it has certainly not been transcended
in our uniquely modern imaginative enactments, or, if it has here been transcended, this has occurred only by profoundly deepening our visions of an
absolute nothingness. If this occurs in virtually all of our deepest modern
poetry, this is a transcending movement in a fully Hegelian sense, for it
negates an absolute nothingness only by way of incorporating or embodying
that negated nothingness into a far richer or deeper or darker body or world.

Thus if we can know or envision an absolute abyss as an absolute nothingness, we thereby can know an absolute nothingness as an absolutely inescapable nothingness, for while such nothingness can be diluted or disguised,
this can occur only by way of a pure passivity, a passivity engulfing our
world, thereby abating or annulling or dissolving what we once knew as the
subject or the center of consciousness. From our uniquely modern historical
perspective, we can know a history of that subject, and one with both an
historical beginning and an historical ending, and the prophetic revolution is
a deep site of that beginning. Only here does an individual faith first appear
in history, one demanding an individual enactment, which itself is only possible by way of moving outside of or away from an encompassing society and
world, a world now known to be under total judgment. Accordingly, only an
ultimate epiphany of the abyss of the world itself makes possible such an
individual enactment; only thereby does a truly individual faith and enactment first become possible, and this very movement will be repeated again
and again in the future. But this very enactment is finally an enacting of its
own ending, an apocalyptic ending, as enacted throughout this history, and
here an apocalyptic enactment is manifest as a profoundly individual
and interior enactment, even if that enactment inevitably brings all interiority
and all individuality to an end.

If we can know our world as the end of history, or the end of everything that we have known as history, this is nevertheless a repetition of a primal movement which has occurred continually in our history, but occurred only by way of an ultimate epiphany of an absolute abyss, an absolute abyss shattering the fullness of history itself. It is not accidental that all of our deep or sacred or ultimate visionaries have been in some fundamental sense apocalyptic visionaries, or have been so in the West if not the East. If only thereby each of them have known an absolute abyss, and an absolute abyss inseparable from their vision. Yet that abyss truly evolves in this history, for even if it is a pure abyss at its very beginning, it becomes ever more comprehensive as it evolves, until in full or late modernity that abyss is all in all. Hence ours is truly a nihilistic age, but it is nonetheless a culmination of a history of almost three thousand years in that very nihilism, so that Nietzsche could choose the ancient Persian name of Zarathustra for his prophet of Eternal Recurrence, a Zarathustra whom he could know as the inaugurator of the prophetic revolution, and a prophetic revolution which only now can be truly reversed. But must not any such reversal inevitably be a repetition of that revolution itself? And above all a repetition of that revolution in ultimately calling forth the absolute abyss of Godhead itself, an abyss certainly known and envisioned in full or late modernity, but now known and envisioned as totality itself.

Perhaps no previous age, or previous Western age, has been at bottom more deeply theological than is our own, even if ours is a purely negative theology, it is nonetheless deeply theological, and just as Mahayana Buddhism knows an absolutely negative totality as an absolutely positive totality, or an absolute samsara as absolute nirvana, our absolutely negative absolute abyss has it least the possibility of being finally realized as an absolutely positive absolute abyss, and it is just such a movement which has, indeed, occurred in our deepest imaginative vision. Already a movement fully parallel to this one has been realized in our deepest mysticism, even as a fully comparable movement has been continually actualized in our deepest prophetic enactments, and if this is the one point at which we can know a deep coincidence between our deeper prophetic and our deeper mystical realizations, a rebirth or renewal of such a movement could be occurring even in our world, although inevitably it could only be deeply disguised or veiled, and most veiled as this movement itself. Both the mystic and the prophet can know world itself as a desert, and desert most deeply in the very glory or splendor of the world. Surely some such image deeply resonates with us, but that very image in our deeper traditions is either a sign of or a call to an absolute transfiguration, and an absolute transfiguration only possible in the depths of abyss.

Now if it is true that our deepest prophetic and apocalyptic traditions have known the deepest abyss as the very enactment of God, an abyss unnamable apart from a naming of God, so that abyss itself is a primary image of God in this tradition, here the naming of the deepest abyss is inevitably a naming of God, and a naming of God inseparable from the deepest naming of abyss. Indeed, it is precisely when an absolute abyss is most fully named and embodied that the most radical and paradoxical naming of God occurs, one dissolving or reversing every name of God that is not the name of absolute abyss. Then the very name of God itself becomes either absolutely empty or absolutely alien, but its primal identity as the name of God resolutely remains itself, and not only remains itself but enacts itself, and enacts itself in a comprehensive universality of naming, wherein everything whatsoever is named and enacted as absolute abyss. "God" is the one name in our history that has been known and enacted as a universal name, that name of names that is the ultimate source of every name, and if this is the very name that is born in the prophetic revolution, and born as the realization of absolute abyss, this is a realization that has been reborn in our history, but now reborn as totality itself.

Already Spinoza could know this totality, and if he could know it only by dissolving every possibility of abyss, that dissolution is progressively reversed in the history following Spinoza. But the totality here known and envisioned becomes an ever more comprehensive totality, and an ever more comprehensive enactment of abyss itself. Yes, this is ever more fully and more finally an enactment of abyss itself, an enactment wherein an original passivity or nothingness of abyss passes into its very opposite. Abyss itself here speaks in its enactment, as is an original silence of abyss truly reverses itself, as is most clearly manifest in our epic tradition from Dante through Joyce. So it is that an absolutely passive nothingness has become an absolutely actual nothingness in our world, and done so in the fullness of naming itself, for even if our naming is most deeply a naming of anonymity, anonymity speaks in that naming, and an absolute anonymity, an anonymity which is the very voice of an absolute nothingness. Now, the name of names is the name of an absolute nothingness or an absolute abyss. If this is the only name that we can most deeply know as the name of God, we thereby do know the name of God, and enact that name in our naming of an absolute abyss or an absolute nothingness, a name which once again is the name both of our deepest origin and of our deepest ending.

A pure theological paradox is embodied in the thinking of Spinoza, Hegel, and Nietzsche, and perhaps in all truly modern thinking, and that is that a deep thinking of God is here necessarily and inevitably an actual unthinking of God, and not only an unthinking of every previous thinking of God, but a profound unthinking or reverse thinking of the thinking of God itself. While this movement may well be paralleled in the negative theology of an apophatic mysticism, Godhead itself never there is actually unthought, or, insofar as it is unthought, this occurs in an iconoclastic movement shattering all images and ideas of God, so as to call forth or give witness to absolute Godhead itself. As opposed to this finally positive theological movement, our uniquely modern theological thinking shatters every possible theological transcendence, dissolving or reversing that transcendence so as to call forth a uniquely modern immanence, but an absolute immanence that is fully and finally a theological immanence, and is so if only because it so fully incorporates or embodies everything that once was realized as absolute transcendence itself. Nietzsche, Hegel, and Spinoza are those very philosophers who most center their thinking upon God. Even if this is a purely negative thinking, it is nonetheless a theological thinking, and a theological thinking precisely in its centering upon God, one that has never so purely or so comprehensively occurred in our theological traditions, so that here a thinking of totality occurs as it never does in those traditions, and a thinking of a theological totality, even if a purely inverted or reversed theological totality.

This is the context in which we can most deeply know ours as a truly theological age, one that for the first time calls forth a truly and fully negative theology, and an absolutely negative theology, and one that is most clearly so in ultimately embodying an absolute abyss. And it is just because our abyss is certainly not simply and only a meaningless surd that we can know it as a theological abyss. Only the name of names could finally be speaking in this abyss, as is decisively manifest in the ultimacy and finality of our deepest naming of abyss, a naming that could only be a theological naming, and even if only a purely negative or purely reverse theological naming, it is clearly thereby a genuine theological naming. Kafka would teach us that the name of God is not to be pronounced among the innocent, and, as a purely iconoclastic writer, Kafka virtually never wrote the name of God. But no other writer has so purely and so finally called forth the absolute negativity of God, a negativity inducing the purest and most total guilt ever evoked in writing. That very guilt is a decisive sign of that absolute abyss which we so deeply know, and just as this is a guilt that we can numb only in our most passive moments, it is a guilt only possible by way of a confrontation with absolute judgment, a judgment that has never been known apart from the presence of "God."

Theological apologists have ever known that it is the activation of the bad conscience that is the most decisive way to "God," and while it is Nietzsche who knows this most deeply, it is also Nietzsche who has most deeply unveiled the totality of the bad conscience or ressentiment. This totality is the totality of an absolute No-saying, and if that No-saying is Nietzsche's deepest name of the Biblical God, and one inaugurated in the "slave revolt" of the prophetic revolution (even if it is not fully embodied until the birth of Christianity), it is an absolute guilt which is the deepest ground of a uniquely Western humanity. Ironically, it is only the death of God that calls forth or makes manifest the totality of ressentiment. It is only when we are stripped of every possible "grace" that we can know the totality of the bad conscience, only then that the world itself becomes a madhouse, straying through an infinite nothing and totally immersed in a truly new and apocalyptic chaos. Now even if that chaos is the very arena of Zarathustra's enactment of Eternal Recurrence, that Eternal Recurrence is most deeply an ultimate transformation of an absolute No-saying into an absolute Yes-saying, and finally an absolute affirmation of that chaos itself. Thereby an absolute abyss truly does become all in all, and even if this is an absolutely transfigured abyss, it is nevertheless abyss itself, and the purest abyss that had thus far been called forth in our naming itself.

Here, and throughout our deepest modern imaginative enactments, an ultimate enactment of absolute abyss is an enactment of an ultimate transfiguration, a transfiguration occurring in that very abyss itself, and a transfiguration inevitably evoked in any full or genuine naming of that abyss. Naming, in the deepest sense, and even a purely negative naming, is necessarily an act of affirmation, an affirmation transforming the passivity of unnaming into its very opposite, and we inevitably hear such naming as an act of grace, an act deeply dissolving or reversing our own passivity, and thereby fully engaging our deepest response. Perhaps this is most clear in late modernity, when we can only fully engage with the most negative voices, negative voices dissolving every positive voice upon our horizon, but therein we are given our deepest release, and our deepest release from an ultimate passivity that otherwise is overwhelming. Now it is just these purely negative voices that most deeply reveal or unveil our deep passivity. We could even understand their very negativity as being absolutely essential to engage such passivity, for even if a pure passivity is finally a pure illusion, such an illusion is universal in our world. This is one of the crucial points at which our deeper prophets are fully united, and just as all genuine prophecy is a truly negative prophecy, this has never been so universally true as it is in full or late modernity, when our purest language has inevitably been a purely negative language, but precisely thereby a language of transfiguration.

Why do we so deeply respond to the language of a Kafka or a Beckett and so lightly to all language of hope? If never before has all open language of transfiguration become so vacuous and empty, just as never before has an actual pronunciation of the name of God become so universally manifest as a deeply pathological and self-lacerating act, could these be decisive signs of the advent of a new transfiguration, and a new transfiguration annulling or reversing every transfiguration that we have known? Not only did Nietzsche know this profoundly, so, too, did Spinoza, and a host of modern visionaries at least from the time of Blake and even until our own day, and if this is a pure reversal of every possible "religious" or "moral" transfiguration, it is nonetheless a pure transfiguration, and a pure transfiguration of our deepest passivity or our deepest abyss. Yet all of this vision knows this transfiguration as occurring within the depths of abyss itself, or in the depths of everything which was once known as "evil" or "abyss," hence these visions have inevitably called forth a profound offense, and the deepest possible offense. That, too, could be a genuine sign of the advent of a new transfiguration, and a new absolute transfiguration, and an absolute transfiguration of everything that we have known as "God."

Waiting for "God" is perhaps our deepest pathological act, that act inducing the deepest passivity, but a passivity that is a truly self-lacerating passivity, and self-lacerating in its very refusal of or flight from an absolute abyss. Already the ancient prophets could know such passivity as a true apostasy, a rebellion against Yahweh, one refusing the absolute judgment of Yahweh, thence issuing in a turning away from Yahweh, and a turning to the manifest power of a now ultimately empty world. A monarchic messianism is a primal consequence of that turning, and just as we now can understand that ancient messianic prophecy is truly alien to the prophetic revolution, and is the consequence of a monarchic and all too worldly Israel, so, too, all messianic prophecy has become deeply alien in our new world, and even if Hegel can be understood as a modern messianic thinker, it is just at this point that Hegel in our world is most alien and unreal. Perhaps the deepest ending of messianism in the ancient world occurred in Jesus himself, and if we now can be assured that Jesus was the very opposite of a messianic prophet, just as was Paul, too, and the gospel traditions as well, then if only at this point an original Christianity has been deeply reborn in our world, and reborn if only by way of the ending of Christendom. Kierkegaard was the first to know this ending profoundly, and if nothing is more alien to Kierkegaard than any form of messianism, this was not only a fundamental ground of his anti-Hegelian thinking, but a ground of his understanding of a truly new objectification of consciousness and society precluding the very possibility of a genuine interiority or subjectivity. While such thinking was deeply alien to Kierkegaard's historical world, it is truly prophetic of ours. If Kierkegaard was the first thinker to know the depths of *Angst*, that is an *Angst* released by the very advent of the modern world, but not universally embodied until the advent of our world.

Such *Angst* cannot be dissociated from the advent of an absolute abyss, an abyss which Kierkegaard could know as the Nothing itself. Just as "the Nothing" is the very opposite of a literal nothingness, an absolute abyss is the very opposite of a pure nothingness, as overwhelmingly manifest when it is universally embodied. Could that embodiment finally be the self-embodiment of God? And a Self-Embodiment of the Self-Saving of God? If our deepest abyss is an absolutely actual abyss, could the pure actuality of that abyss be a contemporary epiphany of what once was known as the pure actuality of God? Now even if such transcendent actuality is alien to all uniquely modern philosophical thinking, if a purely transcendent actuality is open to an absolute transfiguration, and an absolute transfiguration of itself, then if such a transfiguration has, indeed, occurred, it could be known both in and as an absolute reversal of itself. Certainly this is no mere abstract possibility, for this is a paradigm offering a decisive theological way into our uniquely modern thinking, and one unveiling that thinking as a genuinely theological thinking.

Hegel could know Luther as the true inaugurator of modernity, a Luther whom Hegel knew as the first to understand and proclaim an absolute freedom, but that freedom for Luther himself is inseparable from an absolute predestination, an absolute predestination which is an absolute judgment, and even if that judgment is grace and judgment at once, it is an embodiment of the deep abyss of Godhead itself, an abyss only annulled or reversed by that Crucifixion which is the Passion of God. Already Luther could know the Passion of God as an ultimate transfiguration of the Godhead, and perhaps at no other point is he more distant from that Augustinian tradition out of which he arose, but the justification which he proclaimed is inseparable from an ultimate *Anfechtung* or guilt, and one releasing a uniquely modern *Angst*. This is the *Angst* that Kierkegaard was the first to know deeply, and it is finally a consequence of an encounter with that Nothing which is most deeply embodied in God, a Nothing which is the abyss of an absolute No-saying. That No-saying is absolutely inseparable from the Yes-saying of God, a Yes-saying which can only be known by us in the Crucifixion or the Passion of God. Now if the Passion of God is an absolute transfiguration of the Godhead, and one only occurring through the full and final actualization of the deepest and most absolute abyss, here that abyss could only be realized within Godhead itself, a realization which is a truly new creation, and a new creation of Godhead itself.

Our most ultimate modern thinking embodies truly new and even absolutely new ideas of God. Only now does an absolute break occur from all primordial worlds, one shattering all of our theological traditions, so that here the thinking of absolute ground is the unthinking of every previous absolute ground. If such thinking is necessarily the unthinking of God, it is nonetheless a re-thinking of God, one which is luminously present not only in Spinoza, Hegel, and Nietzsche, but even in Kierkegaard himself, who while reversing the thinking of his predecessors, called forth the most abysmal depths of Godhead itself. Alone among these thinkers, Kierkegaard could not actually think redemption, could not think an absolute transfiguration. Perhaps only thereby can that transfiguration be known as grace and as grace alone, but that grace is inseparable from a realization of the absolute abyss of Godhead itself, an abyss only fully known in our world by Kierkegaard and Nietzsche, but one nevertheless comprehensively called forth in our deepest imaginative enactments. Are those enactments finally enactments of the Passion of God, a Passion of God which is the self-embodiment of the deepest and most absolute abyss, and a self-embodiment which is finally a universal embodiment, an embodiment wherein an absolute abyss becomes all in all?

While Christians can know the Passion of God as the absolute event of redemption, is it possible to know that passion in and as an absolute abyss, an abyss ultimately deepening if not reversing every previous abyss, so that an absolute abyss here and now becomes all in all? Then absolute abyss would not only be the Body of God, but absolute Body itself. Further, it would not be an absolutely empty body as in Buddhism, but an absolutely actual body, and actual most openly in its very embodiment of abyss, and an abyss which is finally a redemptive abyss, and redemptive because it is the very Body of God. Surely Nietzsche could know such a body, but he could know it only by knowing the death of God. Yet if the death of God is finally the Passion of God, and a passion of God which apocalyptically is all in all, then here an apocalyptic ending could only be the ending of "God," or the ending of every Godhead that is not the Passion of God. Then bad faith would quite simply be belief in "God," a belief in God refusing the Passion of God, and refusing the Passion of God by only knowing an absolutely transcendent and absolutely sovereign God. But when that sovereignty and transcendence are truly not only emptied but reversed, then there inevitably occurs a realization of the Passion of God, even if that passion can no longer be known or named as "God."

Indeed, it is precisely the deepest realization of the Passion of God, a realization of absolute abyss, which finally ends every possible naming of God, an unnaming which itself is a transfiguring movement, even if a transfiguring movement realizing only abyss. Yet if that abyss is an absolutely transfiguring abyss, and one realized in the deepest depths of abyss itself, then its full embodiment must finally be a transfiguring embodiment, and transfiguring even in its realization of abyss itself. Already this movement is actual in the prophetic revolution, and if that movement has returned again and again in our history, it perhaps only now is fully being universalized. Just as the prophetic revolution is inseparable from the advent of exile, a genuine exile is surely now at hand, an exile that is not only the banishing or perishing of the interior and individual subject, but an exile that is the advent of a universal abyss. Our deeper prophets throughout history have called for a full affirmation of abyss, an affirmation reversing that pure passivity which is an inevitable consequence of the advent of deep abyss, and if this is an affirmation releasing the deepest energy and life, it is an affirmation inseparable from the advent of absolute abyss, and an absolute abyss which is finally an absolutely transfiguring abyss.

Both the "I" of God and the "I" of consciousness perish in that abyss. This perishing is not simply and only an absolutely new perishing, but is the repetition of an original perishing, the perishing of an ancient Israel and an ancient Yahweh. If this is an apocalyptic perishing, it is repeated once again in an original Christian apocalypticism, an apocalypticism ending an old world or an old creation, and only thereby celebrating a new Spirit or I AM that is totality itself. Apocalypticism can truly be known not only as a deeply anarchistic movement, but also as a deeply nihilistic movement. It fully draws forth the absolute nothingness of world itself, a world which it knows as having come to an end, and only that ending is the advent of an apocalyptic totality. Even if that totality is an absolute grace, it is actually real only through the ending of the world. Now just as apocalypticism has deeply been reborn in our world, so, too, has been reborn an ending of the world, an ending of every world upon our horizon, or every world that is not abyss itself. This ending is clearly a repetition of an ancient apocalyptic ending, but now it is an ending that can only know grace itself as a pure abyss. Yet apocalypticism has always known grace as an abyss, for even if this is a transfiguring abyss, it is just thereby abyss itself, an absolute abyss that alone can embody an absolute ending, an ending inseparable from the advent of an apocalyptic grace.

Genuinely apocalyptic enactments are purely positive and purely negative at once, therein embodying a *coincidentia oppositorum* as their center and ground. Here the deepest light is inseparable from the deepest darkness, just as the deepest advent is inseparable from the deepest ending, and it is the very advent of the deepest darkness which is perhaps the most decisive sign of the advent of the deepest light. Now it is precisely when this profoundly negative pole of apocalypticism is abated or dissolved that apocalypticism most clearly dissolves or reverses itself. Then apocalypticism becomes a worldly movement and a worldly movement alone, one truly divorced from a purely negative ground, and open to no ultimate challenge whatsoever. While such transformations have occurred again and again in our history, their demonic ground and consequences are now manifest to all. If we can understand a uniquely modern messianism as such a transformation, the very worldliness of this messianism is a clear sign of a reversal of a genuine apocalypticism, and even if such a reversal can release an enormous power in the world, that power itself is finally a purely negative power, and a negative power which is a truly chaotic power. So it is that apocalypticism has been a profoundly destructive power in history, perhaps the most destructive power, but only when it has undergone a deep reversal of itself, only when it has lost or abated or transformed its original ground, or only when it has dualistically isolated its positive and negative poles, and thereby, and only thereby, released a purely worldly power.

Messianism in one form or another has been a fundamental ground of all historical empires. This is true in both East and West, and even if messianism has been given both sacred and profane expressions, it is inseparable from an all too worldly power, hence it has been assaulted by prophets throughout the world. One such assault has been an unveiling of messianism as an all too human will to power, one originally arising as an ultimate exaltation of monarchic authority and power, and later arising as an ultimate exaltation of totalitarian power. In each there occurs an absolute sanctioning of a purely exterior power, and even if this is done in the name of a universal peace and a universal justice, this is a justice and a peace inseparable from an absolutely sovereign power. While messianism and apocalypticism were virtually inseparable in the historical world of Jesus, there can be little doubt that Jesus was a profoundly anti-messianic prophet. Just as no deeper reversal of Jesus occurred than in the advent of a Christian messianism, this advent itself is a reversal of apocalypticism, and just as the apocalypticism that it reversed was the purest apocalypticism that had thus far existed in the world, the advent of Christian messianism is the advent of a truly new will to power, and one which for the first time was a will to a universal and all comprehensive power. Only this birth made possible a universal messianism, and one which has ravaged the modern world as it has no other world, and even if ours is a truly secularized messianism, it nevertheless is in deep continuity with its historical source and ground.

While our messianism has either come to an end or deeply disguised itself, this ending is finally a delegitimization or profanation of a purely worldly power, a stripping of every ultimate sanction from all worldly power. This first occurs in the prophetic revolution and has occurred again and again throughout our history, but is only truly becoming universal today. So it is that all sacred or "legitimate" authority is now truly vanishing, sanctions are everywhere eroding which are not purely pragmatic sanctions, and if it is fiscal power which is now seemingly the deepest power, this is a power which every real prophet has known as a demonic power, so that the Sermon on the Mount declares that one cannot serve God and mammon. What could be a better symbol of our fiscal power than mammon itself? Hence worldly power today can have no possible sanction, or no possible ultimate sanction. If this is truly unique historically, it can be understood as the consequence of an apocalyptic ending, and the apocalyptic ending of historical worlds in which a truly exterior power was fully sanctioned, a sanctioning which thus far has been an ultimate ground of every historical world.

Surely we stand at the end of an historical era, perhaps of all historical eras. If this can be observed in the deep erosion or collapse of all mythology and all ideology, and if this collapse can seemingly be opposed only by the most primitive fundamentalisms, this is a collapse incorporating a truly new emptiness, and a fully actual emptiness, an emptiness which is the emptiness of every manifest or open power. For the first time a society has come into existence without any deep or ultimate sanctions whatsoever, and if this is truly an embodiment of the death of God, or the death or dissolution of all holiness whatsoever, it is precisely thereby the advent of a new chaos, and of an absolute chaos, and now and for the first time an absolute chaos which is a universal chaos. Yet this is just the condition that an original apocalypticism can know as the advent of apocalypse itself, an apocalypse that is not only an absolute transfiguration, but a universal transfiguration, a transfiguration of everything whatsoever. The truth is that genuine apocalypticism confronts a world that it knows as having already come to an end, and just as this is true of both Jesus and Paul, it likewise is true of both Blake and Nietzsche. It is the "power" of this world which has now truly ended, as manifest for us in the dissolution of all "sacred" power, and with that dissolution both power and sacrality truly become reversed. Of course, this is invisible and unheard in the "world," but now a new world has dawned that is void of all deep seeing and hearing, one that can actually see and hear only chaos itself. If that chaos is a deeply muted or disguised chaos, a deeply veiled chaos accompanying a truly new passivity, that passivity in its ultimate emptiness is an embodiment of chaos itself, and an embodiment of that chaos which is uniquely our own. But that very uniqueness is a decisive sign, one which could be a genuinely apocalyptic sign, and an apocalyptic sign of apocalypse itself. This is a new apocalypse, yes, but just thereby an absolutely transfiguring apocalypse, even if thereby it is only openly manifest as the deepest darkness, and as the most universal darkness yet released in the world.

CHAPTER 10

⤚

The Body of Abyss

Only in Nietzsche and in Mahayana Buddhism can one discover an actual philosophical understanding of abyss, an understanding or a thinking which is here a dissolution or reversal of thinking itself, or of every thinking which is not a pure and total thinking of abyss. Buddhism knows this abyss as *Sunya*, that absolute void or emptiness which is the dialectically negative form of nirvana or Sunyata, whereas Nietzsche knows an absolute abyss as the consequence of the death of God. In both Nietzsche and Buddhism this abyss is an absolute nothingness, and an absolute nothingness that is absolutely negative and absolutely positive simultaneously. But whereas Nietzsche can know absolute abyss as the Will to Power or an apocalyptic Eternal Recurrence, Mahayana Buddhism knows it as absolute emptiness or an absolute quiescence. If these are truly opposite understandings of absolute abyss, this could illuminate a uniquely Western or a uniquely modern transfiguration, a transfiguration inseparable from an absolute act or an absolute actuality. Already Dante's *Commedia* envisions such an actuality, a transfiguration comprehending everything whatsoever, or everything that is not the pure and actual nothingness of Hell itself. Yet even this Hell is essential to the *Purgatorio* and the *Paradiso*, for here an apocalyptic transfiguration is inseparable from the horizon of absolute evil, and all too significantly it is in the *Inferno* and not the *Purgatorio* or the *Paradiso* that the apocalyptic vision and language of the *Commedia* is most realistic. The *Inferno* can be known as the very birth of a uniquely Western realism, or a uniquely Western mimesis, one wholly transforming all ancient allegory, as for the first time the imagination envisions the actually real, and does so far more fully and decisively than is possible in either the *Purgatorio* or the *Paradiso*. But that is just the reason why the *Inferno* is essential to the *Purgatorio* and the *Paradiso*, for apart from the horizon of the *Inferno*, the apocalyptic transfiguration there occurring would be truly unreal.

Now just as such realism is absent in the ancient world both East and West, it is essential to a uniquely apocalyptic transfiguration, and even is so in ancient apocalypticism. This apocalypticism never loses an historical horizon, and therein differs profoundly from its polar counterpart in Gnosticism; as opposed to Gnosticism, ancient apocalypticism is inseparable from its Hebraic or Biblical ground. So, too, a uniquely Christian epic is realistic as ancient epic never could be, as here an epic voyage is a genuinely realistic voyage. It not only occurs in the historical world of its visionaries, but it comprehensively incorporates those historical worlds as does no other imaginative genre or mode of thinking. Here only Hegelian thinking truly challenges the Christian epic, but that thinking can be understood as a genuinely epic thinking, and Hegelian thinking is the first truly apocalyptic thinking, or the first philosophical apocalyptic thinking. But the advent of the Christian epic is the advent of apocalyptic poetry. This apocalyptic poetry becomes ever more fully apocalyptic as it evolves, even as it becomes ever more fully realistic in this evolution, finally giving us, in *Finnegans Wake,* the most realistic language that has ever been written or inscribed. Both *Ulysses* and *Finnegans Wake* are apocalyptic epics, and even as they are in essential continuity with the *Commedia* and *Paradise Lost,* they are wholly inseparable from their ground in Blake's epics, and thus inseparable from a "Self-Annihilation" that is a cosmic, an interior, and an historical self-annihilation, a total self-annihilation that is a total apocalyptic transfiguration.

Not only does that apocalyptic transfiguration, or any full and genuine apocalyptic transfiguration, incorporate the Godhead itself, but it is centered in the Godhead, a Godhead here and now undergoing an ultimate self-transfiguration or self-saving, as Godhead not only absolutely reverses itself, but in that very reversal ever more fully becomes an absolutely new body. This is the apocalyptic body of absolute abyss. This apocalyptic body is luminously drawn forth in *Finnegans Wake*, just as it is in the *Commedia*, but in the *Wake* apocalyptic body is light and darkness simultaneously, or chaos and cosmos at once, whereas in the *Commedia*, apocalyptic body is fully and finally a wholly luminous body, even if it is truly unreal apart from the deep horizon of a pure and total darkness. That is a darkness which dominates the *Wake*, a darkness inseparable from the truly new realism of the *Wake*, and even if this is true of the *Commedia*, too, a far purer realism is embodied in the *Wake*, one reflecting all of that history lying between the *Commedia* and the *Wake*, a realism which is finally pure darkness itself, or that very darkness released by a final apocalyptic ending. No such ending is yet possible in the world of the *Commedia*, although its ground is here fully established, a ground finally realizing itself in the world of the *Wake*, a world which is truly our world, and yet a world only made possible by that epic voyage which is here fulfilled.

Nowhere else in the Christian world is Godhead more fully and more openly embodied than it is in the Christian epic, and nowhere else is Godhead more open or more actual as apocalyptic Godhead, hence the Christian epic tradition is the most Biblical of all Christian traditions, yet it is ultimately realistic precisely through that Biblical ground. At no other point is the Christian epic more distant from Christian mysticism, or even from everything that we have known as Christian theology, as all too paradoxically it is our most realistic poetic genre which is our most Biblical genre, and it is the Christian epic voyage which is our most openly Biblical voyage. Of course, that voyage is a revolutionary voyage, and one revolutionizing even the Bible itself. Yet it incorporates the Bible far more fully than do all other voyages, hence truly realizing the revolutionary ground of the Bible, and doing so far more actually than has ever occurred in any Christian theology. Indeed, it is the apocalyptic ground of the Christian epic that is a truly revolutionary ground, perhaps its most revolutionary ground, but that ground is finally the apocalyptic transfiguration of Godhead itself, one occurring in all of our great Christian epics, even if that transfiguration only becomes fully manifest as the Christian epic voyage evolves. Yet there is a profound continuity in that voyage, one most openly manifest in the deep continuity between Dante and Joyce, but one no less actual in the Christological revolutions of Milton and Blake. These revolutions fully correlate Satan and Christ, and at no point is the evolving continuity of the Christian epic voyage more openly manifest than in its ever fuller enactment of the totality of Satan.

Satan is our fullest image of an absolute darkness, but Satan is not decisively called forth in our history until the advent of apocalypticism, and Satan is our clearest image of an absolutely negative abyss. But only the Christian epic has fully envisioned Satan, and this envisionment only gradually evolves. It is not fully realized until the advent of the modern world, so that in *Paradise Lost* Satan is fully correlated with Christ, and in Blake's *Milton* and *Jerusalem* there occurs an ultimate *coincidentia oppositorum* between Christ and Satan. Only in *Finnegans Wake* is such a *coincidentia* realized comprehensively. This is the consummation of a uniquely Christian epic voyage, a voyage into the depths of an absolute abyss, and that voyage enacts an absolute transfiguration, and finally an absolute transfiguration of Godhead itself. Just as this is a truly forward moving voyage, it is even thereby a genuinely apocalyptic voyage, but an apocalyptic voyage whose very realization of an absolute darkness is precisely thereby a realization of an absolute light. While this is unquestionably a genuine *coincidentia oppositorum*, unlike its Buddhist counterpart it is a truly evolving *coincidentia*, and even a genuinely realistic one, a realism inseparable from that actual history which is here embodied, and a history which is finally the ultimate history of Godhead itself.

Thereby the Christian epic voyage is the most total of all Christian heterodoxies, and even if this is a heterodoxy which only gradually evolves, it is already deeply heterodox in Dante, and most clearly so in Dante's revolutionary correlation of Godhead itself with the very actuality of the world, as for the first time in Christian vision the actualities of Godhead and the world are truly inseparable. While this was made possible by the revolutionary theological thinking of Aquinas, Dante goes far beyond Aquinas in calling forth the actuality of the world. Just as this is inseparable from Dante's assault upon the temporal authority and status of the Church, it is even more deeply inseparable from Dante's revolutionary discovery of a truly new perception, a perception unfolding within us an interior reality, and our interior turning to that reality is the movement of love, a love which is a response to that reality which is finally "isness" and love at once (*Purgatorio*, XVIII, 22–33). This new perception is possible only as a consequence of the Incarnation, but it is unknown in Christianity until the advent of the Gothic world. Although it is fully manifest in Gothic art and architecture, it is only in the *Commedia* that it is poetically and linguistically embodied, and if this is a revolutionary transformation of our language, it is no less so a religious and theological revolution. That revolution is the inauguration of the Christian epic, but it is also a recovery of the original apocalyptic ground of Christianity, one occurring throughout a new Christian apocalypticism, and most forcefully so in that radical or Spiritual Franciscanism which is inseparable from the apocalyptic vision of Joachim of Fiore.

Joachism is most comprehensively reborn in Hegel, but it is reborn in Milton and Blake, too, for Milton can know the authority of the Church as the authority of an age that has now come to an end, just as Milton can know and enact a new revolutionary freedom, and a new freedom inseparable from the advent of a new apocalypse. Only in this apocalypse is Satan fully revealed, but this revelation is inseparable from a new revelation of Christ, as for the first time in Christian vision the Christ of Passion is fully enacted, a full Christ of Passion unknowable apart from a full epiphany of Satan. *Paradise Lost* is our most ecstatic vision of Satan, and our fullest one until Blake, and if it is not until Blake that the totality of Satan is envisioned and enacted, it is not until Blake that a full and total apocalyptic vision occurs, one inseparable from its seeds in Dante, and one only possible by way of a dialectical and apocalyptic reversal of *Paradise Lost*. Once again we are given an apocalyptic vision of history, but now a history openly centering upon the history of the Godhead, and a Godhead whose ultimate apocalypse is only made possible by its original and total fall. Such a total fall is not called forth until the advent of apocalypticism, but only in a uniquely modern apocalypticism is that fall actually the fall of Godhead itself, a radical apocalypticism inaugurated by Blake, and consummated in our own world by Joyce.

Apocalypticism can be known as the most heterodox of all Biblical movements, it surely challenges every orthodoxy that it encounters, and what we know as orthodoxy in Judaism, Christianity, and Islam alike arose as an opposition to and reversal of apocalypticism. So, too, medieval apocalypticism is inevitably heterodox, and is so not only in Christianity but also in Judaism and Islam. But only a uniquely modern apocalypticism is totally heterodox, and not that apocalypticism that is commonly known as such, but rather that apocalypticism occurring in the most powerful expressions of modernity. And that apocalypticism is most radical or most revolutionary in its enactment of Godhead itself, a Godhead undergoing an ultimate reversal of itself, thereby releasing the fullness of an absolute abyss both in historical actuality and in the depths of a truly new interiority. A radically new interiority is born in the very advent of Christianity. This explodes in the Gothic world, thereby inaugurating a Christian epic that is interior and cosmic at once; now an epic voyage is not only a human voyage but a divine one as well, and while this is only gradually called forth in the evolution of the Christian epic, it is nevertheless indubitably real, already occurring in that Beatrice whom Dante knows as the incarnate Christ, and that incarnate Christ who is the deepest ground of the voyage of the *Commedia*. Beatrice is not only the guiding spirit of this voyage, and is so for the most part through Virgil and then finally through herself, but Beatrice is the source or agent of the deepest revelation which here occurs, and that is finally a fully apocalyptic revelation, and a revelation unveiling an absolutely new actuality of the Godhead. Not only is that actuality unknown either to scholasticism or to the hierarchy of the Church, but it cannot be known in any form of Christian orthodoxy, even as it is a driving force in a new Christian heterodoxy, and one most purely embodied in the *Commedia*.

While Dante was condemned by the papacy for his negation of the temporal authority of the Church, that negation is inseparable from Dante's recognition and enactment of a truly new actuality of the world, but a new actuality of the world inseparable from a new actuality of God, for Dante's most revolutionary vision is an enactment of an actuality of God that is inseparable from the actuality of the world. Therefore an apocalyptic transfiguration of the world is inseparable from an apocalyptic transfiguration of the Godhead, and apocalypse itself is finally a total apocalypse that is an apocalyptic realization of Godhead itself. This is most openly manifest in *Finnegans Wake*, but most clearly called forth in *Milton* and *Jerusalem*, just as it is most manifest philosophically in the revolutionary thinking of Hegel and Nietzsche, a thinking reversing the whole history of Western thinking with an apocalyptic finality. Indeed, the very voyage of the Christian epic can be understood as an Hegelian *Aufgehoben*, one truly negating everything that it encounters. But that negation is a dialectical negation, hence it not only incorporates that which it negates, but this is a negation and an apocalyptic

negation realizing that which it negates in a truly new and ever more universal actuality. Here, the forgiveness of sin truly is a transfiguration of sin, just
as evil itself is not dissolved but ultimately transfigured, and the God of wrath
and judgment truly is transfigured into the God of absolute compassion. This
can finally be understood only as an absolute transfiguration of Godhead
itself, and a transfiguration occurring through God's own acts, as most openly
manifest in the Incarnation and the Crucifixion, a Crucifixion and an Incarnation which is a self-emptying of the Godhead, but a self-emptying which
is a profound fulfillment of the Godhead, and a fulfillment actually realizing
an absolute compassion.

Only Christianity knows an ultimate self-negation or self-emptying of
the Godhead, but that is a self-negation inevitably realizing an absolute abyss,
and an absolute abyss of Godhead itself. Therein and thereby the negative
pole of the Godhead fully stands forth, and this is not an illusory negativity
as it finally is in Gnosticism, nor a negative pole that is simply and only the
pure "other" of the positive pole, but far rather a negative pole that is dialectically identical with the positive pole, as Godhead for the first time is fully
actual as an ultimate *coincidentia oppositorum*. If Godhead here undergoes
an absolute self-negation or self-emptying, this is not a primordial self-
emptying, but rather an apocalyptic and historical self-emptying, one realizing itself in the actualities of history and consciousness. Therein it profoundly
transforms both consciousness and history, a transformation inseparable from
the transformation or transfiguration of Godhead itself. Not only does an
absolutely "new" dawn ever more fully, but an absolutely "old" is equally
called forth, an "old" which apocalyptically can be named as the old aeon or
even Satan, but an actualization of Satan and the old aeon or the old creation
only possible as the consequence of an absolutely forward movement. Just as
it was the prophetic revolution which first enacted the absolutely new, this is
a revolution fulfilled in Jesus, and in that Jesus who enacted the final dawning
of the Kingdom of God, a kingdom that is not a primordial or an ancient or
an eternal kingdom, but a kingdom that is and only is an apocalyptic kingdom, or that kingdom which *is* the absolutely new.

But the absolutely new is absolutely other than the absolutely "old," an
"old" only manifest or actual with the advent of the absolutely new, one
which both Paul and the Fourth Gospel can wholly assault, and the advent of
that "old" is an inevitable consequence of Jesus' ultimate enactment of the
Kingdom of God. The very title "Kingdom of God" cannot be found in any
writing until the New Testament, and even if historical Christianity wholly
reversed that Kingdom of God which Jesus enacted, it is above all historical
Christianity, and most decisively ancient and patristic Christianity, which
envisioned and enacted an absolutely primordial Godhead, a primordial
Godhead which for the first time is the very opposite of apocalyptic Godhead.

Not until the advent of Christianity is a primordial Godhead manifest in the West. This primordial Godhead is truly alien to the classical world, and even alien to Israel until the full advent of Hellenistic Judaism, yet it is only in Christianity that primordial Godhead becomes truly primal, or finally and only primordial, and only in that Christianity which is the consequence of the reversal of an original Christian apocalypticism. Hence this is an ultimate epiphany of primordial Godhead, which is the consequence of a negation of apocalyptic Godhead, an absolutely primordial which is the very opposite of the absolutely new, and one only possible as a consequence of a negation and reversal of the absolutely new. A distinctively Christian primordial Godhead, as opposed to a Hindu or purely Neoplatonic primordial Godhead, is the absolutely primordial or the absolute "first" or the absolutely "unoriginate," which orthodox Christianity knows as the Father and the Creator. This makes possible a uniquely Christian Trinity, a Trinity which is an eternal generation, but a uniquely Christian eternal generation in which the Father eternally generates the Son and the Spirit. This eternal generation of the Godhead is possible only because the Father or the Creator is the only person or mode of the Godhead which is "unoriginate," thus the Father is truly other than the second and third persons of the Godhead, thereby giving the Father an absolute sovereignty and transcendence unknown in Hinduism, Judaism, and Islam, or unknown apart from the uniquely Christian Trinity. For as opposed to Brahman-Atman or Sunyata, or even a purely Neoplatonic One, the uniquely Christian Creator is truly other than the other persons or modes of the Godhead itself, and is Himself the source or origin of these modes in a uniquely Christian eternal generation.

Now this is the very Father which a uniquely modern apocalypticism unveils as culminating in a purely abstract Spirit or an absolute No-saying, or that Father which is the purely negative pole of the Godhead. This Father is the very opposite of an absolute Yes-saying, hence a Satan who is the true opposite of Christ, or a totally abstract Spirit which is the true opposite of a fully and totally incarnate Spirit. Yet, as opposed to every possible dualism, a wholly incarnate Spirit is not simply and only the pure "other" of a wholly abstract Spirit, it is dialectically identical with that "other," as manifest in its own actualization as the absolute reversal of abstract Spirit. So, too, the absolutely new is not simply the "other" of the absolutely old or the absolutely primordial, it is a full and total reversal of that absolutely primordial, an absolutely primordial which does not dawn or is not actualized until the advent of the absolutely new. Only Christianity knows that absolutely primordial which is absolutely "first," an absolutely primordial which is absolutely other than the absolutely new, one which could never be manifest or actual apart from the advent of the absolutely new, and one only possible by way of a full and actual negation and reversal of the absolutely new. Here, Godhead itself could only be in profound conflict with itself, a conflict known to Christianity alone, and while wholly alien to orthodox Christianity, it is primal in a purely heterodox Christianity, and the deeper the Christian heterodoxy the more totally this ultimate conflict in the Godhead is drawn forth.

But it is not fully manifest until the full realization of modernity, a modernity alone knowing and realizing an absolute conflict or war in the Godhead, just as it is only that modernity which knows and realizes an absolutely actual abyss, or a body of abyss which is actuality itself, as body itself now undergoes an ultimate transfiguration. Only now does a truly abstract or empty body become manifest and actual, and only now is a bodily energy called forth which is the very opposite of a new empty body. Inevitably such bodily energy is a totality, but a totality inactual and unreal apart from its very opposite. Hence such energy is a truly dichotomous energy, an energy reflecting a new dichotomous body, one wholly alien to every ancient world, but overwhelming in that world released by the advent of Christianity. Only Christianity knows an absolutely dichotomous body, one torn asunder by an ultimate conflict between "flesh" and Spirit, and one releasing a truly new "I," a doubled and self-divided "I" which is truly at war with itself, and only that war makes possible the advent of a truly new self-consciousness. That self-consciousness is inseparable from a new body, a new body as a dichotomous body, a body inseparable from what the Christian uniquely knows as "sin" and "grace," a grace only realizing itself in the depths of sin, and a sin only manifest with the advent of the depths of grace.

Now if it is only Christianity that has undergone an ultimate historical transformation, that transformation is inseparable from the uniquely Christian God, and if it is only Christianity that embodies ultimate historical and interior dichotomies, it is only the Christian God that is a truly dichotomous God. Even orthodox Christianity knows that dichotomy in knowing an eternal predestination, a predestination or election which is inevitably a double predestination; everyone is damned as a consequence of an original and total fall, and only a tiny elect is predestined to a redemption from that fall, with the great mass of humanity being eternally predestined to damnation, and that very damnation is inseparable from the redemption of the elect. So it is that damnation is more overwhelming in Christianity than in any other tradition, only being abated with the secularization of Christianity, but that secularization does not dissolve the dichotomies of a uniquely Western consciousness. It far rather universalizes them, so that Nietzsche could declare that the world itself is now a madhouse. But this is a madhouse reflecting the uniquely Christian God, a God which is absolute light and absolute darkness at once, hence a truly dichotomous God, or a God at absolute war with itself.

If only full modernity makes that war fully manifest, only full modernity is a totally dichotomous world, but that world is an historical consummation of Christianity, and thus an historical consummation of the uniquely Christian God. Blake, Hegel, and Nietzsche all know this profoundly; that knowledge is inseparable from a realization of an absolute dichotomy, and now an absolute dichotomy which is a universal dichotomy, one now inseparable from actuality itself, and one manifest in that new body which is a universally dichotomous body. That body is totality itself, a new and even absolutely new totality, and while it bears innumerable masks, it is finally inescapable, and inescapable as apocalypse itself. Could a truly apocalyptic body be a body of emptiness and darkness? Or could it be anything else if it is truly apocalyptic? For just as apocalypse is an absolute ending, it is the ending of everything whatsoever upon its horizon, certainly including everything that is actual as the body. That is not a dissolution of the body; it is far rather the inversion and reversal of everything that is given or manifest as the body. Hence body as body does not now simply disappear, it becomes wholly other than itself, wholly other than everything most deeply given as the body, and wholly other than everything once namable as the body.

Yet a truly apocalyptic ending is simultaneously an apocalyptic beginning, a beginning of the truly or the absolutely new, as here body itself becomes absolutely new, and absolutely new in a truly new *coincidentia oppositorum.* Just as an absolutely new body could only be an absolutely transfigured body, that transfiguration is impossible apart from its incorporation of that old body or that old world which it absolutely reverses. Only the total actualization of that "old" body makes possible this transfiguration, a transfiguration impossible apart from a transfiguration of that "old" body. Thus not until the "old" body becomes fully actual as an apocalyptic and totally "old" body can a fully apocalyptic transfiguration occur, and even if that actuality bears innumerable masks and is virtually invisible as such, or invisible and unhearable in its full totality, it nevertheless is real in that transfiguration, and so real as to be finally inescapable. But the very advent of that "old" body is a decisive sign of an ultimate and apocalyptic transfiguration, and now a universal apocalyptic transfiguration, for just as this new body is absolutely all encompassing, so, too, is this new transfiguration, as now a universal *coincidentia oppositorum* fully dawns. Of course, the Christian knows that dawning as occurring in the Incarnation and the Crucifixion, one which is truly realized in the Resurrection, but that resurrection is only an initial dawning, and one that was truly reversed by Christianity itself, but with the reversal of that reversal in the uniquely modern realization of the death of God, the possibility and the actuality is established of an apocalyptic dawning that is a universal apocalypse.

Now if historical Christianity is most deeply grounded in primordial Godhead, and an absolutely primordial Godhead, a full and apocalyptic reversal of that Godhead would inevitably reverse the primordial "body" of that

Godhead. Even if that primordial body is a total and all comprehending body, it is precisely that body that is here apocalyptically reversed. Yet that very apocalyptic reversal incorporates that "old" body that it reverses, and therefore incorporates primordial Godhead itself, but it incorporates it only as an absolutely "old" or absolutely primordial Godhead, one embodying a truly and absolutely new transcendence, and absolutely new as an ever increasingly empty or alien transcendence. But this is the very transcendence that is necessary to an ultimate and final negation, a negation which is an apocalyptic negation. Hence it is a negation inseparable from that which it negates, which could only be that Godhead that is the very opposite of apocalyptic Godhead. Only that final embodiment of the Godhead is an embodiment of an absolutely empty and alien Godhead, a truly and wholly negative body which is the consequence of absolute apocalypse itself, an apocalypse wholly unreal apart from this embodiment.

Now if Christianity knows the Crucifixion as an ultimate and final sacrifice, that is a sacrifice releasing an absolutely sacrificial body, a body embodying apocalyptic sacrifice itself. This is a final sacrifice, and precisely thereby an ultimate resolution of primordial sacrifice. Nothing is more invisible or silent in a uniquely Christian enactment of primordial Godhead than is primordial sacrifice. Indeed, no other apprehension of the Godhead is so bereft of even the echoes of primordial sacrifice itself, or so given to apprehending the Godhead as absolute sovereignty and absolute transcendence alone, one foreclosing every possibility of an absolute sacrifice or self-emptying, and every possibility of the transfiguration of Godhead itself. But this enactment of the Godhead is a response to the Crucifixion, and to that uniquely Christian apocalypse embodied in the Crucifixion, one reversing both apocalypse and crucifixion and only thereby enacting a uniquely Christian primordial Godhead. Hence this Godhead and this Godhead alone is the very opposite of an absolutely sacrificial body, and the very opposite of sacrifice itself. Thereby the Christological wars which are inevitable in Christianity are released, wars which are only abated in the most orthodox expressions of Christianity and only stilled in a uniquely Christian passivity. Both that orthodoxy and that passivity are reversals of a uniquely Christian sacrificial body, a body that alone makes possible a revolutionary praxis, or a praxis which is absolute apocalypse.

Yet a totally sacrificial body can be known as an absolutely abysmal body, one incorporating an absolute abyss, an abyss apart from which no absolute sacrifice would be possible, so that sacrificial body is inevitably the body of abyss, and one releasing actual bodies of abyss, and actual bodies of abyss which are the consequence of apocalypse itself. If only the Christian world has realized truly dichotomous bodies, bodies torn asunder by an ultimate conflict between flesh and Spirit, and one in which the body is sin and grace simultaneously, that grace is a uniquely Christian grace in its very embodiment. This is an embodiment of the depths of grace in body itself, and a final embodiment of those depths in a body of total sin and eternal death. Yet that embodiment is the embodiment of the Body of God, a body of God which is the consequence of an absolute sacrifice, a sacrifice in which Godhead itself truly reverses itself, becoming the very opposite of everything whatsoever which is now manifest and real as primordial Godhead. This primordial Godhead only now is an absolutely empty Godhead, a self-emptying inseparable from an absolute and apocalyptic sacrifice. Hence to be open to that sacrifice is to be open to absolute abyss, but an absolute abyss that here is an absolutely sacrificial abyss, and the sacrificial abyss of an absolutely new Godhead. This new Godhead is inseparable from its true opposite, an opposite which could only be an absolutely primordial Godhead, and only now an absolutely primordial Godhead which is an absolutely empty Godhead.

Yet that empty Godhead is not simply and only empty. It is far rather the embodiment of a purely negative abyss, a negative abyss which is an absolutely negative body, so that here an absolute emptiness is an absolutely negative emptiness, one which is the true opposite of an absolutely sacrificial body, but nevertheless one which is essential to the very actuality of an absolute sacrifice. While sacrifice is the most universal of all religious or ultimate movements, and may be understood as the very core of our purest ritual, it is nevertheless most resisted and transformed by our dominant theologies, and most so insofar as these are bound to primordial Godhead itself. That thinking which does most deeply understand sacrifice is inevitably a kenotic or self-emptying thinking, one reflecting in thinking itself the ultimate movement of sacrifice, a sacrifice which is necessarily a self-negation, just as an absolute sacrifice is necessarily an absolute self-negation. Hence if Godhead has, indeed, absolutely sacrificed itself, that could only be an absolute self-negation, and an absolute self-negation of Godhead itself. Only thereby does the purely negative pole or potency of the Godhead become fully actual and real, and actual and real in ultimate disjunction from its own polar contrary. Only now do the negative and the positive poles of the Godhead become actual as true opposites, and opposites in ultimate opposition to each other.

Thus, as wholly opposed to what the mystic knows as the absolute nothingness of primordial Godhead, this pure and absolute negativity is an absolutely alien negativity or an absolutely alien absolute nothingness. Now the Nihil as Nihil and Nihil alone fully stands forth, and even if it is not until full modernity that such a Nihil is either envisioned or understood, its very dawning is ineradicable, hence the advent of a uniquely modern nihilism, and a nihilism more universal today than ever before. Nietzsche could understand that we are finally called upon to sacrifice God to the Nothing, but thereby he is calling forth a sacrifice that has already occurred, and a sacrifice effecting the very advent of the Nihil, a Nihil which is the inevitable consequence of the absolute sacrifice or the absolute self-negation of Godhead itself. Only that self-negation realizes an absolutely actual dichotomy in the Godhead, a dichotomy in which Godhead itself is absolutely torn asunder, now absolutely divided between its positive and its negative poles. A primary reflection of this ultimate division is the ultimate dichotomy now realized between the primordial and the apocalyptic poles of the Godhead, only now does the primordial stand forth as the primordial and the primordial alone, and only now does an absolute omega stand forth which is absolutely liberated from an absolute alpha. Now absolute beginning is and only can be absolute ending, but that absolute transfiguration of the poles of the Godhead releases an absolute negativity which is absolutely new, and absolutely new as an absolutely transfiguring power.

That transfiguring power is inseparable from that Nihil which it embodies, a Nihil which can be named as the dead body of God or the Godhead, an abysmal body of the Godhead which is the inevitable consequence of an absolute sacrifice of the Godhead. Now this is just the sacrifice that is refused in every Christian apprehension of the absolute sovereignty and the absolute transcendence of God. That refusal inevitably impels a radical movement away from that very actuality which is a necessary consequence of the absolute sacrifice of the Godhead, or that actuality which in full modernity realizes itself as an absolute immanence, and an absolute immanence that is the necessary consequence of the pure reversal of an absolute transcendence. That reversal can be understood as occurring in the full sacrifice of the Godhead, for if that sacrifice is the absolute negation of absolute transcendence, its inevitable consequence is the realization of the very opposite of that absolute transcendence, an opposite which is absolute immanence itself, and an immanence only possible by way of the negation and reversal of absolute transcendence. The very advent of that immanence is inseparable from the realization of the full and actual emptiness of absolute transcendence, an emptiness that is a truly alien emptiness, and one which is realized as the Nihil itself.

While it is only in full modernity that the Nihil is fully actual and real, it is nonetheless a necessary consequence of the absolute sacrifice of the Godhead, a sacrifice realizing a truly alien and empty transcendence, and absolute immanence is only possible by way of a realization of that emptiness. If full modernity inevitably has a deep ground in that Nihil, a ground releasing an all pervasive *Angst*, that *Angst* is inseparable from a truly new absolute immanence, which is wholly inseparable from the pure and alien emptiness of an absolute transcendence, or that very alien and empty transcendence released by absolute sacrifice itself. No such transcendence is released by primordial sacrifice, nor is any such transcendence manifest and real before the advent of Christianity. Even if historical Christianity can know absolute transcendence as an absolutely primordial transcendence, that primordial transcendence is ever increasingly an alien transcendence in the historical evolution of Christianity, one deeply known both in the late medieval world and the early Reformation, and these are the worlds that mark the full advent of a profoundly interior *Angst*. Already Paul could know an absolute guilt fully comparable to that *Angst*, one truly reborn in Augustine and the Augustinian tradition, and if that is the very tradition fully reborn in the late medieval world—and one not only shattering all Christian scholasticism, but finally shattering all established ecclesiastical authority as well—this is a reflection of a truly new transcendence, but one inseparable from its origin in the very birth of Christianity.

Thus only Christianity and the Christian world know an actual body of abyss, but that body does not become a universal body until the end of Christendom, and then it is not comprehensively universal until the advent of postmodernity. Postmodernity embodies a fully actual emptiness, and an emptiness of interiority itself, one making possible the advent of a total reification, or a total exteriority, and an exteriority realizing a total exterior realization of what previously was a wholly internal and interior *Angst*. If that earlier *Angst* is a response to a fully actual nothingness of the Godhead, its contemporary counterpart can be understood as an exterior realization of the absymal body of the Godhead, one wherein our absolutely new exteriority is a realization of the dead body of God. Even if that dead body of God is a consequence of the absolute sacrifice of the Godhead, and hence is itself a truly sacrificial body, it is only a sacrificial body as the consequence of absolute sacrifice itself. So it is that Blake could know the Christ of the Church as an actualization or renewal of the dead body of Jesus in the tomb, but that dead body becomes a universal body with the advent of a uniquely modern exteriority, or what Kierkegaard could know as a uniquely modern objectification. This objectification is an objectification of interiority or subjectivity itself; only thereby is it a truly total objectification, and a total objectification which is totality itself.

This is that absolutely new totality which so fully dawns in postmodernity. It can be understood as the very opposite of that totality which Mahayana Buddhism knows as nirvana or sunyata. Whereas sunyata is that absolute emptiness which is absolute compassion, our new emptiness is an absolutely naked or alien emptiness, or an emptiness which is actual as emptiness alone. No such emptiness is possible in Buddhism, or possible in any world other than a uniquely Christian world, unless that world has undergone a total metamorphosis, and a metamorphosis into our new body of abyss. What could be the possible relationship between this new body of abyss and that absolutely original body which Buddhism knows as sunyata? Could they be true opposites, and opposites in a truly dialectical sense, so that each is not only the full opposite of the other, but as a fully dialectical opposition this could only finally be a *coincidentia oppositorum*? If this could be an actual possibility, then it could only be an apocalyptic possibility, but an apocalyptic possibility which is a final realization of the absolute sacrifice of the Godhead. If that sacrifice is the ultimate source of our new emptiness, our emptiness could finally be a sacrificial emptiness, one not only embodying the dead body of God, but embodying that body that is a consequence of the absolute sacrifice of God, and therefore a body of absolute abyss which is an absolutely sacrificial body.

Yet that body is most abysmal precisely in being sacrificial body, and if only an absolute sacrifice can release the full actuality of an absolute abyss, an absolute sacrifice which is an absolute death, that is the death which is an embodiment of absolute abyss, and an absolute abyss which is renewed or resurrected when an absolute death is fully enacted. Only the absolute sacrifice of the Godhead has given us that absolute death, a death which can be known as the most ultimate grace, yet that is the very grace which is inseparable from an absolute body of abyss, a body apart from which such grace would be unincarnate or unembodied. Such grace can be understood as releasing the depths of joy itself, a joy inseparable from that embodiment, but a joy precisely thereby inseparable from an actual body of abyss, or inseparable from the depths of the body itself. Only an absolute abyss embodies those depths, and therefore only that abyss embodies an ultimate joy, and if that joy is inseparable from an ultimate horror, this, too, is a *coincidentia oppositorum*, and a dialectical union inseparable from absolute apocalypse itself. This is that absolute Yes inseparable and finally indistinguishable from an absolute No. Just as the positive and the negative poles of the Godhead are finally indistinguishable from each other, each is fully actual only through the other, just as a uniquely Christian redemption is inseparable and finally indistinguishable from a uniquely Christian judgment or damnation.

Yes, the Nihil, and even an absolute Nihil, is finally not only inseparable but indistinguishable from an absolute Yes. If this occurs and only occurs in the finality of apocalypse itself, that apocalypse is inseparable from an absolutely primordial Godhead, even if it is a final reversal of that Godhead. That is the very reversal giving birth to the absolute Nihil, but that Nihil or that Nothing as an absolute nothingness is not only inseparable from the full actuality of apocalypse itself, it is inseparable from the absolute joy of that apocalypse. Here an absolute No and an absolute Yes wholly coincide. Thus even the dead body of the Godhead, or that body of abyss which is a consequence of absolute sacrifice itself, is not simply and only a dead body, but an absolutely abysmal body truly necessary to absolute apocalypse, and wholly inseparable from the absolute Yes of that apocalypse. Just as that No makes possible this Yes, it is not only inseparable from that Yes, but finally indistinguishable from it as well, and is so because an absolute apocalypse is inevitably an apocalyptic *coincidentia oppositorum*, a final and apocalyptic identity of absolute Yes and absolute No. Already Blake knew this identity in envisioning the final identity of Satan and Christ. Only that identity makes possible his ultimate affirmation of the uniquely Christian God, and if the absolute No-saying of that Godhead is finally an absolute Yes-saying, it is so only because of the full actuality of apocalypse itself.

Yes, a fully actual Nothing is what can be known as the dead body of God, and just as that Nihil is only actually manifest after the Crucifixion, it is only made possible by the Crucifixion. For even if it is an ultimate realization of primordial sacrifice, primordial sacrifice is an eternal movement, whereas the Crucifixion is a once-and-for-all event, and as such the final realization of primordial sacrifice. But Crucifixion is not only crucifixion. It is also and even thereby resurrection itself, and not a resurrection which is a return to a primordial realm or heaven, or even an eternal return at all, but far rather a forward and ultimately apocalyptic movement into that absolute omega which is only possible by way of a negation and reversal of absolute alpha, or the negation and reversal of primordial Godhead itself. If that negation is the realization of the absolute reversal of primordial Godhead, a reversal realizing the Nihil itself, that Nihil is that absolute No which is finally absolute Yes, and inevitably absolute Yes in its realization of apocalypse.

There is no greater ultimate mystery than that absolute No which *is* absolute Yes, but nothing else more fully unveils the death of God, and above all that death of the Godhead which is apocalypse itself. This apocalypse not only embodies an apocalyptic sacrifice, but realizes that sacrifice in the absolutely new, and an absolutely new which is finally all in all. Thus if the deepest depths of the Nihil are an absolute No, that No is finally Yes, and is realized as such in an ultimate response to the Nihil, a response which is finally a total affirmation, and a total affirmation of an absolutely sacrificial Godhead. That Yes releases the deepest possible joy, but a joy only possible through an absolute No. If it is the depths of the Nihil which in our world have evoked the most ultimate call, that call is finally a call to joy itself, or a call to that joy released by the apocalypse of God, and an apocalypse of God only possible by way of the death of Godhead itself. Hence it is absolute death that evokes the deepest call, and if an opening to that death is an opening to the finality of death itself, that finality is an absolutely liberating finality, and it alone can truly be named as resurrection. Yet resurrection can truly be named as resurrection only through crucifixion itself, and an absolute crucifixion, an absolute crucifixion which is absolute death. Not only does that death alone make possible resurrection, but that death *is* finally resurrection, and is resurrection not only as the sacrifice of the Godhead, but as the embodiment of that sacrifice in an absolutely new totality. Yes, that totality is possible only through the Nihil, only through the dead body of God, but this is that abysmal body which is not only a body of nothingness, but a body of nothingness embodying an ultimate sacrifice of itself, and only that sacrifice releases an ultimate and final joy.

INDEX

Made in United States
Orlando, FL
18 August 2024

50496924R00100